No writer...has printed a more living account of human beings who lived and perished, were heroic...weak, bewildered and absurdly brave during months of... Terror.

**BOOTH TARKINGTON**
American Novelist and Two-Time Winner of the
Pulitzer Prize for Fiction

The confusion of the first days of Bolshevism and the dramatic story of her husband's hiding and escape...are well told. ... The calm tone of Woronoff's narrative help to bring out the drama and sad impressiveness of her truthful story.

**ALEXANDER NAZAROFF**
*The New York Times*

Olga Woronoff's memoir *Upheaval* was a moving, must-read for me. Set in the last days of Imperial Russia and during the Bolshevik Revolution, Olga's clear prose not only paints a vivid picture of one of the most turbulent times in modern history but highlights what is really important at the end of the day. I think her story would touch the heart of any reader who is interested in Russian history or indeed in any history.

**ELLA CAREY**
Best-Selling Author

*Upheaval* is an emotionally engaging memoir written by Olga Woronoff, on growing up in Russia, her marriage to Paul Woronoff, who served as a naval officer on Tsar Nicholas II of Russia's yacht, the *Standart*, where he became close to all the members of the Imperial Family, the Revolution, and the Civil War. With additional chapters and notes drawing on new research, written by her granddaughter, Alex de Fircks, *Upheaval* is a testament to the human spirit.

**ELISE MCCUNE**
Historical Author

*Upheaval* offers a new perspective on an extraordinary first-hand account of the life and times of an aristocratic Russian family both before and after the Bolshevik revolution. In *Upheaval* Madame Olga Woronoff (née Countess Kleinmichel) chronicles a life of privilege within the inner circle of the Tsar and Tsarina, the harrowing experience which led to her fleeing her homeland with her husband and finally settling in America. The author's granddaughter, writer Alex de Fircks, contrasts the public story with the opinions Woronoff privately held in her personal diaries. She also helpfully offers background material on the important participants featured in this fascinating and important look back into Russian history.

**CATHY KONING**
Author of *Life Blood: Lessons from one woman
who survived serious illness against the odds*


*Upheaval* provides readers with a detailed and personalised view of epic world events through the eyes of an individual caught up in the world-changing Russian revolution. Being close to the Romanovs gave the original author a unique perspective. Alex has enhanced this work to make it more detailed without detracting from the author's integrity.

**GRAEME LAMBERT**
Retired Secondary School Humanities Teacher


...you, the reader, now have the chance to witness life after the revolution through the eyes of the other Olga, who – along with her husband Pavel – had such a close connection to Russia's last imperial family, and lived through events that most people only learn about from books or films.

**HELEN AZAR**
Romanov Historian, Translator, and Author

# UPHEAVAL

# UPHEAVAL

## A STORY OF RUSSIA, ROMANOVS, AND REVOLUTION

SECOND EDITION

### OLGA WORONOFF

*With new preface, afterword, and notes by her granddaughter*
ALEX DE FIRCKS

*Foreword by*
HELEN AZAR

First published in 1932 by G. P. Putnam's Sons, New York and London.

This revised second edition was first published in October 2025 by Downingfield Press Proprietary Limited, Suite 346 / 585 Little Collins Street, Melbourne, Victoria 3000, Australia. For a comprehensive list of addresses and contact information, please visit www.global.downingfield.com.

Original text copyright © 1932 Olga Woronoff. Revised text, notes, additions to the text, and cover design copyright © 2025 Alex de Fircks. Typesetting and book design copyright © 2025 Downingfield Press Proprietary Limited. The copyright for the cover design is held by Alex de Fircks. The moral rights for the cover design belong to Sophie White. All rights reserved. Cover design by Sophie White. Typesetting design by M. Cheng-Mader. Where mandated by law, the moral rights of the creators have been duly asserted. The frontispiece photograph is from the personal collection of Alex de Fircks and shows Olga Kleinmichel at Evpatoria in 1915, during the final years of Imperial Russia.

Without limiting the rights under copyright reserved above, in accordance with the Copyright Act 1968 (Commonwealth of Australia), no part of this publication may be reproduced, stored in or introduced into a retrieval system, or transmitted, in any form or by any means (electronic, mechanical, xerographic, recording, or otherwise), without the prior written permission of the copyright owner and the publisher of this book, except for brief passages quoted for the purposes of criticism or review.

Every effort has been made to ensure the accuracy of the information contained herein at the time of publication. However, the author and publisher hereby disclaim any and all responsibility for any errors, omissions, or changes that may have occurred after the date of publication. The content is provided solely for general informational purposes and should not be construed as a substitute for professional advice. To the fullest extent permissible by law, the author and publisher expressly disclaim all liability for any loss, damage, or inconvenience, whether direct or indirect, arising from any error or omission in this publication.

Parts of this text were previously utilised by Alex de Fircks in fulfilment of the Master of Research thesis in the Faculty of Arts at Macquarie University, February 2024.

ISBN 9781923513013 (paperback)
ISBN 9781923513037 (e-book)

Downingfield Press undertakes its work on the traditional lands of the Wurundjeri people of the Kulin Nation and pays respect to Elders past, present, and emerging.

**DOWNINGFIELD PRESS PROPRIETARY LIMITED**
MELBOURNE · LONDON AND MONTRÉAL

 A catalogue record for this work is available from the National Library of Australia

*To my daughter, Tatiana.*

OLGA WORONOFF, 1932

*For my sons, who have always indulged my passion for our family history. I hope this gives you greater insight into the lives of your great grandparents.*

ALEX DE FIRCKS, 2025

| | |
|---|---|
| *Forward* | *1* |
| *Preface* | *11* |
| *My Family* | *18* |
| *Our Moscow Home* | *35* |
| *Familiar Faces* | *43* |
| *Ivnya* | *49* |
| *Moscow* | *57* |
| *Happy Days* | *75* |
| *War and Revolultion* | *99* |
| *Facing Danger* | *125* |
| *Hunted* | *142* |
| *A Turn of Events* | *152* |
| *In the Army* | *163* |
| *Before the End* | *174* |
| *Epilogue* | *181* |
| *Afterword* | *186* |
| *Acknowledgements* | *189* |
| *Olga Woronoff's 1919 Diary* | *192* |
| *Correspondence from the Russian State Archives* | *225* |
| *Sources For Notes* | *302* |

# FORWARD
BY HELEN AZAR

The year 1913 is the tercentennial of Romanov dynastic rule, and the eldest daughter of Tsar Nicholas II, the Grand Duchess Olga Nikolaevna, is coming of age, soon to turn eighteen. No one is aware this is Russia's last completely "normal" year – the last of the nation's peace and relative prosperity. The young Grand Duchess's life is full of romance, pageantry and fun: the carefree life of a princess, with just the right amount of excitement and angst typical for a normal seventeen-year-old girl.

Ninety-nine years later, in 2012, I hold scans of the Grand Duchess's original 1913 diary, which I am planning to translate in full and publish.[1] The scans came from GARF – the State Archive of the Russian Federation in Moscow – and it was not an easy task to obtain them. This is the first of several diaries written by members of the last Russian imperial family that I will be translating, and the task initially seems rather daunting.

---

[1] It was published in 2012 in a book entitled *Journal of a Russian Grand Duchess: Complete Annotated 1913 Diary of Olga Romanov, Eldest Daughter of the Last Tsar* .

Previously, I had done much shorter translations of their printed writings, but this diary is written in Cyrillic cursive, which adds a significant layer of difficulty. The Grand Duchess's handwriting is elegant, but often illegible; although after days, weeks and months spent deciphering and transliterating these pages, it becomes much less so.

Among other things, from the first half of her diary, I learn that Olga has a girlish crush on one of several attractive officers from the imperial yacht the *Standart*. She refers to him as "Pavl.Al.". The first time I come across the mysterious Pavl.Al is in Olga's diary entry entitled "Voyage on the *Standart*. Monday. June 10", where she casually writes:

*Excellent transfer [to the yacht]. Did not do anything special, walked around on the deck, sat in the cabin with Pavl.Al., Rodionov and Sablin came [too]. After tea, played [games] with Pavl.Al. and friends, also watched Alexei play with the boys. A little after six arrived at the old nice place and docked on the side. Prayer took place at 8. Balalaikas were played during dinner. After that, held watch with Pavl. Al. on the deck.*

Just ten days later, the name becomes "dear Pavl.Al.", as Olga begins spending more time with its owner.

*Thursday. 20 June... There were boating exercises. Papa kayaked. Cutter-gig escort [was] Pavl.Al.... After dinner T[atiana] and I went to the control room. Dear Pavl.Al. was writing in the log journal. We sat together until 10 o'cl....*

They seem to spend a lot of time together – talking, playing tennis, dice and cards, kayaking, dancing. The Grand Duchess makes it clear that she wants to spend as much time with him as possible, even visiting him in the yacht control room while he is on watch duty, making herself useful by dictating, as he writes notes in the log journal. On 4 July, Olga "sat in control [room] by the window, reading and looking at dear Pavl.Al., who was keeping watch on the deck-bridge." The next day, they "played

Affections with <u>dear sweet</u> Pavl.Al. and it turned out well" (underline is Olga's). She worries about his moods: "Pavl.Al. was a bit sad. He enjoyed himself just a bit today, as he showed me just the tip of his pinkie." She takes every opportunity to sit next to him, which then warrants a diary entry emphasising her delight: "sat with dear Pavl.Al. on a bench. <u>It was so nice!</u>" The reader does not need to guess how Olga feels about Pavl.Al, as she basically spells it out: "sat in the control room with Pavl.Al. He was filling in the log journal. I love being with him <u>so much</u>."

So, who was this enigmatic Pavl.Al? From the second half of 1913, in the imperial daughters' photo albums, a darkly handsome officer with a stylish moustache emerges, often posing with the sisters or their little brother. Here he is, sitting on a see-saw type swing opposite Grand Duchess Olga, while her father and another officer look on from the background. Here he is again, on a deck bench of the imperial yacht, Olga sitting close to his right and her sister Tatiana on his left. And here, yet again, giving little Tsesarevich Alexei a piggyback ride on his shoulders, with the eleven-year-old Grand Duchess Anastasia looking up at him adoringly. There are even photos of him and Grand Duchess Olga posing alone together.

Pavel Alekseevich Voronov (Paul Woronoff) is the name of this handsome officer. Born in 1886 (Russian old calendar), Voronov is nine years Olga's senior, and by 1913 he is already a naval lieutenant, having served on the imperial yacht for several years. He seems to have gone almost unnoticed by Olga until the seventeen-year-old suddenly fell in love with him in 1913. On 12 July, Olga records her feelings of devastation at having to leave the yacht, and between the lines we can read that she is distraught about parting with her beloved.

*Left the yacht around 4:00. So <u>terribly</u> hard to part with the beloved* Standart, *officers and sweetie [text scribbled over]. Lord, save him, everyone... <u>So</u> sad to be without <u>them</u>.*

And of course, we know that by "them", she means "him" – Pavel Voronov.

In the following weeks, Olga's diary entries feel a bit more monotonous than usual, even melancholy. She does not mention Pavel by name, but occasionally wonders about the yacht, clearly thinking of him. Olga reunites with Pavel on 19 August, and in her diary, he is no longer Pavl.Al. but "S." – which stands for *Solntse* (sun) or *Sve* (light). Pavel has become Olga's sun, around whom her life revolves, the one who brings light into it. On that day, her diary entry reads:

*S. finally came for breakfast … For ¼ hour before the walk, sat with S. on Anya's balcony.[2] So happy to see him.*

The next day, Olga watches boating exercises, but her mind is only on him, "Saw boating exercises very far away. How I want to see S." Hence, on 21 August, she again looks through the field glass, and records in delight: "Through the field glass saw S. get into the barge." Finally, the next day, after having once again spotted Pavel from afar through the now ever-present field glass, she gets to spend time with him in person.

*For breakfast we were joined by Rodionov, Father, Stolitsa and S. Awfully happy to see him, missed him so much … The four of us went for a walk with Anya, Rodionov and S. It was so nice. Until 3:30 sat under the balcony on the well with my S. The others were sitting on the bench.*

She now deems him "my S." and "beloved S.", and once again, he starts to make multiple daily appearances in her diary: "…played 1 more set with beloved S. against Papa and Anya and lost – so what. Everything is still the same, as my S. says." She

---

[2] "Anya" is Anna Vyrubova, a close friend of the Empress and the imperial family.

even records when she does not get to see him: "Did not see my S. today", the Grand Duchess writes on 25 August.

Olga is obviously happiest on days when she gets to spend a lot of time with him:

*Stood on the deck with S. Then everyone started dancing, suddenly, on the starboard quarter-deck. It was <u>so much</u> fun. Then [we] went to the cape, rode in the wagon all around it. When we came back, we resumed dancing – I danced a lot with dearest S.*

The days she does not see him, are spent in anticipation of seeing him again, while fighting boredom by trying to catch a glimpse of him through the ever-present field glass: "I am so awfully bored today without S. Saw him in passing, through the field glass on the barge."

Summer of 1913 passes quickly, but early autumn is also spent in sunny Crimea – playing tennis, dancing on the deck, playing games, having tea/breakfast/dinner on the yacht; and all through it, Olga's diary is always about "my S."

She enthusiastically describes those happy days in detail, as if wanting to record them for posterity.

*[We] split into 2 parties, then played Dobchinsky-Bobchinsky, forfeits, turkey; threw a scarf around, hid in dark cabins and laughed a lot.[3] Towards the end [we] played charades. I was in S.'s party every time and was <u>awfully</u> happy. We had the word '<u>sheep</u>'... Laughed so hard, unbelievably wonderful.*

Such days without him are "fun, but empty and sad without my beloved S."

---

[3] Dobchinsky-Bobchinsky is a 19th century, aristocratic parlour game based on the characters from Gogol's *Inspector General*.

Anxiety kicks in when Olga ponders not being able to see him, "I was so worried that I wouldn't see him today", "It is so abominable without my S., so awful." Even the weather seems affected by her mood when she misses him, "[We] were in Oreanda by the sea, watched the surf. Overcast – no sun, no my S.[4] On the way back, a heavy rain started."

On 14 September, for the first time, there is a casual, almost incidental mention of the name "Kleinmichel", together with Voronov's – "Met my S. riding in a motor with the Kleinmichels. I am lonesome when he is not around."

According to Olga Kleinmichel's memoirs, this was the time when she and Pavel were betrothed, although it did not seem to have been made public until a couple of months later. It may have happened on this very day – 14 September 1913 – when Grand Duchess Olga ran into Pavel riding in an automobile with the Kleinmichel family.

During the third week of September, the annual White Flower Festival takes place, along with the traditional Yalta charity bazaar, in which the imperial family is extensively involved. They run their own booth, where they personally sell items made with their own hands. The court members, including the *Standart* officers, all help; and of course, Pavel Voronov is there too, despite having what sounds like a severe cold.

*[We went] to the Festivities Hall to spread out things for the bazaar. My S. and dear friends were helping. He still isn't feeling well, has a cough. I am awfully happy to see him. I was so bored for 2 days without him.*

On 22 September, during the ongoing festival and bazaar, Olga continues to worry about Pavel's health, while herself starting to feel ill. This is also the day when she mentions by name the lady-in-waiting Olga Kleinmichel, along with her sister Natasha:

---

[4] In the Yalta Municipality of the Crimea.

*At 2 o'clock the five of us with Mama, went to the bazaar in Yalta ... Ladies-in-waiting Olga and Tasha Kleinmichel, Marusya and Vera Trepova, as well as Daria Gesse helped.⁵ It was very nice, but exhausting. My head feels empty and hurts. Mama left for the yacht at 4 o'clock. We left at 6. I was sitting on the deck until dinner, and finally my S. came. He has a cold and coughs. So tiresome. At 9 o'clock the 4 of us went to the bazaar again. S. went, too. ... I just wish for S. to get better.*

The rest of the month is spent in a series of the usual fun activities: playing tennis, dancing, watching boat manoeuvres, all the while trying to catch glimpses of her beloved when he isn't present, and worrying about his health.

It seems that even the infamous Rasputin makes an appearance in Crimea that month. On 25 September, Olga and her family see a circus:

*... it was a lot of fun. On the way there saw Grigory Yefimovich [Rasputin]. Cossacks, sailors, soldiers and all of Livadia were there. My <u>beloved</u> S. too. So happy to see him.*

Then, several days later:

*Zeblov, Reverend Father and Kublitsky came for breakfast, but my S. felt sick at the last minute and did not come. Did not see him all day and miss him.*

*My dear S. was not there, and I was angry and bored.*

*It's just so sad that I have not seen S. for two days now.*

On the first day of October, "S. is in Kosmo-Damianovsky, so what.⁶ However, it's awfully boring without him. Want to see him..." At this point, Olga attempts to convince herself that "I

---

⁵ Tasha (Natalie / Tata) Kleinmichel, elder sister of Olga Woronoff neé Kleinmichel.

⁶ A monastery in Alushta in Crimea.

am now used to not seeing S. for so long, and notice his absence less, even though I do miss him a lot."

She finally sees her S. again, albeit from a distance, four days later:

*We watched the saluting navy squadron and I finally saw S., first in a motor, and then with the platoon. He also saw me, my S.*

Some days later, during a dance, Olga apprehensively observes, "Saw my S. once – he was passing in a quadrille [illegible] we met. He seemed kind of sad, I don't know..."

Once again, the name Kleinmichel appears in her diary: "Coming back, ran into the Kleinmichels in a motor. At times I really miss S." Is it a coincidence that she immediately thinks of Pavel when she sees the Kleinmichels? Presumably at this stage Olga was not yet aware of the betrothal, but perhaps she sensed something.

In early winter, back in Tsarskoe Selo, for the first time that year Olga uses a special code she devised for her diary when she refers to Pavel.

*Thursday. 12 December ... We played Dobchinsky-Bobchinsky and Suitcase with T[atiana], Zborovsky and S.[7] [written in code]: I love him terribly much, and it was so hard, I was angry and almost did not speak to him ...*

*Friday. 20 December ... My S. arrived today. May the Lord save him and help him.*

The next day, Olga has to face her heartbreak: Pavel is officially engaged to be married to her namesake, Countess Olga Kleinmichel. She can no longer pretend that Pavel is "hers".

*Saturday. 21 December ... I found out that S. [written in code]: My S. is marrying Olga Kleinmichel. May the Lord send him*

---

[7] Suitcase is a card game.

*happiness, to my beloved S. So hard. So sad. May he be happy.*

*1 January 1914. T.[atiana] was there with my S. [written in code]: in the end he is S. to me, for the bride [has] all of him, but for me [he is] S.*

In her 1914 diary, Olga's sister, Grand Duchess Tatiana Nikolaevna describes the events that took place on 7 February – Pavel Voronov and Olga Kleinmichel's wedding day:[8]

*At 2 o'cl., Mama, Papa, Olga, Alexei rode in one motor, we three with U.[ncle] Sandro in another, to the regiment church for the wedding of Pavel Aleks.[eevich] and Olga K.[onstantinovna]. When we arrived, he was standing alone in the middle of the church. There were masses of people. All the officers of the Guard Eq[uipage], his parents and two sisters who look like him. Then her sisters Tata, [her] Mother, her older [sisters] Clara Martynova and Ella Puschina. Then Olga [Kleinmichel] arrived. She was awfully pretty and sweet. He had two best men: his brother, Nik. Pav., Mishka Khvoschinsky and others. Hers were Dmitry and others. Her brother is not well. From there, when it was over, we went to the Kleinmichels' house. (At the church, the sailors and the boys from Guard E[quipage] sang). Everyone congratulated them there, I was so happy for them and so awfully glad to see them. After some time, we left their house at 3 ½. They departed at 6 oc'l. 45[min] to Nice for three weeks... I was so awfully glad to see the newlyweds.*

This could not have been an easy day for Grand Duchess Olga, but it was her duty to attend the wedding along with her family, and she made a good effort to be happy for Pavel and Olga.

---

[8] Grand Duchess Tatiana was a close friend of Olga Kleinmichel; the latter named her only child, Tatiana, in honour of her murdered friend.

*Friday. 7 February ... At 2 o'clock, S. arrived. Mama and Sandro blessed him. Around ½ of 3 [2:30], the five of us, with Papa and Mama rode to the regimental church for the wedding of P.A. Voronov and O.K. Kleinmichel. May God grant them happiness. Both are nervous, but calm and happy. [We] met S.'s parents and 2 sisters, [who are] adorable, Sh.[vedov?] and Al. P., brothers, etc., [are] the best men. Went to the Kleinmichels' [house], there were felicitations, many people.*

Only five months later, the First World War breaks out, and this is the end of life as Olga and her family know it.

One cannot help but wonder if Olga occasionally thought of her "S." during those dreary days in faraway Siberia. Did she remember that carefree seventeen-year-old girl in love, enjoying the good times and the feelings of exhilaration being around her beloved? Did she wonder if Pavel and his own Olga made it out of Russia safely, after the brutal Bolshevik regime seized the country in late 1917?

Olga and her family would not get the chance to learn of the fate of their loyal friends: the navy officer and the lady-in-waiting. Nor would they know what calamities would befall their much-loved Russia. But you, the reader, now have the chance to witness life after the revolution through the eyes of the other Olga, who – along with her husband Pavel – had such a close connection to Russia's last imperial family, and lived through events that most people only learn about from books or films.

# PREFACE
## BY ALEX DE FIRCKS

It was with some trepidation I began to revisit my grandmother's book, *Upheaval*, in order to include new material and republish it as a second edition. The death of my parents left me with boxes of documents and letters from both sides of the family. In these I discovered a diary written in 1919, much of which my grandmother left out of her original manuscript, as well as notes she had penned for a proposed sequel. After sorting through these documents, I decided there was enough new information to give interested readers a fuller picture of my grandmother's life.

I called my grandparents Babu and Dadu – short for the Russian words *Babushka* (grandmother) and *Dedushka* (grandfather), which I could not pronounce as a child. I have very few memories of them. My grandfather, Paul Woronoff, died when I was nine years old. The clearest memory I have of him is of the two of us playing in the snow outside their apartment. In winter, large icicles would hang down from the roof and my grandfather would chase me under them and then sweep me up, pretending to rescue me from the danger they posed. In the year before he died, whenever I visited their apartment, I remember the door to their bedroom was always closed. With hindsight, I can only assume it was because he was lying sick in bed. My grandfather died on 8 September 1969 of advanced and inoperable stomach cancer.

He was buried at Jordanville, New York. At my grandfather's funeral I followed his coffin, carrying the sword and dirk he had managed to take with him when they escaped Russia. I still have that sword and dirk, as well as the medals he was awarded during his service in the Russian Imperial Navy, they are a reminder both of him and of the life he once led.

I have more memories of my grandmother. I vaguely remember her efforts to teach me Russian when I was seven or eight years old. She would set up an easel with large pieces of paper on which she wrote the alphabet. To this day I can remember how to pronounce the letters, and I can sound out words without knowing their meaning. She also taught me to count to ten. We read children's books in Russian and I recall one of them was about the Russian cosmonaut Yuri Gagarin. Russian lessons were always held after school and I was often joined by one of my friends. My grandmother would make us peanut butter and jelly sandwiches before class. Looking back, I can only imagine how frustrating it would have been for my grandmother who was, by that time, a retired Russian teacher.

Sandwiches were one of the few dishes my grandmother could successfully prepare, along with beef rissoles and mashed potatoes. Cooking was not one of her strengths, which is not surprising as she had no role models from whom to learn. One of my grandmother's entries in her 1919 diary made me laugh when I read of her frustration at losing their cook. My mother also struggled with cooking but, with determination, trial and error, managed to succeed more times than she failed.

As a child I was never told of my grandparents' history. I did not know they were aristocrats; I vaguely knew they had been close to the last Tsar of Russia and his family, but I knew next to nothing about their experiences of revolution, war and eventual escape from the country they loved. The concept of aristocrats and Tsars was also foreign to me. It was not until much later, in my teens, that I read my grandmother's book. By then it was difficult for me to reconcile the frail, elderly people I knew with the elegant aristocrats in the book. It was all too surreal. Later, as an adult, I Googled their names and was both intrigued and shocked at the speculation and amount of interest around my grandfather and the Grand Duchess Olga.

Some of the stories in my grandmother's book were familiar to me. She had often told me about the calves that she and her sisters had looked after and named, and the little dog Sharik, who would ride on the long train of my great-grandmother's dress. My favourite story was of my grandmother's sister Ella who, to show her courage, had pulled out a lock of her own hair. I loved naughty Ella the best.

One of the stories my grandmother told me never made it to the book. My grandmother and her sisters had a long table in their playroom, on which they kept their dolls and toys. Every year, in the weeks before Christmas, they had to decide which of these they no longer wanted to keep. The dolls and toys they selected would then be distributed to the children of the poor families of the district. For my grandmother, this was one of the most difficult things she was asked to do as she loved each one of her dolls and toys. She told me it was as if she were being asked to give away one of her children. Of course, the girls would receive new dolls and toys each Christmas, but my grandmother never got over the sadness she felt at having to decide which of her "babies" she would part with.

But my grandmother's parents and siblings were all just characters in a book to me. I never associated them with real people, or my own family.

If my grandfather ever told me stories about his childhood, I do not remember them. When I was ten years old, I met my Great-Aunt Natasha and my Aunt Olga and Uncle Nick. At the time I had no idea where they fit into our family picture. As an only child I was used to calling many of my parent's friends by the honorary titles of "Aunt" and "Uncle", so I never questioned who they were. It was only years later I learned Great-Aunt Natasha was my grandfather's sister and Aunt Olga was her daughter.

From the time I was ten years old until a few years before she died, my grandmother lived with us. I remember her as quiet and almost fragile. She was also extremely religious. She insisted on wearing clothes which were too big for her, always skirts and tops. She never wore pants and I cannot remember her ever wearing a dress, although judging by old photos she did. Her hair, even in old age, was long and she wore it up in a bun, covered by a hair net. She told me that when she was a girl her hair was long enough to sit on and every evening, before bed, it would be plaited to keep it from becoming too messy overnight.

In this second edition of my grandmother's book, I have included footnotes which will hopefully help the reader to understand more about my grandparents, the places they visited and the events in their lives. I have also added new photographs and, in an appendix, some of the entries from my grandmother's 1919 diary. Reading this diary was eye-opening for me. I had never realised the strength of my grandparents' anti-Semitic views, and definitely do not endorse them. With hindsight their opinions were indicative both of the time and the society they lived in, but neither of these are valid excuses and don't make their anti-Semitism any less wrong.

I also did not appreciate just how normal life could be in the middle of a war. My grandparents still attended performances, visited friends and hosted dinners. They also maintained correspondence with their family and friends.

In another appendix are letters written between my grandmother and the Grand Duchesses Olga and Tatiana, daughters of the last Tsar of Russia. The originals of these letters are stored in the State Archive of the Russian Federation (GARF), which has given me permission to use them.

It has been difficult for me to understand the ins and outs of the Russian Revolution, where it ends, where the Civil War begins and who was fighting who. That part of history is convoluted to say the least. In justice to my grandparents, I can only give their side of the story – but for readers who are interested in exploring that time in history, I highly suggest reading the works of historians of Russian history, such as Orlando Figes, Robert K Massie, Antony Beevor, and Peter Kenez to name a few. I highly recommend Helen Azar's translation of the diaries of the Grand Duchesses, and other works on the Romanovs, some of which she wrote together with Nicholas B.A. Nicholson and George Hawkins, as well as the translations George Hawkins has published himself. It is also useful to read notable Russian writers, such as Tolstoy (a writer my grandmother detested!), Pasternak, and Chekov, among others, in order to gain an idea of Russia and the lives of the Russian people at the time.

As my grandmother predicted in the Epilogue to *Upheaval*, my mother was never able to see the Russia my grandparents knew. My mother never saw Russia at all. My grandparents and parents were always afraid of the threat – real or not – posed by the Bolsheviks and the Communists. They lived in fear that they, or members of their family, would be hunted down and persecuted. That fear was instilled in me from an early age and for this reason I have also never travelled to Russia – although one day I hope to be able to make the journey to the country my grandparents loved so dearly. In the meantime, I continue to search for the history of my family so that my children and grandchildren will be able to understand where they come from.

I have to add a short note about the English spelling of Russian names and words. There are often multiple ways to spell these in English. For authenticity's sake I have chosen to leave the spelling as originally written, so you will find the same word spelt differently throughout.

# FAMILY TREE OF PAUL WORONOFF

# FAMILY TREE OF OLGA KLEINMICHEL

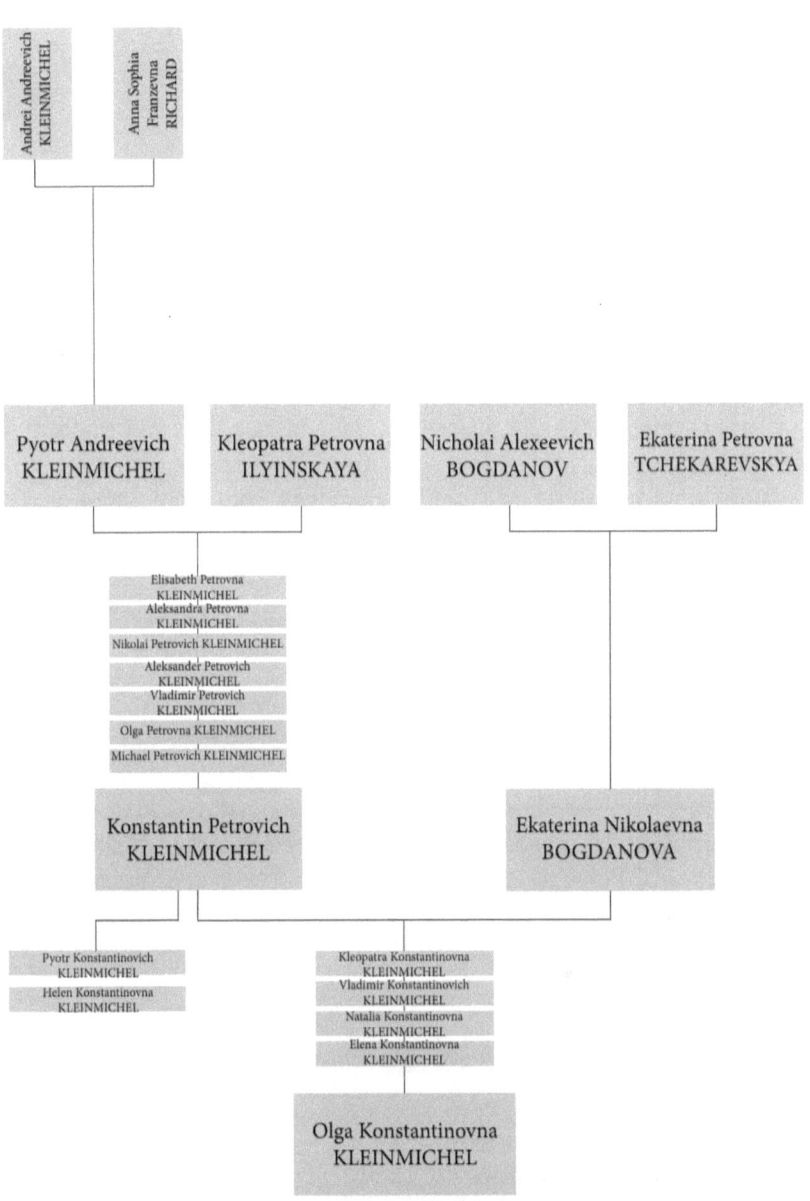

ONE
# MY FAMILY

Events and places that have been part of our lives as children often persist in our memories with a freshness and vividness unrivalled by later scenes and happenings even when these are more striking and more important; and this is especially true, I think, when in our maturity we dwell among surroundings and in circumstances completely different from those of our childhood.

Thus it is with me.

My earliest memories are connected with Potchep, one of our country estates, situated in the picturesque government of Tchernigoff.[1] The place had originally belonged to Count Alexis Razumovsky, morganatic husband of the Empress Elizabeth, daughter of Peter the Great, and in their time had undoubtedly witnessed brilliant receptions and festivities.[2] The house, a building of more than a hundred rooms, had been certainly

---

[1] Today Potchep lies in Russia's Bryansk Oblast, bordering both Belarus and Ukraine.

[2] Olga must have been confused about which Count Razumovsky owned Potchep. It was owned by Count Alexei Kyrillovich Razumovsky and not Count Alexei Grigorievich Razumovsky (morganatic husband of Empress Elizabeth), who was his uncle.

planned to receive and to entertain a great number of guests.³ Besides the numerous bedrooms, drawing rooms, reception rooms and ballrooms, there was also a good-sized theatre.

It was quite the fashion in the eighteenth and in the beginning of the nineteenth centuries to have a ballet troupe and a company of actors on the estate, formed of the most capable and handsome youths and girls among the local peasants. Many a talent was in this way discovered and eventually would shine on the stages of the Imperial Theatres of St. Petersburg. But in the time my family lived there this, of course, was ancient history and the theatre was now used for amateur plays, the actors being members of my family and neighbours. In the park, quite close to the house, was our church, remarkable for its old and quaint *iconostasis*, which had belonged to the church in Moscow where Count Razumovsky and the Empress Elizabeth had been married.⁴ It had been brought by them to Potchep as a pious souvenir of the happy event.⁵

The church, though our own private one, was by the wish of my parents open to everyone so that the services were attended by a great many inhabitants of Potchep itself, as well as of the neighbouring villages. From the earliest days of our childhood my brother, my sisters and I were taken to Mass every Sunday and I still have before my eyes a picture of that brightly dressed crowd of peasant men and women, crossing themselves devoutly in their slow and grave manner, while the air rang with the singing of the responses and the curling clouds of incense slowly rose and dissolved in the oblique rays of sunshine that fell from the tall windows. I can still see Father Alexander, our priest, standing with the chalice in his emaciated hands and my father holding me in his arms while I received the Holy Communion. There was a serene gravity in his face at that moment and a

---

³ Potchep was designed by the French architect La Mothe.

⁴ A screen, bearing icons and religious paintings, separating the altar from the rest of the church.

⁵ This is a legend which could be true.

solemnity that somehow conveyed itself to me. I am happy that my parents, deeply religious themselves, brought us up in their ideas, instilling in us a profound and firm faith in God, for it proved a rock to which we could cling through all the misfortunes and sorrows that befell us later.

My father, Count Constantin Kleinmichel was of Swedish descent and originally the name was spelled differently.[6] In the twelfth century the eastern coast of the Baltic Sea (where now the states of Estonia and Latvia have been established), that until then belonged to the Russian state of Novgorod the Great, was conquered and annexed by Sweden. My father's ancestors settled down in this new Swedish province, which was taken back by Peter the Great in 1710.[7]

In 1812, during the invasion of Russia by Napoleon's army, my grandfather, Peter Kleinmichel, took part as a young officer in the Battle of Borodino.[8] In the reign of the Emperor Nicholas I, he became minister of ways of communication. He was a close personal friend of the Emperor, and the latter would often call unexpectedly upon my grandparents. He usually came alone and would run quickly up the steps in a manner always youthful and brisk. Often, too, he would take my father, his godson, for a drive or to the palace, where they would have tea together and where the child would spend sometimes the greater part of the day; and my father bequeathed to us his love for the courageous and intelligent Nicholas I, a brilliant ruler and an imposing sovereign. The Emperor was very tall and handsome, my father told us; his voice had a metallic sound, which, with its somewhat peremptory note, would carry far, and his glance, the glance of an eagle, was apt to make the guilty tremble.[9]

---

[6] Constantin Petrovich Kleinmichel.

[7] The Kleinmichel family can be traced to the late seventeenth century, to Andreas Kleinmichel, a Lutheran pastor in Riga, Latvia and the great-grandfather of Constantin Petrovich.

[8] Pyotr Andreevich Kleinmichel.

[9] There is perhaps another reason Tsar Nicholas I visited the young Constantin

In the early part of this Emperor's reign, which lasted from 1825 until 1855, riots broke out during an epidemic of cholera in St. Petersburg, and a great and angry crowd had gathered in a square not far from the palace. When a report of this reached the Emperor, he ordered his carriage, telling the horrified members of his Court that he was going to speak to the people.

Then he commanded the coachman to drive forward into the midst of the crowd. There, standing up in his carriage, his eyes blazing with anger, the Tsar told the excited people how foolish and wrong they were to cause trouble, especially when God had allowed such a calamity to befall them. "On your knees" he cried. "And pray to God that He forgive you and stop our misfortune!" The crowd, awestricken by the imposing personality of the Tsar, knelt as a single man! And the Emperor drove away not only unmolested but cheered. Such is the magnetic power, my father used to tell us, that personal fearlessness and courage alone can create.

My grandfather built the first railroad in Russia – the line between St. Petersburg and Moscow, which is still considered the best in the country. By the will of the Tsar the tracks were of a wider gauge than those of other countries, for the purpose of hampering our enemy in case of invasion by making difficult the movement of foreign troops. Needless to say, it likewise made difficult the transportation of our troops onto foreign soil, and

---

Petrovitch. It was known that Constantin's father, Peter, had adopted the illegitimate children of Nicholas I and it is rumoured (although never officially confirmed) that Constantin was one of those children. Peter's first wife had divorced him, citing impotence. His second wife was related to the mistress of Tsar Nicholas I. Allegedly whenever Nicholas I's mistress fell pregnant, Countess Kleinmichel would feign pregnancy. There was a joke at the Russian court that the children of Peter Kleinmichel should change their name to Kleinnicholas. The rumour about Constantin being the illegitimate son of the Tsar was broached in a letter written by Olga Woronoff's sister Elena (Ella) Kleinmichel to her niece Tatiana, Olga's daughter, on 5 March 1974. Elena states the family are not allowed to mention who their real grandfather is, but that many of the officers in the Garde á Cheval regiment, of which the Nicholas I headed, knew the truth – as did the Abbess of the monastery of St Serafin.

thus proves, I think, that the policy of Nicholas I, a policy followed by his descendants, was removed from aggressiveness. When the Tsar was asked through what towns he wanted the railroad to run, he took a pencil and across the map drew a straight line between St. Petersburg and Moscow.[10] The Emperor's wish was carried out, although it presented many difficulties. Maybe because of the lack of swerves and curves, it is so pleasant to travel on that line. Among the delegations that came in turn to thank the Emperor when the railroad was finished, there was one from the peasants of the Moscow government. The monarch, in excellent humour, spoke to every member of the group in particular and asked them how they had liked the trip.

"Very much, indeed!" they said.

"And how long did it take you to get here?" asked the Tsar with a pleasant smile.

"About two weeks, Your Majesty," was the unexpected reply.

The Emperor's face fell, and turning to the engineers who had built the line and to the railroad officials he demanded angrily the meaning of this.

"Your Majesty," ventured at this moment one of the delegates, "we could not have possibly made it any faster; what with the stops for the night and the relay of horses..."

"Horses!" exclaimed the Emperor. "Was that what the railroad was built for?" And, pointing toward the door, he cried, "Get out of my sight this minute."

In 1837 the Winter Palace burned almost to the ground – and it was the Tsar's wish to have it rebuilt within the year exactly to the last detail as it had been; an impossible task, it was supposed. Finding no one willing to undertake it, the Emperor appealed to

---

[10] This is an urban myth.

my grandfather. Exactly a year later the Tsar moved into the perfectly restored Palace.[11]

My father was a boy of fifteen when the Tsar Nicholas I died, and my grandfather, an old man then, bowed under his grief at having lost his dearest friend and beloved sovereign. Feeling that the new generation was not going to understand him, he retired from public work. Soon after he fell ill, and realising that he was going to die, he sent word to the young Tsar, Alexander II. The Emperor came immediately, and, walking straight into the bedroom, locked the door and remained for two hours talking to the dying man, while my father and his brothers waited in the next room. When the Emperor came out his eyes were full of tears, and, looking solemnly at the boys, he said, "I have never until now realised what a man your father is. I am losing my best friend." Then, shaking his finger at them, he exclaimed, "Live to be worthy of your father!" and without another word he strode out of the room.[12]

My father entered the *Preobrazhensky* regiment[13] as an officer when he was sixteen, and his military service did not leave him much time to take care of the estates he had inherited; but when he had attained the rank of colonel he left the army in order to devote all of his time to his lands, and from then on he stayed for the greater part of the year on his estates, only spending three of the winter months in Moscow.[14]

---

[11] The reconstruction apparently was initially less than perfect, had to be redone and cost far more than expected.

[12] Pyotr Andreevitch Kleinmichel was not loved but sometimes hated by Russian society. His role in building the Moscow–St. Petersburg railroad was immortalised by Nicholas Nekrasov in his poem The Railway, which describes the terrible conditions those who worked on its construction were subject to and the many deaths that eventuated. Tsar Alexander II actually dismissed Kleinmichel from office.

[13] One of the oldest and most elite guard regiments of the Russian Imperial Army.

[14] According to Olga, military service – to which all young men of the nobility aspired – was taken very seriously and discipline was very strict. To be an

My mother was my father's second wife; he was her senior by twenty-five years. His first wife, nee Countess Kankrine, had died very young in an accident, leaving two children, a boy and a girl. Soon after, the little girl died; Peter, the boy, was nine years old when my father married again.[15]

I have a vague recollection of my half-brother making me ride on his knee and of how I tugged at his blond moustache and fingered the shining epaulettes of his uniform. He was then already an officer in the *Preobrazhensky* regiment. He died when I was three years old.[16]

My mother was the daughter of Nicholas Bogdanoff, Marshal of the Nobility of the government of Koursk.[17] Her father was spoken of as the handsomest man in the government and his lavish hospitality had become proverbial. He had a genius for friendship and was much regretted at his death.

My grandmother left Koursk after her husband had died and went to live with two of her three sons on her estate twenty miles from

officer of the Imperial Navy of Russia was considered a high honour.

As every member of the Army and Navy wore his uniform all the time, it made him behave the best he could. Of course, some failed to hold their standard high, but then they were excluded from their regiment by the decision of their fellow officers, gathered in a so-called court of honour. This tendency to military service had one serious drawback – an officer had forcibly to neglect his estates.

[15] According to the letter written by Ella Kleinmichel to her niece, Countess Nina Viktorovna Kankrine was a beautiful young woman, but it had not been a happy marriage. She used to slip out of the windows at night to ride off on her horse to places unknown. (It is possible she suffered from depression.) When she was twenty-three she became ill and, while lying down one day, began to play with a toy revolver (or small pistol) given to her as a gift by her husband. No one saw what happened, but the gun went off and she died. Her young daughter, Elena, died from diphtheria not long after.

[16] Peter Constantinovitch died at age twenty-three from inflammation of the lungs (pneumonia), for which there was no cure at the time.

[17] Ekaterina (Catherine) Nicholaievna Bogdanoff.

the city.[18] We visited her every summer for two or three weeks and grandmother spent every spring with us in Moscow. Her birthday happened at that time, too, and we had always the same little ceremony to begin its celebration. She was very fond of flowers and particularly of hyacinths and we used to knock at her door early that day, each of us children carrying a pot of hyacinths and filing into the room by rank of height, I, the smallest, at the head of the procession. Grandmother never failed to express such surprise and delight that we felt quite certain she had not expected it. We loved grandmother dearly for, although over seventy years of age, she understood our youthful dreams and took part in all our joys and sorrows. Often we would sit around her watching her work at some very fine tapestry or embroider with the tiniest coloured beads. We would confide our childish secrets to her while she would listen gravely, looking at us from over her spectacles.

We were a family of five children, each one of us, I think, very different from the other.

Clair, the eldest, was called so in abbreviation for Cleopatra, a name which she cordially detested. She was rather older than her age in mind and manners and, though still a child, could be a friend to a grown-up person. With her very sensitive and kind heart she understood other people's troubles and won their affection by a million delicate and touching attentions.

Straightforward, truthful and kind, she had been ever since her early youth a reliable and trustworthy person. Because of these traits of her character Clair was treated by everyone almost like a grown-up girl and this was perhaps the reason why she called us, her younger sisters, "The Little Ones," and used at times to sermonise us, a treatment we somewhat resented.

She particularly took to heart the task of making a good boy of Dima, my brother. He was just two years younger than Clair and

---

[18] Catherine Petrovna Bogdanoff, nee Tchekarevsky.

was then at the age when boys dislike to be either fondled or preached to. Clair made the mistake of doing both. In the evenings she would go into his room and talk at great length of the defects in his character that he should try to improve and the qualities that he ought to develop. Dima tried to make it perfectly clear to Clair that he was bored. He listened for a while, yawning in a most insulting manner, then pretended to fall asleep. As these visits became more and more frequent, Dima grew so tired of them that one night, on hearing Clair's steps nearing his door, he hid behind it.

She had no sooner entered the room than Dima sprang at her shouting wildly. Clair fled in tears. My brother was punished, but Clair's feelings had been hurt and she never returned to his room.

Clair was almost fanatical in her patriotism. Russia meant everything to her. She disliked going abroad and a few weeks outside of our country was more than she could stand.

She was indignant that we, three younger sisters, had the habit of speaking French among ourselves and one day locked herself up in her room and cried all day because we had teased her by saying that some German people of our acquaintance thought she was the perfect type of a German girl. It was not true, of course, but she was too upset to believe that it had only been a mean joke.

As soon as she was old enough to do it, Clair took courses in nursing at a hospital and during the following summers spent the entire day cleaning out wounds, binding up fingers, distributing medicine, in a word, giving every kind of medical care to the peasants. They came from every part of the neighbourhood, sometimes fifty and sixty a day, until Clair was so exhausted that my mother was obliged to put an end to it.

In later years, Clair rose to biblical heights in her humble acceptance of the great misfortunes that were her tragic lot; although bereft of everyone she had ever loved – having lost her husband and all three of her children in unusually dramatic circumstances – she is the one who consoles and comforts in time of trouble and rejoices with others in their happiness.

Dima (Vladimir) was next in age.[19] He was very reserved and there was a certain aloofness in his manner that came, I think, from his shyness. He was handsome, and extremely intelligent; he had a very artistic disposition and a highly developed sense of beauty, rare for a child of his age. He was very musical and played the piano and the mandolin exquisitely, and, last but not least, he possessed an inimitable sense of humour the like of which I have never met again. He was an inveterate reader and would much rather stay at home buried in a book than go out to play with his friends. Dima and I were extremely fond of each other. He took tender care of me when I was a baby whenever he happened to be with me and used to stay with me hour after hour when I was sick, telling me stories and playing with me. He was sincerely grieved and sorry for me that I did not turn out to be pretty like my sisters.

Natalie – Tata, as she had insisted upon calling herself as a baby – was all imagination and living in a fairyland of her own. Our dolls seemed to come to life in her hands; she often staged whole plays with them. And sometimes, too, she told us long, mysterious, breathtaking stories that held us spellbound for hours at a time. It kept us very still to the great delight of our governesses who would thus get a breathing space from watching us, for this was no sinecure. In our games Tata was always the leader. Her fertile imagination had forever something new in store for us. Taking advantage of the interest and new ideas she brought into our games, Tata invariably took the most enviable and preeminent part in them. If there was to be a queen in the game, Tata was the queen. If a witch was supposed to live in the woods catching children for her meals, she was the witch and we two younger sisters were the children. She was an autocrat in our

---

[19] "i" in Russian names and words is pronounced like "ee" and "a" like "ah", thus Dima sounds like Deema and Tata like Tahta.

little world, and it seemed so natural that it should be so that we did not demur.

One day Tata conceived the unfortunate idea of playing at being Christian martyrs. Of course, we were the martyrs and she – the executioner. She flogged us with a skipping rope, inflicting on us quite bad bruises. The important part of the game was to stand this without any outward sign of suffering, and I must admit with a certain amount of pride that not a single sound escaped our lips, though Tata was thorough in her methods. That night the traces of our tortures, numerous red and swollen stripes across our backs, appeared to the horrified gaze of our maid. She reported to "Higher Quarters" and the game of martyrs was forever banished from our repertoire.

Ella (Elena) was nicknamed "Quicksilver" by our governesses and teachers; she gave them the most trouble. Extremely gay, alive, always up to some mischief without meaning to be bad, always caught at it and punished; forgetting it the next minute, good humoured and unselfish, teasing her teachers, but still loved by them – that was Ella. One day my mother came as usual to see us in our nursery and asked Nurse if we had been behaving. Nurse, who had a weakness for Ella, remarked that she was particularly good and quiet today and had been sitting by her side for a long while. Alas, that good behaviour was soon to be explained. Ella had been busy cutting out the pretty designs in Nurse's printed dress, while Nurse was for once peacefully knitting her stocking.

Ella never cried when she was hurt. To prove her courage, she once deliberately pulled out a big lock of hair right above her forehead and did it without wincing. This unnecessary feat brought annoying results. The new hair grew now perpendicularly to her brow and ever since, to look tidy, she has been obliged to have it curled. To punish Ella was very easy, the main idea was to keep her quiet. She was usually given some crocheting to do. Seated by a window, her legs twisted around the legs of her chair, she would do row after row of that endless work. Holding it close to her eyes and squinting in the process, she would stick her tongue out and the bunch of new hair, standing out in a straight line, would follow the movement of the crochet as it progressed along the woollen band.

I was the cry-baby. I seemed to have an inexhaustible source of tears, always ready to be let out. Anything might start the flood, but usually I was sorry for somebody and sometimes for myself. I never cried aloud – the tears would just stream down my cheeks until I felt relieved. Tata and Ella loved to tease me and then would exclaim gleefully, "Look, her nose is turning green already. Beware of the flood!" That was enough. I would sneak into a corner and surely enough the dam was broken. I never admitted why I was crying and everybody else felt annoyed at me for having those frequent crying spells.[20]

My greatest ambition as a child was to learn how to read. Having reached the age of three, I started to beg everyone I could get hold of to teach me, but my parents had strictly forbidden this to be done, so that all my attempts were thwarted. It was thought at that time that a child's mind should not be developed too early. Little by little, though, with ruse and perseverance, and letter by letter, I picked up all the alphabet and by four years of age could read in Russian and knew most of the Latin letters. I then began to read everything I could lay my hands upon, so that our governesses, in whose charge we were in the daytime, hid all

---

[20] This is one of the stories I discovered amongst Olga's memories:

I remember quite clearly how at the age of one and a half or two years old; I was sitting on an ottoman in our playroom in Moscow, my legs stretched out in front of me. My nurse was busying herself with something, the door opened and Nikolai, the man whose duty it was to stoke the stoves, peeped in and, seeing but the nurse and me, entered the room. I was told in later years he adored children and took every opportunity to have a look at us. He came over, knelt by the ottoman and spoke to me. And for some reason (was it shyness?) I could not make myself speak to him – though it made me unhappy. Nurse came and told me I should say something to Nikolai, who was so nice to me, but the more she coaxed me, the more tongue-tied I felt. This I remember as clearly as day. I asked myself, "Why can't I say something, why, why?" And I was ready to cry.

books away from me on the top of the bookcases, where I could not reach them. Thus I was often left to stand with hands clasped behind my back, face upturned, gazing wistfully at the spot where the object of my dreams had disappeared.

Tata, Ella and I were reared together ever since I was transferred to the care of Nurse from the hands of my wet-nurse, Anna. A wet-nurse in those days was quite an important person. She wore the national Russian costume with a great number of coloured ribbons and beads; everybody tried to fulfill her caprices and to keep her in good humour; her meals were served to her in her room.

This last privilege almost led to a drama in my wet-nurse's case. Anna was one day caught feeding me, then a baby seven months old, with *borscht*, a heavy beet and cabbage soup. My mother nearly fainted, though I seemed to relish our national dish. Questioned, my wet-nurse confessed that she had been doing this for nearly three months already. I am not sure if this settled the question of Anna's departure, but I know that I will like *borscht* until the end of my days – maybe because I tasted it so early.

Soon after that I was moved into the big nursery with Tata and Ella, under the rule of our German nurse. Nurse was kindness and gentleness personified and we adored her. I can still hear her greeting us every morning with the same words. Lifting her hands as if in benediction, she would say:

"God bless you and send His holy angels to your side that they might protect and guide you in your life!"

Then she would kiss each of us fondly and we felt that the day had started right.[21]

---

[21] It was due to this German nurse that German was the first foreign language the children learnt. In her unpublished memories, Olga wrote:

I shall always remember when, having put us to bed, she would go to each of us in turn, put her dry and bony hand on our head and say: "God bless you, and

In the morning we used to take a ride on the back of a meek old pony in a saddle that looked not unlike a comfortable little wicker chair. It was padded and covered with red velvet. In my case, the

send his holy angels around you, that they watch over you." This blessing and prayer brought such a feeling of peace and security to us, we fell asleep relaxed and happy.

Nyanechka (Nanny) always wore grey and a little black lace affair pinned on the top of her head. She never raised her voice or got angry or even looked strict. There was always an aura of quiet calmness about her. Even naughty Ella obeyed her without a murmur. We all adored her.

One day, I must have been four or five years old, we were having a doll's tea party in our playroom. Nyanechka was sitting by the window. I glanced at her from time to time, she was wiping the little teacups we had been using and I felt a pang of guilt that here we were having a good time but creating more work for Nyanechka. The next time I glanced up my heart stood still. Nyanechka was looking out of the window with unseeing eyes. I had never seen her look so terribly serious and sad. Her hands holding the tea towel and a little cup lay motionless in her lap. Her mind was far away on something that filled her with grief. I dropped everything, ran across to her and, burying my face in her lap, burst into tears. At once she was there again. She stroked my hair and spoke gently to me, "What is it Olgachen? Why are you crying? Go and play with the others. See what a good time they are having?" But my heart was breaking and I could not tell Nyanechka why, she would have blamed herself for letting her feelings show.

It was only many years later we found out how unspeakably mean her two daughters (who lived in Kiev) were to her. Ella heard about it first. The two daughters with whom Nyanechka had gone to live after we grew up, were making her life miserable and one winter night they turned her out into the street with no place to go. She wandered out into the dark, snowy night holding a little bundle of clothes. Somebody must have notified Ella (Nyanechka would never have said a word herself). Ella took Tata with her, arranged for room and board in an old people's home outside of St. Petersburg and went to Kiev. She told the two mean women what she thought of them, picked up Nyanechka and installed her in her new abode. Poor Nyanechka was very, very old by then, this was just before World War I broke out, I do not think she realised where she was or what was happening to her, but she was her old gentle, loving self as before. The war pretty soon broke out and Ella's husband left for the front. Ella would go and sit at Nyanechka's knee, put her head against it and cry her heart out. And dear old Nyanechka stroked Ella's head with her withered hand and tried to comfort her, not knowing what was happening. A few short months afterward she quietly went to heaven.

pony was led by the bridle by one of the grooms, my nurse holding me with both hands – an unnecessary precaution as I was strapped in. Tata and Ella, respectively three years and eighteen months my seniors, awaiting their turn, closed the procession, envy written all over their faces. We would thus proceed along a path that ran the whole length of the house. It was quite a ride for me for the house, as I said before, was a large one. Arriving at the end of the path, I had to give up my place to the next lucky sister.

During the day, my father took one of us sometimes with him to inspect the work done in the various parts of the estate. As this was considered a special favour, we felt very proud of it. Off we would go, seated side by side in the wide-open carriage driven by four horses, with Yegor, my father's personal coachman, on the box.

Yegor was an ex-serf that, like the rest of the serfs on our lands, had expressed the desire to stay in my father's service. He was a very dignified, handsome old man, with silver white curly hair and large dark eyes. He considered us almost like his grandchildren. Although addressing us in a very formal way, he often used to pat us on the head and made me climb on his shoulders when we came to see the horses in the stable.

As we drove along, my father used to explain to me everything that was being done on the several *khutor* or farms into which the estate had been divided to make the management easier. My father had been awarded gold medals by the Ministry of Agriculture for the model management of his land, and his breeding farms of cattle, fowl, pigs and sheep received the highest awards at both national and local exhibitions. He took an equal interest in the little town of Potchep, that with the years had spread out almost to the gates of our park. Through his pains, a railroad now connected Potchep with large commercial centres, and in the business section of the little town he built an entire block of stores, which he rented to the local merchants at a ridiculously low price. How often I heard the manager blame my father for what he called an unnecessary generosity, but he received the same reply:

"Let them be – I want them to make good."

A great number of the houses that my father owned in Potchep, he gave into the lifelong possession of his old employees' families, as we found out after his death.[22]

Potchep having no regular fire company, my father donated the whole equipment: fire engines, trucks and firemen's apparel for twenty men, who were trained in this line at his expense. It was a great day when everything was ready and there was a demonstration of the fire company's work. All our family drove out in several carriages to the spot where the demonstration was to take place. A large and excited crowd had already gathered at some distance from the barn that my father had sacrificed for this occasion. As soon as we had settled in our places, the signal was given and up thundered the fire engine and the trucks all spick and span, the firemen in their new uniforms, their casques dazzlingly bright in the sunshine. The men attacked the barn, as if a fierce fire were raging in it. They showed agility and presence of mind. The crowd cheered. When all was over a delegation from the inhabitants of Potchep thanked my father and we drove home very happy and excited.

Alas, the next year, while we were as usual spending the winter in Moscow, our house in Potchep caught fire. The firemen, I am afraid, did not show as much efficiency. A great part of the rooms were badly damaged. We never returned to Potchep in the summer, but afterwards spent the summer months in Ivnya, an estate in the government of Koursk.

---

[22] During the time Constantin owned Potchep it was, by all accounts, a thriving town with many small businesses, craftspeople and factories which produced a variety of products. Constantin also built a brick factory and the bricks were used for many local products.

My parents, though, used to go to Potchep alone two or three times during the summer and these were gloomy days for me. I particularly missed my mother, who represented for me everything that is good, just and beautiful. She somehow knew how to be strict and yet caressing, firm but at the same time loving and tender.

My father, reserved and particularly exacting, inspired a certain amount of fear in us; but he had, I think, a weakness for me as the youngest, although he would not admit it. Many times I interceded with him for my sisters and brother and, invariably, when I began to plead for them, his face would light up into one of his kindly smiles and I knew that I had won a pardon. My friendship with my father grew so strong as time went on that even after the long years that he has been dead, I miss him more than I can tell.

TWO
# OUR MOSCOW HOME
*Constructed from the unpublished memories of Olga Woronoff*

I was only eleven months old when my family moved to Moscow, where we lived for many years. I was told that, when my family were leaving Koursk, many friends came to see us off, bringing bouquets and baskets of flowers (which were placed in the entrance to the car and the corridor), one of which caught fire, endangering all of us. I was handed out of the train window to some friends outside, and the fire was put out quickly.

I wish to add here that the day I was born, my parents were visited by Father John of Kronstadt, a priest of a saintly life (and now proclaimed a saint for his ascetic and saintly life, his complete dedication to his calling and the many, many miracles that happened through his intercession).[1] I feel humbly grateful that this saintly man picked me up in his arms that day, prayed for me and my family and gave me his blessing. Father John became well-known for his untiring efforts and prayers among the poor, the unbelievers – everyone who came for his help and intercession. Even foreigners would write to him asking him for his prayers. In Kronstadt, a city near St. Petersburg where he

---

[1] Father John of Kronstadt was a member of an ultra right-wing organisation in Russia which was well known for its anti-Semitic views. He was canonised in 1964 by the Russian Orthodox Church Abroad and in 1990 by the Russian Orthodox Church.

lived and worked, he had created houses for the poor. Many people, at one time unbelievers, or outcasts of all kinds, found faith through him and spiritual and material help. The church of which he was the priest was always crowded to capacity. The miracles he performed and his insight into people's minds and hearts were truly wonderful. I must have been about twelve years old when Father John came to Moscow and visited us to celebrate a *moleben* (prayer).

Perhaps my earliest memories are connected with Moscow, where our family occupied a very large old house belonging to Count Bobrinsky who had kept for himself a small apartment on the ground floor, where he very seldom stayed.[2] I had only one brief glance into it one day and remember that it was crowded with antiques of every kind. Count Bobrinsky was a passionate collector of antiques and travelled around a lot in Russia and abroad.

The house was large and had four wings; it should have been kept as a museum after we left. Count Bobrinsky had told my father that he would have leased it to no one but him and, after the death of my father and our move to Tsarskoye Selo, he closed down the house and gave all the furniture to the museum of Alexander III. We occupied the two upper floors as well as additional rooms for the seamstresses and maid quarters. The second floor was truly palatial now that I think of it. In my childhood I took it for granted. The house was old and I remember being told that some of Napoleon's generals had been housed in it when he was in Moscow.

In front was a big yard fenced off from the street. In the spring we sometimes played tennis in it. As you entered the front door you found yourself in a vestibule whose ceiling was supported by four (if my memory serves me right) fat columns. To the right a door led to the apartment of the doorman – always in his dark blue coat with silver buttons and a dark blue cap – to the left was

---

[2] Alexei Alekseevich Bobrinsky, the address was Malaya Nikitskaya Street 12, Moscow.

the door to Count Bobrinsky's apartment. Straight ahead a few carpeted steps led to a glass door which led to the garden. The stairs were separated to the right and left, and at each turning met again on a landing, then rose in a wider sweep to the second floor. Along the railings pots of green plants gave a look of freshness to the top landing which ran right and left to two doors. The one on the left was always closed. Behind it were my father's rooms. Since the ceilings were high, the doors were high. They were decorated in muted, gilded wood designs. One entered through the door at the right into a second vestibule which had three doors. The left-most one, straight ahead as you entered the vestibule, opened into a secondary dining room, the one on the right closed off the stairs that led to the third floor. The middle one opened onto the end of a corridor, which one crossed to open another door into the dining room proper. It is amazing to me now, when I look back on our life in that house, how impeccably everything was kept, just as it had been one hundred years ago. I mean by that not the cleanliness, which goes without saying, but for example the draperies at the windows were the same – a soft red in heavy silk. Under them were curtains of creamy white silk bordered by a string of gilt wood pompoms. The furniture was also covered with that subdued red silk.

Near the windows was the door into the ballroom. Another door opened into the small dining room, which really served as a buffet, where the dishes and glassware were kept. The ballroom was large, or so it seemed to me. Its walls looked like marble. One end opened onto a balcony that looked out onto the front yard. At the far end there was a small room with an elongated opening high up in the wall under the ceiling, like a very wide window without glass. It was called *hore* (chorus) and had heavy yellow silk draperies to match the upholstery of the ballroom furniture. Once or twice as a child, I climbed up the steps leading to that little room to have a peep at the dancers from behind the musicians. Supper was served from the small dining room around midnight, when there was a break in the dancing and many tables were set up in the ballroom for the guests.

There was no electricity in the house until my parents had it put in much later and I remember the balls given for my eldest sister by candlelight. It made no difference in the quantity of light of course, only it made the room somewhat warmer, but I liked it so much better than electricity, especially in that old house.

At the age of seventeen we made our debut at a ball given by our parents. It was the first time we appeared in a long dress with a train. Imagine my disappointment when my mother told me I would not wear a long dress at my debut as it would look funny on me. I was then very thin and slight and had such a mass of hair that, when it was coiled at the back of my head, it made my head look enormous. I had not been allowed to wear my hair up until seventeen, as my mother thought I looked ridiculous and I had to have it in a long braid down my back. And now, this second blow, just the thing I had wished for most and looked forward to with joy. I implored my mother in vain but she was as firm as a rock. Then, for the first time in my life, I decided to disobey. I begged our dressmaker to arrange the dress I was going to wear and when it was all ready, to add a train. Dresses were rather complicated at that time, but it was easy to add an extra frill or something of that kind. However, as I was going against my mother's wishes, I had a hard time to persuade our dressmaker to do it.

Of course, this was done secretly – and it was with a thumping heart that I appeared before my mother half an hour before the guests began to arrive. My skirt lay a few inches on the ground and my mother was amused and indignant at the same time. "I wanted to save you from ridicule," she said. "You look like a dressed-up monkey! Now bear it as you can."

But I was so happy nothing could spoil the joy I felt at hearing the lovely little rustle of my dress trailing behind me.

At that time only quadrilles, cotillions, mazurka and waltzes were danced, and it was considered most improper to waltz around the room more than once with the same man. We were not allowed to talk with our partner except during quadrilles. But the greatest dance of the ball was the mazurka (a type of quadrille, only longer and more complicated), and you had supper with the partner you danced mazurka with.[3]

The figures (or parts) of this quadrille are interrupted by mazurka and waltzes, which you can dance with different partners, and this is the moment when it is easy to see when a girl has success. Large baskets of flowers are distributed between the men, and they offer a bunch of them to the girl they invite to dance. If a girl is popular, the flowers pile up in a huge heap on a chair placed near hers. My two middle sisters, who were extremely pretty, would come home from a ball and fill their bathtub with flowers, until they were put into vases in the morning. Flowers were ordered in huge quantity from Nice, usually of one or two colours, roses and carnations prevailing. They were brought in at different times during the mazurka and cotillion.

I remember a ball where a cart full of the most beautiful pink carnations was brought in pulled by a big dog. The hall entry was a huge shield of white carnations in the shape of a fan. Three men had to carry it, and by the end of the dance the room looked like one big flower garden. Balls rarely started before 11pm and often ended at 6 or 7 in the morning.

My husband told me how often, as a young officer, he had had no time to sleep after leaving a ball, but took a shower and went to his service – at which no excuse was accepted if you were even a few minutes late.

Opposite the door leading to the dining room was the door to the living room, which should really be called the salon. What a beautiful room it was! The walls were covered with blue silk framed in gilt wood. The colour was a wonderful, subdued blue, neither too dark nor light, and the silk had a satin and a dull stripe. The ceiling was decorated with paintings of *amours* with

---

[3] Most likely this was Durang's Russian Mazurka Quadrille, which was more complicated than a normal mazurka.

bows and arrows. I am not sure, but I think there were five windows. In the middle of the room, against the wall and between each pair of windows, two sandy-coloured, marble-topped tables stood. They formed a triangle, with the wall being the third side, encircling a group of palm trees and lower green plants. On these tables stood the most beautiful, delicately wrought china statuettes (quite definitely French). I remember in particular a couple dancing – the lady holding up her dress with one hand, just enough to reveal the dainty lace (how artistically fine this work was) trimming her skirt under it.

Beyond the salon was a sort of in-between small room, through which one passed straight ahead into my mother's bedroom. From this small room there was a door led into the corridor, across which were my father's rooms. The small room served as a sort of library or more intimate small living-room. My mother's bedroom, the walls of which were covered with green satin and silk, striped as the salon's blue, held some beautiful antique French furniture – for example some cupboards of black wood ornamented in relief with the figures of small birds, leaves, cherries and such, made of marble of various colours. Of course, they must have been French for they were in excellent taste. I wish I had thought of taking pictures of all these things and of the rooms – but they would probably have perished anyway in the great debacle. Probably the most remarkable feature of all these front rooms were the parquets, which were a work of art. They were laid out in designs of black, white, brown and beige wood. Each room had squares of different designs.

My mother's bed was enormous – we children would climb on it and it easily held four of us in a row. It was covered with a very soft and pale-coloured satin – somewhere between pink and mauve. A small door led into the corridor at the left end of it, which was Mother's maid's room and a large bathroom. As I said before, my father's rooms were on the other side of the corridor and they looked out onto the garden.

I wish I had pictures of the garden. It was fairly large for a city. A shady walk with tall trees ran on three sides of it. Beyond the wall was a side-street, but the wall was high enough to give us complete privacy. In the middle were sandy paths around flower beds. My father, who was very fond of flowers (in Ivnya he had the rarest kinds of French roses), had filled the shady parts under the trees with a profusion of lilies-of-the-valley. It was a delight when their aroma filled my father's rooms in the spring. His rooms were strictly a man's rooms. From the corridor one had to pass through a small, windowless room where his clothes closets and bureaus stood, then into a room holding a leather-covered divan, a desk and assorted chairs and small tables. It was not a large room. My father never used it himself as far as I remember. He preferred his large desk in the bedroom, next to a fireplace. Above the desk hung a portrait of the Emperor Nicholas I. Opposite the fireplace was a davenport covered with dark green leather and embellished with fine and sober bronze ornamentation – quite *Directoire*. Other furniture (easy chairs, a *table de toilette* in the same style) supplied his needs. Along another wall stood my father's bed, in which he spent, due to his gout, a great deal of his time. Behind the head of the bed was a *kiot*, a shrine for his icons, before which an oil-lamp always burned. My father was a very poor sleeper and he spent most of the night reading. Besides conservative Russian newspapers, he subscribed to French newspapers and to several historical Russian magazines. He was immensely well-read and his memory was fabulous. I remember how we listened open-mouthed one day when he and his old friend threw out questions at each other, for example on history, to see who remembered best. His friend, too, was a prodigious reader, and their erudition was amazing. It was truly stimulating to listen to them and I often wondered if I ever could acquire so much knowledge.

Between the front rooms and those at the back of the house there was a long corridor. One end led to my mother's maid's room; the other, to the right, was the door to the dining room, and on the left the upper vestibule. Straight ahead was a big mirror. In the middle of the corridor hung one of the big bronze chandeliers with (I suppose of course glass) delicate crystal chains.

From the second floor vestibule a door opened onto a staircase that led to the third floor, which was mostly the children's kingdom. At the top of the flight of steps, there was a door on the left, which opened upon a landing at which the stairs separated into two flights, one right and one left. Straight ahead was an alcove, where we children used to hide in (until forbidden to) in order to jump out and scare the wits out of people coming down one of the flights of steps. The steps led to a corridor which ran almost the length of the house. From one flight of steps to the other in the corridor there was a handrail.

Our children's rooms looked out front. In early childhood Tata, Ella and I slept in the same room, although I remember an earlier period where I slept apart from the others in a bed with netting on both sides.

THREE
# FAMILIAR FACES

While in the country we were very much together, in town we saw our parents much less frequently. Though they continued to guide every detail of our lives and education, our daily lives were quite separate from theirs. We were not often allowed out of our quarters, except when we were to kiss our parents good morning or good night, or on those occasions when we were sent for. I did not particularly like being told to come down to the drawing room. It happened as a rule when one of my mother's guests had asked to see us. It was annoying to be kissed by a lot of people, patted on the cheek, admired and asked a number of questions that were sometimes not so easy to answer.

We were not supposed to talk unless spoken to, but Ella often kept my mother on tenterhooks for, if she felt she was seeing something unusual, Ella simply could not help asking questions. It happened once that when we came down to the drawing room, there was among others a man who was entirely bald. He had not a single hair on his head.

Ella, with a finger in her mouth, observed him for a while with a perplexed air. Then, before my mother could interfere, she asked in a stage whisper,

"Mamma, where in the world does Mr L's forehead end?"

Thus, as soon as my mother would see Ella staring at one of the guests, she used to send us upstairs on some pretext.

Every Sunday we were taken to church to the Nikitsky Monastery which was close to our house.[1] We were very much impressed by the atmosphere of the place. We watched with awe the black figures of the nuns gliding noiselessly through the church and were fascinated by their pale, austere faces, with eyes rarely raised from the ground. We loved the grave notes of the church bells and the severely monotonous monastic singing. Life in a convent seemed to us the ideal thing.

But, on the other hand, we were very much attracted by the ballet, to which we were taken quite often. This was fairyland to us. *The Sleeping Beauty*, *The Swan's Lake*, *Coppélia* and many other exquisite ballets held us entranced throughout the performance and we lived under their spell for weeks after.

One day all three of us, Tata, Ella and I, set off to find my mother and told her that we had something important to talk over with her. We asked her if she would let us enter the Nikitsky Monastery as nuns. My mother answered that, being five, six and eight years old, we were just a trifle too young to take such a serious step.

"Then," we said, "maybe we can join the Moscow ballet?"

About this time, my life was already peopled with many familiar faces outside the nursery. Among them were Ivan, the butler, and Nicanorytch, my father's personal valet. Both were ex-serfs. It was only our family that called Ivan by his first name alone. His long service in the house had made him something more than a servant and the rest of the household spoke of him as Ivan Mikhailovitch. He was a quiet, meek old man, and somehow I felt always sorry for him.

---

[1] Possibly Nikitsky Monastery in Kashira, 124 km from Moscow.

Nicanorytch's first name was Alexander, but we gave him a more familiar appellation (Nicanorytch means, son of Nicanor), because we were very fond of him. He never let anyone else wait on my father, although he spoke to him in a gruff manner and often grumbled at him. I think Nicanorytch was the only being on earth from whom my father accepted such treatment. He knew that the old man was heart and soul devoted to him and repaid him by a deep affection. Whenever my father told him to take a rest, the old servant looked at him with hurt eyes and replied, "If you want to get rid of me, say so." Nicanorytch had a set, serious expression on his face – it was almost like a mask. I saw him smile only when he bent down to talk to me, calling me "Little Countess Olga". I let him carry me in his arms down to my father's room, for I felt that it made him happy, although I rather enjoyed the pleasure of walking down the many steps. Nicanorytch was always around whenever my father wanted him, so, when it one day happened that he failed to answer the bell, my father grew worried and sent another servant to the old man's room, where Nicanorytch was found dead.

There was also Grisha, whose sole duty was to heat the stoves. He had been brought over by my mother from my grandmother's estate. In his native village he had been known as "Grisha the Storm," for the way he walked along the street, as if a strong wind were blowing him along. Due to his slow wits, he was the laughingstock of the peasants. But the climax came when Dima, having found out the poor fellow's lifelong desire to own a watch, made him a present of a large alarm clock. The same day, Grisha was seen parading through the streets of his village with the alarm clock hanging from his neck on a string and loudly ticking away on his chest. After that, life became miserable for Grisha and my mother offered to let him enter our service.

Early one dark winter morning, Grisha was, according to his habit, lying on his stomach across the corridor, starting a fire in one of the stoves, when my mother came hurrying along. One of my sisters had fallen ill and she had been called to her bedside. Unaware of Grisha's long body barring her way, she tripped over him in the darkness and fell. Grisha explained afterwards that he had been so startled by my mother's unexpected appearance that instead of getting up, he covered his eyes with both hands and lay still.

Then there were Mademoiselle Keller, the housekeeper, and her ninety-five-year-old mother, Madame Keller. They belonged to a good family but had lost their fortune. They were very well educated and spoke several languages. Madame Keller was a frail, little, old woman, dried up with age; she used to hold on to the wall when she walked – it seemed almost that the slightest breeze might blow her away like a feather, but she had the most lucid mind and not only remembered every detail of her past life, but was absolutely conscious of her present surroundings. She was always busy at some mending and most surprisingly was in no need of spectacles. She had occupied the same position in my Grandmother Kleinmichel's house as her daughter did in ours, and it was she who told us of the Emperor Nicholas's frequent visits, of his fondness for my father, of his great charm and magnetic personality.[2]

When we listened to her it was as if we walked back through many years into the faraway time of my father's childhood. We could almost see him taking a brisk walk with his brothers and tutor in the big garden of my grandparent's place in St. Petersburg, during a particularly cold winter when the air was so sharp that crows dropped down dead in their flight. We could picture grandmother embroidering by the window, then turning to her housekeeper and companion, and saying, "I see the Emperor driving up to our door – leave us now, my dear."

And how stricken they all were by the Tsar's unexpected and untimely death, and how grandfather told his family that the Emperor's last words to his son and heir had been, "Serve Russia!"

---

[2] Countess Kleopatra Petrovna Kleinmichel nee Ilyinskaya was Olga's paternal grandmother. See Chapter 1, footnote 9 regarding the Emperor and Constantin.

Aline Keller, her daughter, was an old spinster who had not married so as to keep company with her mother. Apart from a certain bitterness that this sacrifice had left in her, she was the gayest, most companionable person. She was considered a member of the family and took my mother's place when my parents were away. We thought she was old-fashioned in her ideas, for she often proclaimed herself shocked at what she called our "modern ways."

"Young ladies," she would exclaim reprovingly, lifting her eyes to the ceiling, "in my days, young girls used not to sit with their legs crossed. I am ashamed of you."

There was our family doctor, too, whom we very informally called "Vassiliok," (his first name was Vassily). He had known us ever since I was a few months old and we could not imagine a day to pass without seeing him. He had taught us little songs and nursery rhymes, which we sang to him in chorus as soon as he appeared in the door of our nursery. Under his very morose and reserved manner, he hid a very affectionate heart and a world of idealism.

I was his favourite, and regularly every year since I was old enough, he took me, with my parent's permission, to the circus. I think he enjoyed it just as much as I did and we both reacted to it in the same way. Off we would go gravely, hand in hand, and watch the performance intently and silently to the end, and nobody could tell from the expression of our faces that we had had the excitement of our lives; but at home I squeezed him in my arms and murmured a heartfelt "thank you" into his ear.

Vassiliok had liberal ideas and, dropping his usual taciturnity, he often got into heated political arguments with my father. But while my father was excited and angry, Vassiliok became only a shade paler and his low voice trembled in wrath. Vassiliok believed in the benefit of great changes but, when the revolution came, with all its blood and ruthless cruelty, he was shaken to the depths of his soul. He did not want that.

As we grew up, Nurse's place was taken by Mrs Monton, an English nursery governess. With her was her daughter Jessie, who I thought was a beauty. She was tall, dark skinned and had fuzzy black hair. Now we had a governess for each language, English, French and German, in turn for a day. They all lived in the house.

We took our dancing lessons in the ballroom. Our teacher was considered the best ballet-master in Moscow. He had once been an outstanding dancer on the stage of the Moscow Great Theatre, but although he had still kept a great agility, he looked like a well-preserved mummy. His lessons were so interesting and he was so exacting that we soon began to dance very well and developed a real passion for it. From time to time, we learned some "character dance" and performed it before our family.

The Grand Duke Serge, then Governor General of Moscow, who loved children and who, with his wife, the Grand Duchess Elizabeth, sister of the Empress Alexandra, often saw my parents, expressed the desire to see them. So one day, at a big party that my parents gave for them, each one of us performed a dance as a surprise to the guests of honour. I was eight years old and had two dances to do. In the first one, I represented a snowflake and came out on the stage clapping my hands together as if in cold. I was dressed in white with bits of white down flying around me at the end of invisible threads. I circled the stage in little jumping steps and came to a stop facing the audience – about four hundred people – then I grew really cold with stage fright and all of a sudden forgot the whole dance. In vain did my mother and our teacher show me from the side scenes in explanatory gestures how to go on. I gave up and flew off the stage and into their arms weeping, while a thunder of applause accompanied my exit. The Grand Duke asked to see me. He told me how much he had loved my dance and how sorry he was that it had been so short. My mother made me do the other one, a Japanese dance, and this went off smoothly for I had regained some of my confidence – I was certain now that no one had noticed how miserably I had failed.

FOUR
# IVNYA

In Moscow, our days were very busy. A priest taught us the Holy Scripture and the history of the Church and besides the lessons in languages and all the other subjects, we had music and drawing lessons.

In the first warm days of the spring, when we used to get ready for our examinations (which we passed at one of the Moscow schools), we would begin to dream of the yearly journey to our summer home, Ivnya. This journey could warrant the term of migration, perhaps; for, besides our parents, my brother, my three sisters and myself, there were our three governesses, our Russian teacher, Mrs Monton and Jessie, a Russian and a Swiss tutor for my brother, a doctor, two dressmakers and some of the servants. The bustle and excitement of many people traveling was so thrilling to us children.

It was a great moment for us when our train finally stopped at our station, and we hurried toward the carriages waiting for us there. Each of them was pulled by four horses harnessed side by side; the coachmen wore their sleeveless, black velvet coats, close-fitting from shoulders to waist, thence falling in many folds like a skirt, and worn over a silk shirt of a bright colour. On their heads sat their small, round, black felt caps crowned with peacock feathers. As soon as we were settled in our respective carriages, we set off upon the fifteen-mile drive to Ivnya.

Once outside the little town we would fly along at an invigorating speed, the two horses in the middle of the team at a wide trot, the horses on either side galloping, carrying their necks arched and their heads gracefully turned to their own side of the road as had been the fashion in Russia for ages. A long training is required for the horses to run in this manner, and a horse schooled for the left flank of a team cannot be harnessed on the right flank.

Usually it would be close upon sunset when we started on these drives, and darkness gathered quickly; but about four miles from Ivnya, where, atop of a hill, a windmill reaches its long arms up to the dark sky, we would be met by several men on horseback carrying burning torches. Keeping in line with our carriages, they would accompany us at a gallop, holding the long torches in outstretched hands, the butt ends resting on their stirrups. Two miles farther, where the road turns at the edge of a wood, we could catch our first sight of the glittering, lighted windows of our house, still far away on a hill and surrounded by masses of black trees. Then downhill we galloped, the horses' hoofs thundered over the bridge across the pond; suddenly a mysterious silence was about us as we drove into the park, rolling noiselessly over the sand-strewn driveway until we arrived in front of the church that stood just opposite the house. Invariably we stopped there first to hear a *Te Deum* and to offer thanksgiving prayers for the end of our happy journey.[1] The church was brightly lighted inside, and the priest met us, cross in hand, with a few words of greeting. Outside of the church the head gardener stood with his help waiting for us to come out and, after my parents had been greeted, they offered each of us a bouquet of flowers. The director of the sugar factory, the manager of the estate and the chief superintendent presented their greetings in turn.

We children then hurried to our rooms on the other side of the house. It was a great joy for us to be here again. Everything

---

[1] A *Te Deum* is a hymn or prayer.

appeared wonderful to us. There seemed even to be a particularly lovely odour in the rooms; was it just the fragrance of the spring air, heavy with the scent of lilacs that grew in abundance in the park, or was there also a touch of something indefinable, maybe of fresh paint, recently waxed floors and sheets that smelled slightly of mint and wormwood? I would lean out of the window, rapturously taking in the beauty of the familiar scenery; the wide lawn, bright green in the moonlight, the heavy, mysterious clusters of trees crowding around it, the dark sky with stars as clear and sparkling as tears. I would wonder at the peaceful quiet, would listen to the cricket in the grass, to the far away hooting of an owl and would turn away reluctantly to follow my sisters into the dining room. There, the candles would be shedding their mellow glow from the tall old-fashioned candelabra onto the flower-bedecked table and from their dimmed gilded frames the old portraits seemed to watch us with mysterious smiles.

After a long dinner, during which the grownup people talked of things concerning the estate and I nodded drowsily over my plate, I would be sent to bed. Cosily tucked in, I would watch the flickering flame of the *lampada* burning before the icons in a corner of the nursery until my eyes would close of themselves and I would wander away into the land of happy dreams.[2]

It was our parents' wish that every morning, even before we had breakfast, we should go to pray for the dead in our cemetery, on the other side of the church, where several members of our family had been put to eternal rest. There were the graves of my father's first wife and of his eldest sister, of my half-brother, Peter, and of other relatives, as well as of several persons that had not belonged to our family. Among them was that of my mother's Swiss governess who had spent nearly all of her life in my mother's family and who had died in our house; and that of an old gardener who had expressed the desire to be buried near the graves of those whom he had served.

---

[2] A lampada is a little oil lamp of coloured glass.

One of my father's ancestors by the name of Nicanor Pereversev, who had lived in the eighteenth century, was also buried there.³ I often stood before his portrait, that hung in the dining room, studying it and trying to imagine from the jovial countenance and somewhat sarcastic smile what it must be like to live exactly as one pleased – for my father had told me many stories of this ancestor's extravagance and of his gay resolve never to have a caprice, or to let his friends have a caprice, that he would not immediately gratify. To test the strength of this resolve, his friends are said to have demanded tauntingly that he take them for a drive in a sledge, despite the fact that it was a warm day in mid-July. Nicanor Pereversev laughed. "You are all invited to a sledge drive in three days from today!" he cried. Three days later, on a particularly hot July morning, his friends woke to find the ground covered, apparently, with snow, sledges waiting at the front door, and their host chuckling with delight. With salt, carloads of which had secretly been brought to the estate, he had turned a whole countryside from summer into winter. Nicanor Pereversev was true to his eccentric nature to the end. His last wish, which was duly executed, was that at the moment when his coffin was lowered into the grave a salute should be fired from a cannon he had ordered brought there for the purpose.

Among other portraits that adorned the walls of that dining room, and which I particularly admired, there was one of my father's great-great-aunt, the graceful Countess Wolkenstein, wearing a white satin dress and a powdered wig.⁴ There was also a family group of my Grandmother Kleinmichel with three of her eight children, and a splendid life-sized portrait of my grandfather in full dress, by the well-known portraitist Krieger, wearing all his decorations and the pale blue ribbon of the Order of St. Andrew (the highest order of the Empire) across his uniform.

Our house, like the one in Potchep, had been built by Rastrelli, the famous Italian architect of the time of the Empress

---

³ Olga's paternal great-great-grandfather.

⁴ Countess Wolkenstein was the sister of Nicanor Pereversev.

Elizabeth.[5] It was not as large as the other one, containing sixty-five rooms. Around it was a large park that ran down to a wide pond, on the other side of which was a sugar factory. We spent the greatest part of the day playing in the park. Part of it was especially reserved as a playground for us and here was an open-air gymnasium where we tried to compete in skill and agility. Tata was particularly good in gymnastics for she was naturally as nimble as a monkey. In a few seconds she could climb to the very top of a smooth-polished pole, while we could scarcely struggle up to the middle.

We sisters also had each of us a garden of our own, where we raised vegetables and flowers, and proud was the one who was first to serve her very own radishes on the luncheon table or offer the first flowers from her garden to our mother.

In the morning we used to go to the farm that supplied our house with its products. It was just outside the park. My father had made a present of a calf to each of us three younger sisters. We loved to give them their morning portion of milk, holding our hands in the pail while they sucked and pressed our fingers between their rough tongues and palates. They knew their names and our voices, and even when they had become full grown cows, they would leave the herd at our call and come to us, each one to its own mistress, to rub their soft noses against our cheeks. One night we were coming home from a long walk in the woods when we caught sight of the cows returning home for the night. In the quiet of this evening hour, when a peaceful stillness descends upon the earth, we could hear the muffled thud of their feet on the soft road, and the dust that rose under their lazy steps had a tinge of pink in the rays of the setting sun.

We called our cows by their names. They stopped at once and looked around, then, seeing us, they left the rest of the herd to

---

[5] It would have been impossible for Ivnya to have been built by Rastrelli, as he died in 1771, well before Ivnya was built in 1854. He had also never travelled to Koursk. Many of the estate mansions built between 1850–70 were designed in the Rastrelli fashion, to look like Russian baroque. Ivnya was built in the style of the Winter Palace.

continue on their way, and galloped toward us. Our governess, who was seeing this for the first time, was so terrified that she jumped over a fence, dragging us along with her. Then, all flustered, she hurried us home, scolding us for what she called our foolhardiness. But we felt aggrieved to have been forced to show such lack of confidence in our pets. We turned our heads at every step to glance back at the three cows that were watching our disgraceful retreat from over the fence with what we thought was a look of reproach and disappointment in their large and gentle eyes.

In the afternoon, we sometimes used to go out in the forest for a picnic, taking with us a samovar and basketfuls of sandwiches and cakes. We would find a clearing where we would settle down on a large carpet. At some distance we then made a fire and when the crackling branches had turned to glowing ashes we baked potatoes. We children would then play hide-and-seek and gather wild strawberries and pick armfuls of wild flowers. After dinner, while there was still light enough, we played games in front of the house, at which all our numerous teachers and tutors took part, and the air rang with excited shouts and laughter.

Here, like in Potchep, my father took us with him to the different parts of the estate. We sometimes stopped at the new school that he had built for the peasants of Ivnya, and loved to watch the children at their lessons, their flaxen heads bent over their books, eyebrows knitted and lips pouting, diligently busy with their work. My father had also built and was supporting a hospital for his peasants and had often helped them with cattle, grain, seed and machinery. The peasants who made a success of their farms were many and I personally knew several in Ivnya and other places who owned at least four or five hundred acres of land. It is these thrifty farmers, now called *kulaks* in Soviet Russia, against whom the government is fighting fiercely in every way.

The people believed in my father's good judgement and justice, and came often to him for advice and help. At Ivnya, as it had been in Potchep, we frequently saw groups of peasants advancing to the "palace", as they called it, and asking for him.

He always came out to them and had chairs brought, but only the older men sat down – the younger ones stood respectfully behind their chairs. At these councils, many things were decided, mostly concerning their livelihood, and my father helped them out of their troubles. But they also often turned to him for settlement of their family quarrels.

When the revolution broke out and reached the remotest places, the peasants of Ivnya came in crowds to my eldest sister, who was then staying there with her husband and children, and begged her to remain where they could be protected from all the evil people who were spreading in the country.[6] They also begged her to write to us to come and stay in Ivnya until the "madness", as they expressed it, was over. "The Count took care of us as of his own children – it is our turn now to take care of his children," they said.

But happy as the summer was for us, I still preferred the autumn months, when the sky was of an intense blue and the dimmed horizon of a summer day became clear and did not seem so distant. Perhaps because of the great variety of trees, the forests acquired a richness in colour that I have seen in no country outside of Russia. From dark to bright red, mellowing down to copper, and suddenly splashed with the purest gold, the woods in the autumn were a joy to the eye. The fields, bare of their crop, became a dull yellow, while the roads stretched through them like shiny black ribbons; and over the patches of ploughed-up dark, rich earth, long glistening gossamer threads weaved fantastic designs. In the woods, mushrooms were plentiful and we brought basketfuls of them home where the preparations of preserves for the winter were in full activity.

About that time Uncle Andrew, my mother's youngest brother, a passionate hunter, arrived for the hunting season with his pack of about a hundred *borzoi* hounds to hunt wolves, foxes and hares

---

[6] Olga's eldest sister Cleopatra (Clair) and her husband George Victorovich Martynov became the last owners of Ivnya, after the deaths of both Constantin and his son Dima.

in our forests. The wolf is a cunning, fierce and unimaginably strong beast. In the space of a moment, he can shake off two or three dogs that have a tight grip on him. He also can jump high and far.

There was once an old and vicious one living in one of the forests of Ivnya. The peasants, whom wolves annoyed from time to time by carrying away sheep, had been trying to get him, for they knew him by his broken tail. They traced him one day in a field of wheat, where he was temporarily camping at a short distance from the road. The peasants left their carts along the road and surrounded the animal's abode with pitchforks, hatchets and knives in their hands. What was their amazement and anger when, with one magnificent leap, their old enemy cleared the strip of field as well as the cart that barred his way and disappeared in the woods. It took my uncle two seasons to run the sly old thing down.

The first frosts would be there, when the ground was white in the early morning and on the terrace we could break ice in the marble vases, which had earlier contained flowers. We would shuffle through the heaps of dead leaves that rustled under our steps and exhaled a delightful scent of mouldiness and damp earth.

The sugar factory would begin to work after an inauguration with a *Te Deum*; and we would watch the finely cut beets travel on the long leather straps and be engulfed by one of the roaring monsters to suffer many changes until we were offered little packages of ready, snow-white sugar.

We stayed at home after dinner now, busy with some handwork while our teachers read to us aloud; sometimes we organised little concerts, for Ella had a magnificent, naturally set voice and the four of us sisters had formed a little choir of our own. Ella and Dima also played the mandolin while one of the grown-up people accompanied them on the piano.

FIVE
# MOSCOW

We were such a big and united family of children that we had not many playmates outside; indeed, we preferred to play by ourselves. One winter in Moscow, however, we met the Grand Duchess Marie and her brother, the Grand Duke Dmitri.[1] They were near the ages of Tata and Ella, and a great friendship soon sprang up between us. At that time, they were living with their uncle, the Grand Duke Serge, and his wife, the Grand Duchess Elizabeth.[2]

We children began seeing one another by taking dancing lessons together; but these were soon interrupted by the tragic death of the Grand Duke Serge when a bomb was thrown at his carriage as he was driving through the Kremlin. The Grand Duke was literally torn to pieces, some of which were said to have been found on the roof of a four-storey house nearby. His coachman

---

[1] Grand Duchess Maria Pavlovna and Grand Duke Dmitri Pavlovich were the children of Grand Duke Paul Alexandrovich and grandchildren of Tsar Alexander II.

[2] Grand Duke Sergei Alexandrovich, fifth son and seventh child of Tsar Alexander II. He married Princess Elisabeth of Hesse. They had no children of their own but were guardians of his brother's two children. The sister of Grand Duchess Elisabeth, Princess Alix of Hesse, married Tsar Nicholas II, the last Tsar of Russia.

also was killed, and an old woman who was passing by was wounded.

My three sisters and I were having a lesson in our classroom when this terrible explosion took place; and, though our house was quite two miles away from the Kremlin, the air about us shook violently with the sound. We were silent for a minute and alarmed; but far from guessing the truth. Some time later, my brother Dima walked into the room and sat down gloomily in a corner. Our teacher asked him why he was so glum. "One would be that at least," he answered. "The Grand Duke Serge has been killed by a bomb. Didn't you hear the explosion?"

I felt my heart sink and my hands and feet grow cold – realising that the detonation we had just heard had meant the death of somebody, somebody we knew and loved. As soon as we recovered from the first shock, we asked our teacher if she would permit us to run down to our parents; but Dima told us they had left for the palace. That same evening we were taken to the first *panikhida* (service for the dead). The Nikolaevsky Palace,[3] occupied then by the Grand Duchess, had a passage that led straight to the church of the Tchoudoff monastery,[4] where the coffin had been placed. A great many people were already assembled when we arrived; we took our places among them, and soon there was a hush.

The Grand Duchess appeared from the passage, the ribbon of the Order of Saint Catherine making a red streak across her black dress. I was afraid to look at her face; but, in spite of myself, I glanced up. She was very pale but composed. Our young friends, the Grand Duchess Marie and her brother, Dmitri, followed. They looked as if they had been crying a great deal, but now their faces were only very serious. The nervous tension I was in broke

---

[3] The Small Nikolaevsky Palace, part of the Kremlin, was destroyed in 1929.

[4] Chudov Monastery, part of the Kremlin, closed in 1918 and was dismantled in 1929.

down when the service began, and I cried as I had never done before. The dignity and Christian humility with which the Grand Duchess Elizabeth bore her grief filled my youthful heart with overpowering emotion, especially when I heard that she had gone so far in her forgiveness as to visit the assassin in prison and even to implore the Emperor, Nicholas II, to mitigate his sentence.

The tragedy of the Grand Duke's death for a long time cast a shadow on our lives, and it most decidedly changed the face of Moscow, releasing much disorder, though I was too young then to understand why. There were days when we were not allowed to go out, because bullets came whistling every once in a while through our yard. A wounded man was picked up one day in front of our house and Clair, who had become a trained nurse, had him brought in and dressed his wound. Another man was killed just outside our gate. One day a notice, signed by the revolutionary committee, was posted about the streets, warning the inhabitants to have no lights in their houses at night. The disobedient would have their lights blown out by a bullet. I suppose this was intended to make it easier for them to put up their barricades at night and to escape from the troops. As a measure of precaution, heavy curtains were hung at all of our windows; but my father declined to keep the curtains drawn in his room, and we did not dare insist. He had the habit of reading in bed the greater part of the night, and he went on doing it just as usual. One evening a group of armed men came to our door and ordered us to put that light out. Of course, my father would not hear of it; he sent them about their business and, much to our surprise, the incident was thus closed.

In the spring of that same year, my grandmother, who was as usual visiting us in Moscow, fell ill. My parents looked worried and we were told not to make any noise and to walk on tiptoe when passing grandmother's door. I spent my birthday very quietly as the atmosphere of the house was not a joyous one. In the morning I was told that Grandmother wanted to see me, and I crept gently into her room. She was propped up high on her pillows and looked pale and grave. Seeing me she motioned to me to come nearer to her. "My little girl," she said, "I wanted to give you this New Testament as a present on your birthday. I want you to promise me that you will read a chapter of it every day, as long as you live. I was going to write this on the top leaf, but I am too weak to do it. If I ever get well, I will do it later. But do you promise this to me, now, just the same?"

"I promise, Grandmother," I whispered through my tears, as from her words I realised how ill she was.

Then she smiled and drawing me to her, she kissed me on the forehead.

Easter came a week later, but the usually joyful holiday was mournful for us this time. Grandmother's health was growing rapidly worse. We had not the heart to play and wandered aimlessly from room to room. In the evening, my sisters and I sat down to dinner. A profusion of flowers, as well as the dishes of dyed eggs and the tall *koulitch* and *paskha,* crowned with little bunches of roses, made the dinner table look gay; but somehow we did not even feel like eating.[5] In the morning we had seen the priest go up to Grandmother's room, leaving behind him a faint odour of incense. And now the door suddenly opened and my father appeared on the threshold.

"Children," he announced gravely, "Grandmother has passed away. Get up and pray for the repose of her soul."

We arose and turning to face the icons, we made the sign of the cross, but my mind was in a tumult and I could not pray.

"What is death?" I asked of myself, "What is exactly the passing of a soul? Where is Grandmother now and what does that, which has been Grandmother, look like there, upstairs?"

---

[5] Koulitch and paskha are Russian Easter dishes. Koulitch is a tall, rather dry cake and paskha is a dessert made predominantly from quark (or cottage cheese) and eggs.

I felt chilled to the bones, afraid of the unknown. I took refuge in my mother's room and there, huddled up in a corner of a big armchair, I stayed for a long while with fingers tightly clasped, staring in front of me, while the light outside grew dimmer and dimmer until darkness closed in about me. Presently my mother came in and, finding me in her room, she took me by the hand and told me to come and say good-bye to my grandmother. I dared not tell her that I was afraid, for fear of hurting her feelings, and I silently walked beside her though my heart was stricken with terror. So much the greater was my relief at seeing Grandmother seemingly peacefully asleep on a bed of flowers. I forgot all my fears, but the mystery of death hovered about me for weeks after. My mother exerted herself in giving me all the entertainment she could think of, although being in mourning, she could not do much.

In the evenings we went out for long drives in the country and one night on our way home, as we were coming through a park just outside Moscow, we met a man carrying several puppies in his arms. We stopped and my mother bought one of them for me.[6] It was the nicest looking little dog with fluffy white and brown hair and huge brown eyes; he was just as fat and round as a little ball, so we named him Sharik.

The man had sworn that it was a St. Bernard, but it was in vain that we waited for Sharik to grow up. He turned out to be a middle-sized, curly-tailed, vulgar little mongrel. But his common looks were generously repaid by his almost uncanny intelligence. He understood not only the words that were uttered with a certain

---

[6] According to Olga's unpublished memoirs, she and her mother were driving through Petrovsky Park. As they were passing by, the man held out the puppy saying that the little dog was for sale. It was a mongrel, but the look in his enormous black eyes was so intelligent that they stopped to see him closer. My grandmother wrote: "The new arrival created a great deal of excitement among my sisters. In our playroom there was a big round table, on which we placed the puppy. He ran from one to another of us, slipping and gliding over the polished surface, just like a little ball. And that was the name we gave him – Sharik (little ball). Eminently intelligent and loving, he soon became a member of our family, a true friend."

inflection of the voice, but almost anything you told him. Sharik brought a new interest into my life and with his arrival my sombre moods vanished like smoke. My parents used to have as much fun out of him as we children had. Sharik, my mother would say, "go and call Fenia" (the maid), or Clair, or Olga, whatever the case might have been, and Sharik would at once depart in a businesslike trot, find the person and bring her back, tugging gently with his teeth at the hem of her dress. He slept in my room and was so fond of me that he felt unhappy and lost whenever I was away. When I started to go to school, Sharik spent hours on a windowsill waiting for me to come home and, catching sight of me, he would rush down to meet me almost knocking me down with the unrestrained manifestations of his joy.

My mother always used to come to our rooms to kiss us goodnight in the evening and we eagerly awaited that moment, for this was the time when we had her all to ourselves to tell her all that had happened to us during the day, to seek encouragement or advice, or simply to hug her in our arms. Sharik's eyes would light up with excitement at the sight of her long train, upon which he would comfortably settle down while my mother bent down to kiss us. Then he would ride triumphantly out of the room, while we clapped our hands in delight.

Sharik felt keenly if there was anything out of the ordinary in the atmosphere of the house. If excitement reigned in the air, he was sure to be running in and out between us, yapping joyfully and getting under our feet in a most exasperating manner. On these occasions his good-natured countenance wore the likeness of a smile.

But at the time my father was severely ill, Sharik showed signs of a deep grief; his head bowed to the ground and with a drooping tail, he slowly roamed through the house, looking at us with mournful eyes. When my father died, although Sharik was in another part of the house, he crawled under my bed and nothing could induce him to come out. There he lay motionless for many hours, refusing food, refusing even to respond to our caresses by wagging his tail, and heaving from time to time a deep, tremulous sigh. Sharik died when he was twelve years old and I do not feel that I exaggerate in stating that I felt I had lost a friend.

The summer following the Grand Duke Serge's and my grandmother's deaths, Tata, Ella and I spent with our friends the Grand Duchess Marie and her brother at the Grand Duke's estate near Moscow. Our unhappy war with Japan was going on, and the Grand Duchess Elizabeth had organised on the estate a hospital for wounded soldiers. She visited it every day and often took all of us along with her in the afternoon. We played games with the convalescents, and sometimes one of our Russian teachers would read aloud Chekov's funny stories to amuse them. We all took some kind of handwork and sat in a circle to listen, and even the Grand Duchess could not help smiling at the soldiers, who were laughing until tears rolled down their cheeks. Often, too, the Grand Duchess had an entertainment for the soldiers in her house.

On Sundays the Grand Duchess Marie, Tata, Ella and I joined the choir to sing in church. On my name-day, too, Mass was said, and on this occasion the Grand Duchess was a few minutes late; but when I returned home, I knew why. I found that the table in my room was covered with presents, and a huge bunch of roses and a cake! She had arranged this surprise herself with infinite kindness and care, giving me the things I would like most. She treated us in the same motherly way that she did her own nephew and niece, and gained our entire confidence and deep affection.

The Grand Duchess Elizabeth was very fond of my parents and in the winter she often came to see them without announcing her visit beforehand. Sometimes while we studied in the morning in our classroom, she would come in with our mother to kiss us good morning. Once a week in Moscow, too, we spent the afternoon at the Nikolaevsky Palace, where the Grand Duchess had organised a committee for helping the poor of Moscow.

Young girls gathered there to make clothes for them, which were then distributed in their homes. A short prayer was first said by the priest attached to the palace church and then we all sat down, needle in hand, to sew the garments that had been already cut out for us. The Grand Duchess, always busy, came and went, and sometimes sat down to work with us.

Later, in 1911, she founded a religious community for women, buying a piece of ground in the city and transforming the several buildings into living quarters for the Sisters, a hospital for the poor and a dispensary, where people who had had accidents in the street were brought to have their wounds dressed and where poor people received free medical care. A church also was built on the place. The Grand Duchess left her palace and went to live as the prioress of this community – "Martha and Mary" – and she was the heart and soul of the organisation. From early morning till night, she was helping the poor, comforting the unfortunate and sick, assisting at operations, and listening with kindness and patience to all those who came to her for comfort and help. She not only gave herself to charity within the walls of the community, but often went out secretly, with one of the Sisters, to help and give medical care to the poor in the worst and most wretched parts of the city. Here she was known as "Sister Elizabeth" and she worked with love and care amidst the horrible dirt and odours, bringing comfort and peace wherever she went. Those who needed hospital care she took along with her. Soon a home for incurable tubercular patients was founded by her and later a school for different handicrafts. Even at night she did not stop her activity, but visited the dying in her hospitals trying to bring them comfort in their last moments.

In the summer she sometimes made trips to different monasteries, and she never failed to visit my father upon her return. He was then laid up most of the time with gout that made him suffer terribly. The Grand Duchess brought him either an icon or holy water or something from the place she had been to, and she would stay with him a long time, telling him of what she had seen, and leaving behind her an atmosphere of serenity and peace. She was the first one to come when my father died, and her angelic presence did much to help us through the first days.

At the age of seventeen, the Grand Duchess Marie married Prince William of Sweden, the marriage being celebrated at Tsarskoe Selo, the Emperor's residence. Tata, who was nearest to her in age, was the only one of us sisters to assist at the wedding. Although Tata had not yet been presented at court, the Grand Duchess Marie obtained permission from the Empress for her to be present at the ceremony. This was one of the occasions when the so-called Russian dresses were worn. These were court dresses in the old Russian style, made of brocade, velvet or silk and trimmed with fur. A *kokoshnik*, a head dress with a long veil, accompanied it. Soon after the wedding, the couple left Russia, and the Grand Duke Dmitri shortly after left Moscow, though he went only to live with the Imperial family at Tsarskoe Selo.

My sister Ella and I, the two younger ones of our family, were going to school now; Ella, being very sociable, always wanted to go. As for me, my mother hoped that in this way I would get rid of my timidity, which she thought was too great. I entered a private school that was quite close to our house, so that I could come over for lunch. My schoolmates belonged to the middle-class and took almost at once a defensive position towards me. Their friendly attitude had lasted only as long as they did not know who I was. But as soon as they found out that I was a member of another social class, they began to suspect each other of trying to enter into my good graces because of my title, and, out of pride, one by one they dropped away from me. I felt miserably isolated.

When I one day ventured to ask a girl why, after having been so nice, she had turned a cold shoulder on me, I received the following answer: "Oh, you are all right, but if I began to be friendly with you, the rest of them would imagine that I want to be invited to your house."

Thus I was left alone and shrank deeper into my shell. Several times I had asked my mother if she would not change her mind and let me continue my studies at home, but she always replied that she still firmly believed that the school would do nothing but good for me.

"It depends upon you," she would say, "to be happy in any circumstances where you happen to be placed in life. Take yourself in hand and decide that you will go through with it."

Each time I bowed to her final word, so firmly did I believe in my mother's good judgment and so well was I trained to discipline my will. I went through the four years of school that were left to complete my education, although it never ceased to be a source of suffering to me. I even stayed for another year to take up a special subject and I do not think that this effort has been wasted, for I believe I can say that it helped me to build up a certain strength of character that proved useful in the years that followed.

When Ella graduated from school, my mother took her and Tata to St. Petersburg to "go out". Moscow, after the death of the Grand Duke Serge, had become a very quiet place; the society had dwindled to a small group of people. Most of the boys, immediately upon their graduation from the university or the military schools in Moscow, left for St. Petersburg to take up diplomatic service or to enter one of the regiments of the guards, and young girls also made their debut in the capital.

My eldest sister, Clair, had married and was living at her husband's country place near Moscow, so that I was left alone with my father, who was nearly seventy years old and had not been feeling well for a long time. That winter, when just we two were together, is one of my fondest memories. Often after my studies, which took me until ten o'clock at night, I stayed up with him and he used to tell me of his childhood and youth; he also explained to me much about the management of our property and gave me advice as to life in general.

I can still hear his voice telling me to hold tight to three things in life – faith in God, truth and mercy. "God is powerful enough to lead you out of any situation... Tell the truth always – a truthful person may sometimes be disliked but will always be trusted and respected, and you can do great things in life if you feel that people trust you and depend upon you. Be merciful. Give and forget that you have given. If people are grateful to you, so much the better; but you must not expect it. Do not be afraid to be generous – God will never abandon those who help others."

Thus the winter months passed, and the spring brought a new marriage in our family! Ella had become engaged in the winter, and her wedding was celebrated in Moscow, which left but a small family of us to spend the summer at our beloved country place, Ivnya, especially as even my mother did not go but remained in Moscow with my father.[7] Tata and I, indeed, left for Ivnya alone, with a dame de compagnie; but later two friends of ours, girls of our age, came to stay with us there; and my brother, who by then was already an officer, brought over a friend of his, whom we had known for a very long time and whom we thought of as a second brother, so we had a happy time. When our guests left, one of the girls asked me to spend the autumn with her at Yalta, a seaside resort in the Crimea; and, as soon as I had obtained my parents' consent, I started on the journey, accompanied only by my mother's old and very respectable maid. I felt very much excited at being so grown-up and independent, as I was very young and childish in many ways.[8]

The Emperor, Nicholas II, and his family were staying at their residence, *Livadia*, just outside Yalta. I had seen the Tsar on

---

[7] Ella, Countess Helene Kleinmichel, married Vsevolod Vsevolodovich Puschin – a lieutenant in the Life Guards Cavalry Regiment.

[8] In her unpublished memories Olga writes that the mother of her friend (Sophie Ivanenko) asked them if they would like to go to Yalta, a seaside resort in the Crimea, which was very fashionable in the fall because of its wonderful climate and the beauty of the scenery. She says that she and her friend "jumped at the suggestion with delight". They drove over by car, which took several hours to Sevastopol, the well-known port in the Crimea.

several occasions at military parades but always at a distance, and I was exceedingly glad to see him one day in Yalta driving slowly along the quay in an open car. He was accompanied by two generals and another car followed with several officers of the Imperial suite. The Tsar was saluting in answer to the people's greetings, the attentive and kindly gaze of his immense grey eyes seemed to rest on each person in particular as he drove past them. After this I often saw the Emperor drive through the streets of Yalta, either with his daughters or the Tsarevitch. Sometimes the young Grand Duchesses went shopping in the morning with one of the ladies-in-waiting to the Empress. They delighted in that because they could mix with the crowd and buy things just as everyone else did, and they were so pleased if they were not recognised at once.

Soon, at a dance at the Princess Bariatinsky's, I was presented to the Emperor and to two of the young Grand Duchesses, Olga and Tatiana. The latter, to my idea, was the prettier of the two; but both had the simplicity of manner that is the greatest charm in every person and especially in anyone who holds such a position as theirs. They were not *blasé* in the least, and their faces shone with pleasure and excitement. At this party I also met my future husband, Paul Woronoff[9], who was then an officer on Their Majesties' yacht, the *Standart*.[10] A legend is attached to his name – *voron* means raven in Russian; it was a nickname given in the fifteenth century to three brothers, Tartar princes, who settled along the Volga River after the great Tartar invasion. It was said of these brothers that they "flew on their prey like ravens!" This nickname became their Russian name, while the Tartar name was never used by them again.

Of his four years' service in the proximity of the Imperial Family, Paul kept a sacred memory. The little Grand Duke Alexis, heir-apparent to the throne, was particularly fond of him – the

---

[9] Pavel Alexievich Voronov.

[10] Standart meaning "banner" – the *Standart* was named after the famous frigate of Peter the Great.

Empress told me once that he always had my husband's photograph by his bedside – and, of course, my husband was completely devoted to the little boy. No one, I think, could help loving that child, who, besides his natural charm, won everybody by the kindness of his heart, his responsiveness to other people's troubles – he was always first to help and comfort – and the patience with which he bore the terrible disease that made him a martyr from time to time.

This illness, called haemophilia, is a change in the blood, which more or less loses the power to congeal. The slightest incautiousness, blow, fall or violent effort may cause a terrible haemorrhage. When the haemorrhage is internal it is almost impossible to stop, and frequently the little Tsarevitch was brought close to death's door. This terrible illness is hereditary and is transmitted through women to their sons. Only men are victims of it. The house of the Princes of Hesse was subject to this disease, and when the Empress Alexandra, formerly Princess of Hesse, discovered one day that she had given it to her only and adored son, it was to her utter despair. It is easy to understand, I think, that when the most famous physicians called to his bedside declared the illness incurable, she sought help elsewhere.

There were many more parties at Yalta where I met again the young officer, Paul Woronoff, to whom I was to be married before many years had passed; but the evening that still remains delightfully in my memory is that of the celebration of the Grand Duchess Olga's sixteenth birthday.[11] A dance in her honour was given at Livadia. It began with a dinner served at little tables, five of which were presided over by the Emperor and his four

---

[11] Apparently the Grand Duchess Olga had a "crush" on Paul Woronoff. Many articles have been written about this and it has been mentioned in several books. In her translation of Grand Duchess Olga's diary, parts of which are included in the introduction to this book, Helen Azar gives more information about this infatuation. To my knowledge, my grandfather never spoke of this time in his life, and I have never found any documents or letters regarding it. He was close to all the members of the Imperial Family and it is possible he did not know about the Grand Duchess's "crush" on him.

daughters. The beauty of the Crimean scenery, with the high and rocky mountains outlining their rugged silhouettes against the deep, southern sky, glittering with myriads of stars; the gardens full of blooming roses, the distant murmur of the waves somewhere below, and the pretty young Princess, her eyes sparkling with pleasure and a flush of excitement on her cheeks – it was like a fairy-tale that miraculously had come true, and, unbelievably, I was in it.

The Empress appeared only after dinner. She suffered frequently from her heart, receptions were a strain on her, and the eternal anxiety about her son made her long to avoid appearing in public. Her face usually wore an expression of weariness and sadness which "society" took for coldness and haughtiness on her part and sulked. This caused much of her unpopularity, which natural timidity increased, and misunderstanding led to a feeling of bitterness on each side. At the time of which I am speaking, however, I did not grasp the situation; but unmindful of it, I let myself live and took in all the joy that I could.

In the winter that followed, my mother took Tata and me to St. Petersburg, and I was officially presented at Court, which meant to be presented to the Dowager Empress and young Empress, and to all the Grand Duchesses. We stayed in the capital for several weeks, during which we were often invited to take tea at Tsarskoe Selo and spend the afternoon with the young Grand Duchesses. It was then that I was struck by the difference I saw in the Empress Alexandra. At home, in the intimate circle of her family, she was an entirely different person. She was gay and happy, and even took part in the quieter of our games. She displayed the greatest interest in everything and often laughed to tears at her children's pranks.

The four sisters were all very different. The eldest, Olga, was very intelligent and gay and had a heart of gold; but she was also rather timid, so that her sister Tatiana, who was much more sociable, was easier to get on with at first.[12] Marie was kindness and unselfishness personified; but Anastasia was the most amusing – she was always full of mischief.

"Anastasia is our family clown!" the Emperor once exclaimed, laughing, to my mother.

All four of the girls were essentially Russian, and they suffered at the very idea of marrying outside their country. Each time there was a question of marrying a member of a foreign royal house, Olga implored her parents to give no serious thought to it, as she wanted to stay in Russia. They all had an adoration for their parents, and each time I saw them I had the renewed feeling of being in a happy, friendly, very Russian family.[13]

In September 1912, Tata and I left for Stockholm, with a *dame de compagnie*, for we had been invited to visit the Grand Duchess Marie, now Princess of Sweden.[14] Princess Marie met us at the pier, and it was in the highest spirits that we drove to her house, which was just outside Stockholm. She had then already a three-year-old son, such a nice little fellow, with rosy cheeks and huge eyes like his mother's. He spoke only Swedish, however, and to our great regret we could not understand all the funny things he said that made the others laugh.

Princess Marie and her husband did everything to give us a good time; they showed us the most interesting and oldest cities and the loveliest spots in the country; we went out to dances with them and they had parties for us at their home.

---

[12] My mother's name was Tatiana and, while I do not have any proof, I assume she was named after the Grand Duchess, just as I assume I was named after the Empress – although the name Alexandra can also be found throughout my father's family.

[13] Later, Olga often corresponded with several of the Grand Duchesses. The surviving letters are in the State Archive of Russia (GARF) and some are copied here in the Appendices, with their permission.

[14] A dame de compagnie is a female companion.

It was nice to see how much the Grand Duchess Marie was liked in Sweden and that the Royal Family was so fond of her. Several days had not passed after our arrival in Sweden, before the King expressed the desire to make the acquaintance of his daughter-in-law's Russian friends. He came over alone for tea one day. We were both charmed by his simple and friendly manner, and that interview remains one of the most pleasant memories of our sojourn in Sweden.

Time was flying quickly for us, but before the end of our visit had come, we received news that my father was ill. We left for Moscow at once. My father had pneumonia. He looked so changed that my heart stood still when I saw him. The doctors told us there was no hope for his recovery, for he was then seventy-two. His firm faith in God made him face death without the slightest fear. Each day that brought him nearer to his grave took some life out of me, too.

A short time before the end came, my father received the Extreme Unction and said good-bye to all of us in turn. We were all around him when the last minute came. The priest had said the prayers for the dying and had quietly left the room – after my father had, in a last, supreme effort, turned his head to kiss the cross that the priest held out to his lips. The shadows of an autumn night were slowly gathering in the room; only the lampada, burning in front of the holy icons, spread a soft light about my father's bed. In spite of the agonising feeling of losing a being who had meant so much to me, there was a great peace in me.

I was thinking that, like the servant in the parable, my father had traded with his talents and done his best and was leaving the rest in the hands and to the sublime mercy of his Lord. When my father had stepped over the threshold of this world, we remained for a while in deep silence. I could not cry. Far more than my grief, I was overwhelmed by the majesty and beauty of this calm, fearless, Christian death. It was as if I had myself approached the fatal door, and had been conscious of something supernaturally great that eclipsed my own human feelings.

My father's desire had been to be buried at a convent where he had often been and to which he had taken us several times. It was a very poor convent, which he had helped very much, and he had told us that he would be sure that we would not forget to continue to help them if his grave were there. A funeral service was said in Moscow, to which hundreds of people came. The convent to which we then took my father was far from Moscow and fifty miles away from the nearest railroad. It was towards midnight that the funeral procession was at last in sight of the monastery. The numerous church bells began to ring at once and their deep grave notes were carried far across the vast and empty plains. Out of the gates there appeared another procession. Priests, in their shimmering robes, advanced at the head of it, followed by the Prioress and over a thousand nuns holding lighted wax candles in their hands and singing the funeral chants. In the darkness of the night, it looked like a stream of light pouring out from behind the white walls and widening into a flood that soon surrounded the hearse. The prayer rose, too, like a huge and mighty wave and it was thus that, moving slowly and in great solemnity, my father entered his last place of rest.

As the shock of my father's death had badly shaken my health, my mother decided to send me abroad for several months, and I went first to the French Riviera with the same *dame de compagnie* who had accompanied us to Sweden. But the radiant sunshine, the gay singing under our windows, the noisy and boisterous life in the streets – everything seemed to strike a discordant note with my state of mind and at the end of six weeks I was only worse. Upon hearing this, my brother – always there when one of us and particularly when I was in grief or in trouble – took a leave of absence and three days later he was with me. His arrival brought me no end of joy. When he had to return, my sister, Tata, joined us and we started on a trip through Italy. Just before we left the Riviera, however, an entertainment was given in our hotel and among other features of it there was a clairvoyant. She told my fortune by the lines of the hand, informing me that I was going to be married in the winter of the following year, and that soon after I would lose all my possessions and would have to live modestly for many years. Part of her prediction has still to materialise: that I will recover my fortune when I am forty years old!

When we returned from Italy it was not to Moscow but to Tsarskoe Selo, to which place my mother had moved. My brother was living there, and my two married sisters were close by in St. Petersburg, and thus we were all of us together again.

SIX
# HAPPY DAYS

In the spring I became Maid of Honour to Their Majesties, the two Empresses.[1] This is a title carrying no duties with it except those of being in attendance twice a year if there are official receptions. As an outward sign of the honour bestowed, on official occasions a Maid of Honour wears the diamond initials of Their Majesties, fixed on the light blue ribbon of the order of St. Andrew. These appointments generally took place on the respective name-days of the Dowager Empress and young Empress. The Empress Alexandra's name-day was on the sixth of May, but as my birthday was on the fourth I had the surprise of receiving the initials as a birthday present two days ahead of time – which is a small yet, I think, a significant instance of the Empress's kind thoughtfulness. We spent the next summer in Ivnya, and in the autumn I went once more to the Crimea, where I met my future husband again, and became engaged to him.[2] I also recommenced, reluctantly at first it is true, to take part in festivities – to "go out," as it is called.

---

[1] Tsar Nicholas II's mother, the Dowager Empress Marie Feodorovna, and wife, the Empress Alexandra.

[2] Autumn, 1913.

A charity sale was organised in Yalta by the Empress Alexandra, and she and her daughters sold at a stand. Crowds of all sorts and conditions of people thronged the room, for everyone who wanted to was allowed to enter, and, as each person naturally wished to buy something from the Empress's own hands, she was feverishly busy during the several days of the sale.

I was astonished to see how animated and pleased she looked in spite of her great fatigue. Everything sold at her stand had been made either by her personally or by her children, and they had worked for months before the sale. As I was selling at the same stand, I could see all of the people who crowded about it – among them a number of peasants – and I particularly remember one old woman who caught the Empress's hand and kissed it reverently.

"I have dreamed all my life of seeing you," she said, "and here you are now – let me look at you well! I have no money to buy things; but I wanted to see you. God has granted me this joy. God bless you and all your family."

Soon after this charity sale, the Princess Bariatinsky organised a show for the benefit of some charity cause. It was to be a play, followed by living pictures. Tata and I took part in both. The plot of the play was the following: in an ancient and deserted castle the old portraits come to life on the night when the descendant of its original owners comes back to his family place. This theme gave a vast field for the display of the actors' various abilities. Some of them sang, others recited poetry – Tata and I danced the minuet.

The rehearsals were a source of great excitement and pleasure to us, particularly as the performance was going to take place in a real theatre and we knew that not only all Yalta was going to be present, but also the Imperial Family. Finally the night of the show came and we were all in a state of feverish expectancy. Through a little hole in the curtain we watched the people pouring into the house. Soon every box and every seat was occupied and there was a continuous murmur of voices, an exchange of greetings, bows and smiles, until there suddenly was a hush and the whole audience stood up – the Emperor had entered his box, followed by his four daughters.

Almost at once the curtain rose. Some of the actors were dreadfully nervous and one girl, who had to sing, could hardly control her voice, so that the first note that she managed to produce was an absurd little squeak. I saw the Emperor put a warning finger on his eldest daughter's knee, for she was on the point of being shaken by an irrepressible giggle. She straightened out her face at once.

When our turn came and the gauze hanging that had concealed us from view noiselessly slid aside, and the first chords of Mozart's Minuet floated in the air, I felt as if I were rooted to the spot and almost wished the stage would open under my feet and swallow me up. My heart was beating so loudly that it seemed to me to drown the music. Still, we managed to step out of our frame and to begin our dance. When it was over the Emperor clapped and nodded smilingly in acknowledgment of our low curtsey. The house rang with unanimous applause. But we were disappointed that the Emperor had not had our dance repeated. We saw the young Grand Duchesses turn interrogative glances on their father, who bent down and spoke to them with a smile. They told us later that the Emperor had noticed how our knees trembled during our performance, and, much as he had liked the dance, he had not had the heart to make us go through it again.

At Christmas we were home again and the preparations for my marriage began, for I was insistent that I had never seen the point in long betrothals, and my mother agreed to let the marriage take place before Lent. My fiancé came to see me every day, and, as was the custom, sent me huge baskets of flowers – occupied as I was, I had no more idea than any other of the young girls in Europe that 1914 was to be a year, for sinister reasons, long to be remembered. Just before my wedding, one of my aunts gave a fancy dress ball for me in St. Petersburg.³ It was the last ball at which I danced before the terrible, sustained catastrophes of the war and the revolution.

An old Russian custom decrees that a bride and bridegroom shall each have two friends, a man and a woman, representing their parents, to give them the blessing before the marriage and to assist at their wedding. These pseudo parents had to be selected among persons not closely related to each other, and could not be a husband and wife. Originally, the true father and mother were not even allowed to be present at the wedding, so that the affianced couple should feel free from the weight of their filial obeisance and thus answer honestly the priest's question as to their desire to be married to someone who had been chosen by their parents.

Though without any real meaning now, the custom persists, and, on the occasion of my wedding, both the Tsar (Nicholas II) and the Empress (Alexandra) expressed their desire to give my fiancé the blessing – but added smilingly that since husband and wife both were not allowed to give it, he would have to choose between them. This was certainly very embarrassing, and Paul answered that he wished he could have both Their Majesties to bless him; but, since he could not, he would ask Her Majesty the Empress to act as his "Mother". The Grand Duke Alexander agreed to act as his "Father".⁴

The wedding was to take place at 2:30 in the afternoon.⁵ Paul had to go first to the Palace to receive Her Majesty's blessing and thence to the church where, following an old custom, he would give a bouquet of white flowers to his best man, who would bring

---

³ According to MacMillan in *The War that Ended Peace*, over 300 invitations were sent out (pg 164).

⁴ Grand Duke Alexander Mikhailovitch, grandson of Tsar Nicholas I and brother-in-law of Tsar Nicholas II.

⁵ The wedding was held at the Feodorovsky Cathedral in Tsarskoe Selo on 7 February 1914.

it to me as a sign that my betrothed was waiting for me. In the morning, a package was brought to me; it contained a golden lampada (oil lamp) in the shape of three Imperial eagles supporting a pink crystal bowl with their wings. A note from the Grand Duchess Tatiana said that this was a present to me from the Empress, who wished that it would burn before the icon with which she was going to give the blessing to my future husband.

My two married sisters and their husbands arrived from St. Petersburg in the morning, too, and a great excitement reigned in the house. I managed, however, to run over to my brother's apartment, for he was ill with a bad cold. Both he and I were terribly upset that he would not be able to assist at my wedding, particularly as he was going to be my best man – to the last minute we hoped that the doctor would let him come.

At 2 o'clock I was dressed, the veil pinned on my hair; and there was nothing to do but wait. At 2:30 Paul's brother arrived with a bouquet of white lilacs and roses; but he told us that we would have to wait a little while longer to give the Imperial Family time to arrive in church before me. When the message came that Their Majesties had left for the church, one of my aunts gave me the traditional blessing, my mother kissed and blessed me over and over again, and I got into the car with my aunt and drove to the Feodorovsky Cathedral. It was snowing heavily. One of my cousins, who was going to give me away, was awaiting me on the steps, and he led me into the church, the choir singing a psalm of greeting. I had grown completely calm and, although I did not turn my head, I seemed to take in every detail. Paul, my fiancé, was standing alone in the middle. To his right stood Their Majesties and their four daughters, also several members of the Imperial Family.[6] The Tsar wore the uniform of the Navy Guards, to which Paul belonged. I caught sight of the little Tsarevitch peeping and smiling from the flowers that adorned the Imperial

---

[6] Including Grand Duke Cyrill Vladimirovitch, aide-de-camp to the Emperor, among others.

family's place in the church, and there was an immense crowd of relatives and friends.

Then the priest came up to me. Putting my hand in Paul's, he led us into the centre of the church, and the ceremony began.[7] The marriage service consists of two parts, the betrothal and the wedding. Formerly the first part took place soon after the engagement and was quite independent of the wedding, and so it still can be, but as a rule the two ceremonies are united. During the betrothal prayers the couple exchange rings, for in our church both husband and wife are supposed to wear wedding rings and to wear them on the right hand. After the betrothal was over, the priest led us nearer to the altar onto a piece of pink satin, which symbolises the life we should have to go through hand in hand, and on this we stood for the rest of the ceremony. A superstition exists that the first who steps upon it will have the upper hand in married life, and most bridegrooms gallantly pause in order to let the bride step on it first.

During the marriage ceremony crowns are held over the heads of the bride and groom as a symbol of God's blessing. The crowns are supposed to be worn during the ceremony; but they are usually so heavy that the "best men" in turn hold them above the heads of the bride and bridegroom. There are, therefore, always several best men, and we had eight for each of us. As my brother was ill, the Grand Duke Dmitri was my first best man.

In our church we are supposed to stand all through the religious services, unless we feel faint or ill, and we have chairs along the walls, whence we can get them if needed; but we have no pews. It is rare that anyone sits down. We are so used to it from childhood that we can stand in church for hours without feeling the least tired. My mother told me later that at my wedding her emotional agitation must have been visible because the Empress,

---

[7] In her unpublished memoirs, Olga noted that the four Grand Duchesses seemed to be just as moved as the bride and groom. She wrote, "Their Majesties were watching the young couple with tenderness as if they had been their own children.".

who was looking at her with sympathy, motioned her to sit down. My mother bowed but shook her head – she could not think of taking a seat while the Empress was standing. The Tsar, who had observed this little scene, at once walked away and brought a chair for the Empress, who then smilingly invited my mother to follow her example and sit down, which my mother gladly did.

The wedding ceremony is followed by a *Te Deum*, and then the young couple may be congratulated by their friends and relatives. Russian men kiss a married woman's hand instead of shaking hands with her, and I felt a very responsible matron when this tribute was paid to my new position. A most unexpected honour, however, was paid to me that day. As I curtseyed low before the Emperor, in a gracious and spontaneous gesture he raised my fingers to his lips.[8] Then he drew Paul towards him and kissed him.

My husband and I drove home together from the church, and when we walked into our drawing room, we found the Empress and the Grand Duke Alexander standing there, holding an icon and the traditional large, round, loaf of black bread crowned by a silver dish filled with salt, the symbols of prosperity and welfare. Behind them stood the Emperor and his children.[9] We knelt down to receive the blessing from the Holy Icon, which was then handed to my husband along with the bread and salt.[10] When the Imperial Family had gone,[11] we went to greet our other guests,

---

[8] According to Olga's unpublished memories this "provoked a low murmur among the ladies".

[9] The Empress had asked Pavel and Olga to stay a little longer in the church in order for the Imperial Family to arrive at the house before them.

[10] It is an old Russian wedding tradition to give bread and salt to the newly married couple.

[11] The members of the Imperial Family noted the occasion in their diaries and journals. Tsar Nicholas II wrote "Came back to Tsarskoye at 2pm, got my clothes changed and went with Alix and Sandro (Grand Duke Alexander Mikhailovitch) to the regiment's church to attend the wedding of PA Voronov and Olga Kleinmichel. After the service we went to Countess Kleinmichel to congratulate the newlyweds and to drink to their health. Дневник Николая II (1913–1918). Russia: Захаров, 2021.

and a few hours later, after another visit to my brother, we left for a trip abroad.[12] An officer was not supposed to take long leaves of absence, so we had to be content with twenty-eight days; but we were happy, and those few weeks stand out in radiant compensation for the gloom of the ensuing years.[13]

In July of that same year, 1914, President Poincaré came to Russia and my husband was appointed to accompany him, during his stay in our country, upon each of his trips on the sea. While the President of France was in Russia strikes unfortunately broke out in St. Petersburg, which made a painful impression on everybody, and there were disorders. Our carriage, going from the suburb of Peterhof into St. Petersburg to meet some friends of ours, was smashed to pieces by rioters; the horses were wounded and the coachman saved his life only by running. We were convinced, later, that these disorders had been fomented by

---

[12] An article about the wedding appeared in France in Le Figaro, 2 March 1914, which noted the marriage took place two days before the wedding of Princess Irina Alexandrovna with Prince Felix Felixovich Yusupov. The article stated it was a *mariage d'amour* – a marriage of love and described the guests as including the Imperial Family. According to the article a special train had been organised to take the many guests to St. Petersburg.

[13] In her unpublished memories, Olga noted that spring in St. Petersburg that year was bright and warm. She wrote, "Tata was still not used to my absence and missed me very much as previously we had always been together. I made plans to stay with her in the country for the summer. Spring brought with it a flurry of social engagements. We had a season ticket to the Arts Theatre and often enjoyed plays there. The last play of the season was *A Thought* by Andreev [sic], the cast performed wonderfully and we felt sad that we would not see them any more this year. When Paul was on duty, I joined friends for drives to the countryside, where we would picnic or attend musical events. I even hosted my first evening party, which was organised for Tata. We invited several friends and the singer Mororessy, who has a very pleasant voice and a huge repertoire of various beautiful lyrical songs. I was worried that our guests would be bored but fortunately it seems everyone had a good time. In the meantime, my mother was suffering from bad health and it was recommended that she go to one of the spa resorts in Germany."

Leonid Nikolaievich Andreyev was a Russian writer of novels, short stories and plays. *A Thought* was written about a murder from the viewpoint of the murderer.

propaganda paid for with "German money", but nothing in the atmosphere at that time predicted to us that the horror of the war was so close at hand. My brother was at Ivnya inspecting his estates there, and, toward the last of July, perfectly easy in mind, I set out to join him there for a short visit, leaving my husband at Peterhof.

When I arrived at our station, however, it was only to learn that my brother, called back by a telegram, had left an hour before for St. Petersburg. He had given no reasons, but the station master told me that he had looked grave and worried. A premonition that something dreadful was on the point of happening swept over me and I wanted to return at once; but, since there was no express to St. Petersburg until the next morning I decided to go on to Ivnya. My sister, Tata, met me on the steps of the house. My brother, she said, had been ordered back to his regiment. He thought it meant mobilisation! A war seemed so incredible that I stood there speechless, thinking how my husband would have to go too and how I had left him for a pleasure trip! I could not forgive myself. Without taking my things off, I went into the house, and we tried to plan on the quickest way to return to St. Petersburg. We decided to drive in the automobile that the factory had for its needs, straight to Koursk, fifty miles away, and try to catch a train there.

I had no heart to go out to any spot I loved in the park or even to my room; half an hour later we were on our way. I had spent exactly forty minutes in Ivnya; and it was the last time I ever saw it.

Four years later, I heard from a former employee – who had joined General Denikin's army – that Ivnya had been presented to Trotsky by the Soviet government. He had come to stay there for a short time but, finding the place too far from Moscow, he took possession of another place close to the capital, having previously moved our furniture from Ivnya to his new quarters.[14]

---

[14] It has not been possible to verify whether this is true or not.

After that, some Bolshevik troops, sent out to the south front against the White Army, were quartered in our house in Ivnya for two weeks. They had amused themselves by shooting down the stucco ornaments from the ceilings and poking holes with their bayonets in the floors. The family portraits, which had been hidden by our servants – of their own initiative – in the cellars of the sugar factory, were found by these troops and wantonly torn to shreds.[15]

---

[15] At around the same time, Olga was concerned about her mother, who had not been in contact with the family since her arrival in Germany. They finally received news from her from London at the end of July. She was unable to leave and was very worried about the situation. However, the family was happy she had managed to get out of Germany, which at the time was very difficult.

Count Pyotr (Peter) Andreevich Kleinmichel, Olga's grandfather

Count Vladimir Konstantinovich Kleinmichel, brother of Olga

Paul Woronoff as a naval cadet in autumn 1901, age 13

Countess Olga Konstantinovna Kleinmichel with her father Count Konstantin Petrovich Kleinmichel

Olga Kleinmichel with her sister Natalie (Tata) Kleinmichel

Left to right: Olga Kleinmichel, Natalie (Tata) Kleinmichel, Claire (Clara) Kleinmichel, Grand Duke Dmitri Pavlovich and Helen (Ella) Kleinmichel

Olga Kleinmichel with unknown partner at a fancy dress ball

Paul Woronoff 1908

Olga and Paul Woronoff on their honeymoon in Nice 1914

Paul Woronoff

Olga Woronoff November 1914

The back of the photo reads: 'Us at Evpatoria, near the sanatorium'

Olga Woronoff on the Kuban River

Unidentified man and Paul Woronoff on the Kuban River

Grand Duchess Anastasia, Grand Duchess Olga, Paul Woronoff, Grand Duchess Tatiana

The Imperial Yacht *Standart*

On the Imperial Yacht *Standart;* Paul Woronoff seated (middle of front row) in front of Empress Alexandra, 1913

The gardens at Ivnya

Paul Woronoff and Tsarevich Alexei on board the *Standart*

The last Imperial Family of Russia: Tsar Nicholas II, Empress Alexandra, Grand Duchesses Tatiana, Olga, Maria, Anastasia and Tsarevich Alexei

The back of the Kleinmichel's country house, Ivnya

Paul Woronoff (front row, 2nd from right) during the First World War

Olga Woronoff

SEVEN
# WAR AND REVOLULTION

When we arrived from this last anxious, nervous visit to Ivnya, my husband met Tata and me at the station in St. Petersburg and comforted me with the news that the Navy Guards had not yet received any orders to go. I hurried at once to Tsarskoe Selo to see my brother. He tried to calm me by saying that mobilisation did not necessarily mean war, but he was to leave St. Petersburg with his regiment the next day! I took from the chain I wore about my neck the little icon that the Grand Duchess Elizabeth had given me when I was a child and attached it to his chain as we said farewell to each other.

The next day Germany declared war upon Russia.[1] The Emperor and his family came to St. Petersburg from Peterhof. It was my husband who was at the steering-wheel of the Imperial steam barge that brought them from their yacht to the Winter Palace on the Neva. Delegations from all classes and organisations had gathered in the Palace at the Emperor's desire. I here quote the Emperor's words, which he addressed to the delegations:

"It is with calm and dignity that our Mother, the Great Russia, has received the news of the declaration of war. I am convinced that it is with the same feeling of calmness that we will lead it to the

---

[1] 1 August 1914.

end, whatever this war may be. I here solemnly declare that I will not sign the peace, until the last soldier of the enemy's army has left our soil. And it is through you, representatives of the troops that are so dear to me, and are assembled here; representatives of the guard and of the military district of St. Petersburg, it is through you that I address myself to my entire army which is animated by the same spirit and is as strong as granite, and that I bless it for the hard task that it has to accomplish."

Everyone knows how desire to serve their country united all Russians in that memorable moment. I was among the colossal crowd of at least 20,000 people who had gathered before the Winter Palace to express their loyalty to the Emperor and to Russia in this tragical crisis.

A great silence seemed to hold us all in a tense suffocation, when suddenly the Tsar stepped out onto the balcony above us. He was terribly pale. At the sight of him a tremendous cheer shook the air, then, moved by the same impulse, the whole immense crowd sank to their knees and began to sing the National Anthem – "God save the Tsar." I looked about me and saw that many people were crying; I myself could not stop the tears that were running down my cheeks. The Emperor did not speak, appearing to be greatly moved; he made the sign of the cross and left the balcony. The Empress had appeared for several moments at his side.

That same evening, I walked with my husband through the streets of St. Petersburg; traffic had practically stopped on the Nevsky Prospect, where long processions carrying icons and the national flags moved slowly along, chanting prayers or the National Anthem. Officers were caught up and carried by the cheering people. With a feeling of awe, and a heavy weight on our hearts, we paused in front of the Kazansky Cathedral, and listened to the ecstatic, mournful sounds – an enormous crowd praying fervently and singing the responses of a *Te Deum*. These demonstrations of religious and patriotic feelings that swept the nation like a tidal wave, lasted in the capital, on that memorable date, almost throughout the night, and for many days after.

The battleships had their full crew, and therefore all the officers and sailors from the Imperial yachts were perforce left behind; but they impatiently longed to go to the war too, and soon, in the absence of battleships, the order was given for them to form two battalions to fight on land.[2] Thus it was that on a rainy night in the first days of September, I had to say goodbye to my husband. Before his departure, the Grand Duchess Olga gave each of us a little icon, which we always wore thereafter. This is the only material memory of the Imperial family that we were able to save through the years of revolution.

My mother and Tata went with me to see Paul off.[3] The train was standing far off the platform, and we had to splash through pools of water until we found it. Sailors, all in khaki uniforms, like soldiers, were busily moving around with lanterns in their hands. I earnestly tried to smile at my husband and hide my feelings, knowing how unkind it would be to upset him at such a moment. Then the signal of departure was given. My husband hugged me for the last time, and jumped into the train, and, with a grunt, it began to move. The sailors were crying "Hurray," and my husband was waving to me until the train disappeared in the dripping darkness.

The weary, worrying months passed. Ella's husband had gone to the front and so had Clair's.

---

[2] On 30 August 1914 Pavel wrote to his parents, "My dear beloved Mama and Papa! Please forgive me that I have not written to you recently, we were very busy preparing for the campaign. Today at 8:50am we are marching off to the front. I am asking you, my dears, to bless me in your thoughts from afar, and I firmly believe that your blessing will be for me the same as if we were together now. I hug you warmly, very much loving you, your Pavlik." The address was: The Volunteer Army, 2nd Battalion of the Naval Guards.

[3] Olga's mother had finally returned from London.

In the daytime, Tata and I took courses in a hospital, studying to be trained nurses, and in the evenings we made warm things for the soldiers, and were sometimes able to forget our anxiety with Clair's babies.[4]

The Emperor had given the Winter Palace over for the needs of the army, and the Empress formed there a committee for supplying the army with warm clothes. She had also organised hospital trains, for which everything was prepared at the Palace. A great many women of all classes worked there from morning till night and trains full with articles were sent regularly to the front. Another part of the Winter Palace was transformed into a hospital for soldiers. The Grand Duchess Olga was at the head of a committee organising help for the soldiers' families, and her sister Tatiana took upon herself the organisation of help for the refugees who were pouring in from the front. One of the palaces at Tsarskoe Selo was turned into a hospital where the Empress and her two eldest daughters took a course in nursing the wounded.

After our brilliant advance in the Carpathian Mountains, we began to suffer reverses at the front. Towards the end of August 1915, we heard that the Germans had captured Brest-Litovsk and that our army was retreating toward Minsk. The losses of the Russian army had been colossal – more than a million and a half men since the first defeat. Most of the regiments of the guard had lost a large number of their officers, in some cases sixty out of eighty, and scarcely any of those who had remained alive had escaped being wounded. Of course, the losses among the men had been even heavier. The Tsar, who from the first had wished to be at the head of his army, felt that the moment had come for him to do so. On 31 August the Grand Duke Nicholas was relieved of his supreme command and given instead the command of the army of the Caucasus; on 5 September, the Tsar, having left Tsarskoe Selo, took over the command of all military

---

[4] In a letter written to Grand Duchess Tatiana on 22 September 1914, Olga mentions she had to quit the course for health reasons.

and naval forces at General Headquarters. This news was received by some with joy, by others with apprehension. Many superstitious people, too, had acquired the belief that the Emperor had "no luck".

But disappointment at the beloved Grand Duke's being relegated to a distant and comparatively unimportant front was keen and widely spread; for the Grand Duke, in spite of the recent retreat, had remained as popular as ever. There was a feeling of depression throughout all Russia, and a rumbling discontent that was at once made use of by Germany, turned to propaganda and exploited in the highest degree.

In October 1915, Ella's husband was killed. It was a terrible shock to all of us. We had been very fond of him, and Ella had been so happy with her husband. His body was brought to St. Petersburg, and Ella had him buried at the same monastery where our father had been buried several years before. Then she and her baby daughter went to live near that convent, and they remained there until the revolution broke out.

In the course of that same winter – in February 1916 – I had a brief happiness that made Ella's tragic loss seem even greater, for my husband was transferred to the *Svodny Polk* – a regiment of officers and soldiers chosen for a short service every two years from those regiments having a member of the Imperial Family for honorary commander. The *Svodny Polk*, with other troops, formed the bodyguard of the Tsar and his family. This transfer, however, gave my husband to me for but a short time; after a few months, Paul left St. Petersburg – or Petrograd as it was now called by the Tsar's decree, in order to abolish the German suffix – and I was again one of the innumerable anxious women with a husband at the front.

Meanwhile, ugly things were being whispered more and more openly about Rasputin's influence over the Empress. It was said, indeed, that he was even all-powerful in Russian politics – that with the Tsar at General Headquarters, the Palace would be wholly under the will of Rasputin and the very Ministers would hold office only upon the latter's sufferance.

It was said that Rasputin was a tool of Germany. I do not know if this was true; but he was certainly used by our enemy to discredit the Imperial couple and to foment those disorders so helpful to Germany. Rasputin has been called a monk, but he had never been one. He was a peasant, who had been at first supposed to lead a saintly life, and he undoubtedly had a strange power of magnetism. To the Empress's religious and somewhat mystically inclined nature he embodied her last and only hope of preserving the life of the Tsarevitch. And her trust is not to be wondered at, since every time Rasputin was called to the unfortunate child's bedside, he was able to check the hideous bleeding – whether by coincidence or not.

In reality, Rasputin was torn between depravity and repentance of his sins; but he masked this skilfully and any attempt to disclose his debauchery to the Empress was naturally regarded by the poor mother as the persecution of a saintly man by those jealous of him. It was soon true, however, that Rasputin became unanimously hated by all classes of Russians, with the exception of a very small group. When, on 30 December 1916, Rasputin was murdered at the Yusupov Palace, under circumstances that have been widely written of, the general rejoicing that ensued was very subdued.[5] It was subdued for two reasons: first, the murder of Rasputin had necessarily to be considered somewhat as an act of rebellion against Their Majesties; second, there was an uneasy, vague feeling that a door had been opened into the unknown – something had happened that might bring the brooding revolution from the dark into the open. Although no one at that moment could imagine what was to come.

---

[5] The conspiracy to murder Rasputin was orchestrated by Prince Felix Yusupov and Grand Duke Dmitri Pavlovich – the same young man who had been a childhood playmate of Olga and her siblings, and Olga's first best man at her wedding.

The Russian people were divided into distinct social classes. The greater part of the population consisted of the peasants, and with the peasants the infinitely small class of the nobility were mostly on good terms. They understood each other well, which of course was the result of common interests in the land.

There were the merchants, forming a very large, wealthy, united and strong class with the several old and very wealthy families at their head – an aristocracy of their own, proud of their names, and whose fortunes were handed down from generation to generation.

I can cite examples of individuals belonging to this, or indeed any of the classes, who were granted titles by the Tsar for services rendered to the State. In the army, too, anyone could become an officer – in the Guard alone, the officers had to be of noble birth. Then there was the relatively much smaller class of tradesmen and the workmen; then the clergy, who had everyone's consideration and came in frequent contact with all classes of the population, though less frequently with the middle class, the so-called *intelligentsia*, than with any other group.

The *intelligentsia* – lawyers, doctors, teachers – were very much under the influence of advanced ideas coming from abroad. At first only dreamers aspiring to build paradise on earth, when the moment came actually to create the ideal life, they showed their incapacity and power was not left in their hands for long – it was taken by the small but fiercely compact organisation of the communists.

Reading could be called a passion of almost all literate Russians, I think. We do not read a book for "amusement", but searchingly, keenly anxious to seize upon understanding of the ideas therein. Each new book is excitedly discussed, and there used to be the most agitated debates even in schools between the pupils of higher grades, as to just what the author intended to say and if he were right or not. Novels did not mean much to us, but we were greatly interested in philosophy, religion and history. I remember

Ella writing a composition in school on Fichte's *The Destiny of Man*, at the age of fifteen.⁶ At the numerous lectures given by writers or professors of literature, the talk would usually be followed by a debate in which anyone might take part. It was interesting to see how much excitement this always provoked, how crowded the audience was and how great a number of opponents would speak up.

I remember one lecture given by the well-known writer, Merezhkovsky; he had chosen to speak of the godliness in man's nature.⁷ A very young man was the first one to combat the famous writer's opinion, doing so in words that implied much thinking, reading and feeling. Merezhkovsky grew keenly interested, as he proved by defending his ideas quite as earnestly as he would have done with a man of his own age and experience.

Unfortunately, the Slav nature is apt to fall into extremes. Too much thinking and not sufficient physical culture is as bad as the reverse, and excessive development of the mind may lead sometimes to exaggerated and wrong ideas. The younger Russians studied sociological problems with enthusiasm. Quickly inflamed by "high ideals" they did not stop to think whether they could adapt these ideals to life in a practical way; and, to my idea, this was one of the reasons why the leaders of the revolution – who did sincerely believe that universal happiness could come through revolution – proved later so pathetically inadequate and childishly helpless before the situation they themselves had provoked. Many brilliant speeches were made and a lot of beautiful words wasted. How bitterly some of these men regretted their own destructive work can be seen from the words of one of the socialist leaders, Mr Tchaikovsky.⁸ At one of the meetings of his party on 9 July 1917, he said:

---

⁶ In the original edition of *Upheaval*, Olga mistakenly attributes the authorship of this book to Nietzsche.

⁷ Russian poet, novelist, critic and thinker.

⁸ Possibly Nikolai Tchaikovsky, a Russian scientist turned socialist.

"On us socialists lies the responsibility for the ruin of the army ... the soldier, who went to war out of the simple feeling, natural to every man, of defending his land, his home, his family, was destroyed by our inculcating in him the idea that he went to war to fill the pockets of the capitalists..."

I could cite many more such statements, but I shall return to the story of the revolution as it affected my own individual life. In January 1917, my husband was taken ill with his heart and sent back from the front to St. Petersburg – Petrograd, I should say. Examined by a committee of doctors at the Naval hospital, he was instructed to go for two months to make a cure at a watering resort in the Caucasus.[9] Before our departure, we were invited to spend the evening with the Empress and her children. I had not seen them for some time, and I found a great change in the Grand Duke Alexis. The last time I had been to the Palace the Empress had received me in one of the children's rooms and the Tsarevitch had been wheeled in there in his bed. He was then recovering from one of the attacks of his terrible illness, and he looked very thin and pale. Everyone tried to amuse him, and it was touching with what tender care his sisters played with and looked after him. The Empress was knitting something for the Grand Duchess Tatiana's committee, and now and again she would smile at her son, though her eyes did not lose their sad and preoccupied expression.

This time, however, the Grand Duke Alexis looked as I had never seen him before. He had grown a great deal and the transparence in his face had disappeared, he was rosy-cheeked and really healthy looking. Each time the Empress looked at him her face beamed in a happy smile. The Tsarevitch kept always close to her, kissing her face and hands from time to time and stroking her hair. This picture of a closely united and happy family will always stay in my mind. It was the last time I was to see it.

---

[9] I have as yet been unable to find documentation confirming this.

In the beginning of February 1917, we left on our four-day journey to Kislovodsk, a place in the Caucasian Mountains, where there are springs of mineral water that come hot from the ground and bubble like champagne.[10] My husband's health was in a very poor condition and for some time we lived a very secluded life. When he began to feel better, however, we went occasionally to see our friends, of whom there was quite a number in Kislovodsk, and we gathered most often at the house of Madame Orlov – where we talked over the reports from the front. My husband began to speak of going back to the front when we had been in Kislovodsk only a month; but his doctor would not hear of it yet. Everything seemed peaceful here, and, if the war had not been on our minds all the time, we would have enjoyed our stay very much.

Then, one day, our morning paper, which was edited in another city, failed to arrive, and there were faint rumours that something very unusual was going on in Petrograd. We hurried to our friend Madame Orlov's house to discover if she had any news, and we found nearly all our party assembled there, all talking in a very excited way. Nobody knew exactly what had happened; but everyone was pale and serious. One of the men had been to the station – no trains were running – and on the wall there he had seen a notice signed by the Commissaire of the Committee of the Duma calling upon all persons to be calm and continue in their respective occupations, then stating vaguely that events of great importance had happened in Petrograd.

What actually had happened was the famous mutiny of the *Volynsky* battalion on 12 March (27 February by our Russian calendar). This reserve battalion consisted of men being trained to complete the *Volynsky* regiment, ravaged at the front. By an order of the General Staff – a sadly unwise order – its men were drawn, in the greater part, from residents of the city – mostly workmen from the Petrograd factories, not soldiers but recently mobilised civilians of the capital, corrupted by propaganda.

---

[10] Kislovodsk is in the south of Russia, near the border with Georgia.

My mother, Clair and Tata were in Petrograd at this time, and my brother, who had been injured in the leg, had recently been sent to one of the capital's suburbs in charge of the sick soldiers of his regiment. My husband's family was, as we knew, safe on their estate near the Ural Mountains. Of course, I was very much worried about my family, and the scarcity of news increased my anxiety. A few days passed in awful anguish, the vague tidings growing worse and worse. Then, one morning we were awakened by a knock on the door and a telegram was handed to us. It was from Tata – a brief announcement that my brother had been killed. On learning what had befallen me, all our friends came to see us. Among them was Countess Anastasie Hendrikoff, Nastinka as we called her, who was lady-in-waiting to the Empress. By that time we had heard of the abdication of the Emperor, and the news was spreading that the entire Imperial Family was about to be arrested. Poor Nastinka was terribly affected; she was heart and soul devoted to the Empress and her family and she suffered agony at the bare thought of what they were going through. She left for Tsarskoe Selo on the first train that was available and, joining the Imperial Family, accompanied them when they were deported to Tobolsk. She would never have left them; but at Ekaterinburg she was forcibly taken from them, put into prison, and, shortly afterward, shot. Rumours of murders in Petrograd were now circulating wildly in Kislovodsk, and already meetings were being held in the streets and revolutionary speeches were to be heard here and there.

One day a man wearing a huge red bow on his coat stopped me in the street, and, holding out one of those boxes used for collecting donations for charity, he addressed me as "comrade" and asked me to give something for "liberty". To be sure it sounded to me as a queer object for donations, and if the so-called liberty was used to kill people, impunity guaranteed, I certainly did not feel like helping in any way. I walked on without a word, the man following me closely and uttering threats because I had refused to give to "the cause". The idea of being forced into doing something for "Liberty's" sake struck me as being quite entertaining and I turned an amused face upon him. I suppose he realised the absurdity of the situation, for he stopped in the middle of a sentence, and, stepping back, let me go on my way without further words.

My husband, who had wanted to join his battalion at once, had received a telegram from his commander telling him to stay where he was. There was no word of explanation, but we learned the reason for this later. At the end of February, the Navy Guards had been called back from the front to reenforce the Imperial bodyguard at Tsarskoe Selo. When the revolution broke out, the reserve detachment quartered at Petrograd joined the rebels, and sailors came to Tsarskoe Selo to induce the men of the battalion to do likewise. Despite the efforts of their officers, the sailors began to desert in groups. Though threatened by the men, the officers remained at their posts. The Empress knew of this and was deeply moved by their devotion; but after several days she summoned the officers, and, thanking them, bade them leave Tsarskoe Selo, for she feared the situation might lead to bloodshed if they remained.

To their protests, the Empress replied that she ordered them to leave; and she added that they must not worry because the Temporary Government had taken measures to guard the Imperial Family. Thus the battalion had fallen to pieces, so to speak, and it was at this moment that the commander wired Paul to stay where he was – there was nothing for him to come back to.

The days dragged on. People had already been arrested in Kislovodsk, and we all had the uneasy feeling that we were being watched. Several men were always hanging about our hotel and we felt their eyes upon us every time we looked away from them. People stayed mostly at home now, and we saw little of our friends. In the meantime, I had received another wire from Tata, telling me that an important letter had been sent to me in care of her maid. We would have left Kislovodsk, where it had now become very disagreeable, if we had not been expecting this letter. At last, Tata's maid arrived. As soon as she had asked the hotel clerk for us, two men who had been standing at the door walked up to her.

"So, you are the carrier of that important letter," they said. "You will have to give it to us and if we find something suspicious in it, you, as well as your masters, will be arrested."

The girl, keeping her presence of mind, answered them that the letter had been in her handbag; but she had lost it and she was wondering what fib to tell us so that we should not scold her for her carelessness. The men, luckily enough, believed her, for to persuade them she turned out the contents of her suitcase and there was no letter there. They laughed and gave her plenty of advice regarding the way to deceive us.

The letter, which the girl was wearing on her person, contained details of my brother's death, on which I shall not dwell here, and it also told us of what was going on in Petrograd.

In its naivete, thinking that in the twinkling of an eye and thanks to the revolution, all the criminals had become good, the government had committed a blunder in the very first days of its power. The prison doors had been opened and the capital flooded by individuals whose first act was to burn all the documents concerning their crimes. Sure of their impunity, they broke into houses, robbing and killing right and left. As an example of the awful deeds of those days, I can cite the death of General Giers, whom we personally knew. The mob burst into his apartment in the middle of the night and pulled the General out of bed. In the presence of his wife and daughter, who were firmly held at a distance, one of the men picked up a penknife on the desk and put the General's eyes out. Then he was dragged by his feet out to the street and thrown into one of the canals that run through the city.

We felt that we could not stay any longer in Kislovodsk. We wanted to leave for Petrograd immediately; but Anna, my sister's maid, strongly advised us to do nothing of the sort. She was sure that if we made preparations to leave Kislovodsk for good, we would be arrested on the spot. We then decided to leave most of our belongings at the hotel in order to suggest that we were merely going to some place in the neighbourhood for a couple of days. In truth, we planned to go for a short time to Tiflis and from there on to Petrograd, hoping in this way our traces would be lost.[11] Anna persuaded us to let her stay in Kislovodsk, from where she would go back to the capital with our things as soon as she felt she could do it safely. We felt worried about leaving her behind; but she laughed our fears away, telling us she could very well take care of herself. We gave her all the money we could spare, enough to live upon for several months, and we begged her to go home as soon as she could. The next day we left for Tiflis.

Tiflis is a quaint, very oriental looking, old city and in any other circumstances we should have enjoyed being there; but it, too, had the unpleasant atmosphere of suspicion and mystery. At our hotel we met, by chance, my husband's uncle, General Paul P Woronoff; up to the last few days he had been attached to the person of the Grand Duke Nicholas, on whom the Temporary Government had called to take again the chief command of the armies.[12]

Huge crowds had gathered at every station to cheer the Grand Duke on his way from the Caucasus to General Headquarters, and he spoke to them, entreating them to serve their country loyally, as the Tsar had asked them to do, and to continue the war until victory. Halfway to Headquarters, however, the Grand Duke received a message from the Temporary Government that his services would not be needed. The Grand Duke, upon whom all Russia had looked as the only man equal of taking the firm lead, was thus deprived of power, and the country was left in the hands

---

[11] Tiflis is present day Tbilisi, in Georgia.

[12] Probably Major General Pavel Pavlovich, who fought in the Persian campaign on the Caucasian front during World War I. Grand Duke Nikolai Nikolaevich (the Younger) was the Supreme Commander of the Russian Imperial Army from July 1914 to August 1915, then Viceroy of the Caucasus and Commander in Chief of the Caucasian army and was returned briefly to the role of Supreme Commander in March 1917.

of a group of men weak and entirely unprepared for such a difficult task. Robbed of all they had been accustomed to believe in, and left to themselves to analyse the events, the people's minds were thrown into tumult.

It is a mistake to think that the revolution came from below. It was the educated, the so-called *intelligentsia* who started it and were then swept away on the surge they themselves had raised. How many times I heard peasants and working people say, "We did not want or make the revolution. It was the higher class that made it, and now see what the country has come to. Yes, we joined it later; but who would not have lost his mind in such circumstances."

Two or three days after our arrival in Tiflis when we rang the bell for breakfast, it was to no avail. We went out to discover what might be amiss and found the hotel absolutely empty. From a window we saw masses of people walking down the street, carrying red banners – though very pompous, they seemed peaceful.

The hotel servants were all outside, gaping at the procession, and we soon learned that no meals would be served either that day or the morrow, or the next day. All the stores also would be closed for three days on account of the people feting the revolution. Even bread would not be sold. So now we had to start enjoying the new regime by fasting three days.

We went to church, since it was Sunday, and when Mass was over and we were wondering what to do instead of having luncheon, we luckily happened to meet an acquaintance of ours, Prince Galitzin, who, it turned out, had been living with his family for some time in Tiflis.[13] He said his wife would be delighted to see us and would not we come to lunch. Thank goodness, we would

---

[13] Most likely Prince Vladimir Emmanuilovich Golitsyn / Galitzin. His wife, Princess Catherine, was born Countess Catherine of Carlow, she was the great-granddaughter of Grand Duke Mikhail Pavlovich, the youngest son of Emperor Paul of Russia.

not only be saved from starving but see friendly faces around us! Our friends insisted that we come every day for our meals, for they had known through their servants what was coming and laid in a sufficient supply of provisions.

The day did not end as peacefully as it had begun. As we were returning from the Galitzins', we saw a crowd pulling down the tomb of one of the former governors of Georgia. They dug out his coffin, and, putting his skeleton against a wall, shot at it. Unable to kill a dead man, they found satisfaction in this sacrilege.

My husband's uncle then left us, and we parted from him with heavy hearts, though we did not know it was to be the last time we should ever see him. Two years later, fighting against the Bolsheviks, he was surrounded by the enemy, and blew his own brains out with his last bullet.

Finally we, too, left Tiflis, having at last succeeded in getting tickets. By this time, the army was breaking up and the soldiers were leaving the front for their homes in spite of desperate efforts on the part of officers to keep them in the trenches. The station was a picture of terrible disorder and untidiness. Crowds of soldiers with their rifles and wearing red bows were filling the place. The platform looked as if it had not been swept for a year, scraps of paper and cigarette ends were lying all over the place. Loud talk, laughter, songs and awful language filled the air. Soldiers crammed not only the compartments, but also all the aisles of the trains, and even roofs of the carriages were crowded with them. Our places were already taken by several people; but the conductor only shrugged his shoulders and told us to try to make the best of it for there was no way of getting them out. We lifted the top berth and climbed up there with our suitcases.

The compartment, made for two persons, was occupied now by eight people – two women, three soldiers, a young Sart from Turkestan, in his picturesque costume and turban, and Paul and me. The Sart was in the last stage of consumption; he was moaning continuously and spitting every now and then on the floor. The time for our departure came at last! But we still remained, while new groups of soldiers packed themselves into the already overloaded train. In about an hour the train gave a desperate jerk, another, and again another – and stopped. Our engine was not sufficient to pull such a weight.

Another half hour passed on conjectures whether we would be able to move; then, at last, a second engine being added to the train, we slowly left the station. The noise over our heads was terrific, the beating of heavy boots, screams and laughter did not stop for a minute.

The air in the compartment was so close we could scarcely breathe and our companions refused to open the window. Most of them were smoking cigarette after cigarette, the Sart was moaning feebly and spitting continually on the floor.

After four days of this pleasant traveling, we reached Petrograd and went straight home to our apartment on the Neva in view of the fortress of St Peter and Paul. Crowds of workmen and soldiers, with red bows pinned to their coats, were strolling aimlessly along the unswept sidewalks and in the middle of the streets. Occasionally a tram would painfully make its way through the crowds. Processions with red flags were progressing along the Nevsky Prospect, men and women singing revolutionary songs in shrill voices, and shouting such words as "Down with the bloody Tsar," and "Death to the bourgeois," with cheerful faces.

These peaceful rejoicings were now and again interrupted by the passing of armed automobiles. Some of them were trucks, crammed with soldiers and sailors pointing their rifles recklessly in every direction, and some were "nationalised" private cars loaded with armed men. Two brave warriors would inevitably be lying on their stomachs on the front fenders, with their fingers on the triggers of their rifles. These cars always went at a maddening speed, whistling and shouting, the people scattering out of their way as fast as possible, for they were on their way either to arrest a "dirty bourgeois" or to "nationalise" his belongings.

The revolution had not touched our servants and we were joyfully met by them. "Indeed, I am glad to see you, Sir," Paul's orderly said to him. "Everybody has gone insane here, and you will find great changes."

"I hear," my husband said, "that officers now are supposed to say 'you' to the men, instead of the familiar '*thou*'. I just don't know how I will manage that with you. I am afraid I will be making a mistake all the time."

"You can say 'you' or '*thou*' to me, whichever you please," he answered. "That makes no difference to me. All this is so silly, I simply cannot get over it."

In Russia to say *thou* to a person is not in the least insulting. Peasants always said *thou* to us and we liked it. In a speech to the Tsar himself *thou* was very often used. It was a friendly and familiar manner of address and truly Russian; the imposed "you" sounded very foreign, affected and cold.

The next day was a great day for the revolutionaries.[14] They had been preparing for it for some time. It was the funeral of the "victims" of the revolution, meaning by victims, of course, those who had died for "the cause". It was to be an imposing ceremony; but as there had been but very few "victims", a number of bodies of murdered policemen, of tramps and unidentified men had been borrowed to make up the appointed number that were to be given the honour of being buried in the middle of the city, amidst speeches and the singing of the Marseillaise. On the Champs de Mars, a huge place where military parades used to take place, one big grave was dug and then marked by high poles with red flags waving from their tops. From the early morning tremendous crowds were gathering to watch the performance, and about noon the procession appeared. We could see from our windows the

---

[14] 23 March 1917.

coffins, draped in bright red cloth, borne slowly through the masses of people. Banners bearing insulting inscriptions against the bourgeois and appeals for justice dangled in the sun.

Later that afternoon I drove past the grave of the "victims". I had taken a cab, thinking it safer not to use our car. When we were opposite the grave my cabman took off his hat and crossed himself with devotion. "Oh God!" he murmured. "To think that my poor brother has been buried without even a prayer, in red rags, and to the sound of those horrid songs!"

"Was your brother a revolutionary?" I asked.

"Oh, no!" he exclaimed. "God forbid! He was a policeman and was killed by these cowards. My mother went to the morgue to get his body; but although she begged and wept, they would not give it to her. They said they needed it for this funeral. Funeral indeed!" he continued furiously, "Just buried like a dog!" And, pulling up the reins, he drove me away at a brisk pace.

Soon after this I went to my brother's grave. Tata went with me to show it to me, for no name had been placed on it lest his tomb be violated as so many graves had been. There was nothing to mark his resting place but a heap of sand with some pine branches on top of it to keep the sand from blowing off, and a wooden cross. I had brought some flowers to put on the grave; but I found already there a tiny bouquet of field flowers, brought, as I learned later, by some poor children whom Dima had befriended. I am sure my brother appreciated this tribute paid to his memory more than any beautiful flowers I could bring.

Just before the revolution broke out, Ella had come to visit my brother for a few days. She was still there when Dima was killed. On the night of 14 March, a group of soldiers looking sombre and determined tramped up to his house and rang the bell. They told my brother that a large number of men had assembled near the officers' mess and were waiting to talk to him.

Maybe he felt that he was not going to see Ella again, for, as he was leaving, Dima took her in his arms and kissed her tenderly though he promised to be back soon.

She watched him descend the several steps and limp along the street, painfully dragging his injured leg, the soldiers surrounding him in ominous silence; with a sinking heart she saw them disappear in the darkness. For a while she could still hear the heavy beat of the boots on the snow. Some time passed, then the doorbell rang again, the same soldiers were there. They told Ella that my brother had been put under arrest and had sent them to his home to get some wine and victuals.

"If my brother has been arrested," Ella replied, "he surely has not sent you for wine. There, take this holy water to him."

The men glanced sheepishly at each other, then one of them nudged the fellow who appeared to be at the head of the group with a gesture that seemed to convey the meaning, "We'd better tell her."

His comrade understood it for he said, "It's like this, ma'am, the Count has been killed."

My sister then asked them to take her at once to the mess, which they willingly agreed to do, telling her on the way what had happened. Dima and two officers had been arrested and shortly after released. It was just as they were coming out of the house that Count M, one of the officers, an elderly man, had the imprudence to give way to his temper and to tell the soldiers just what he thought of this unmotivated arrest.[15] Somebody in the crowd cried, "If the Count M speaks his mind so fearlessly, it means that he probably has machine-guns ready for us somewhere around this place." Absurd as this was, the minds were in such a state of excitement, that it needed but a spark to produce a flame. Cries of "To death with them!" and a general disorderly shooting followed these words and bayonets went into

---

[15] Count George Georgievich Mengden.

action. Count M and Colonel E were hideously mutilated, their faces were chopped to masses of shapeless flesh.[16] My brother was spared these tortures, thank God, for he met his death calmly and in prayer, the soldiers told Ella.[17]

They had by this time reached the garden that enclosed the mess. It was a very still, frosty night. The snow-covered lawn glittered coldly under the moonlight. The soldiers asked Ella not to enter the garden, but to let them bring my brother's body out. They explained that the sight of the other atrociously mutilated bodies was not fit for her eyes. Then they brought Dima out and carried him home with every sign of respect and contrition and, as they laid him on his bed, they took their caps off and stood in reverent silence, while Ella knelt down to pray. They came back later in the night to warn Ella that her death had just been decided at a meeting and begged her to leave the place at once. My sister then sent Dima's orderly to Petrograd with a message to my mother and decided to return to her little daughter.

The local soviet had forbidden the bodies to be buried. They were to be thrown into a ditch and no one was to touch them; soldiers were placed on guard at the door of the room where the murdered men's bodies lay. In vain did my mother, who had come at once, beg to have Dima's body delivered to her. She then bribed the guard and stole the body away.[18] In the middle of the night, with the aid of his orderly, she took him on a sledge to this distant cemetery, where at dawn a funeral service was said, and his body put to eternal rest.

---

[16] Colonel Egerstrom.

[17] Every account of the murders in Luga on 1 March 1917 states that, while Mengden was killed immediately by a rifle butt to the head, both Colonel Egerstrom and Count Vladimir Kleinmichel, were first bayonetted and then finished off with rifle butts.

[18] This was confusing as at first it appears Dima's body was at his home, but the passages are as Olga originally wrote them.

In Petrograd, Kerensky was gaining a great popularity. He was the only member of the government who seemed to have a certain energy amidst the general confusion and flabbiness, and his democratic ways had won him the sympathies of the lower classes. In the morning when he arrived at his office, he shook hands with every employee, beginning with the doorman, the janitor, the couriers and so forth. Women repeated with tears of emotion in their eyes, that "the poor dear" had shaken so many hands in the past weeks that he was now obliged to wear his benumbed arm in a sling.

We stayed in Petrograd about two weeks, in the course of which I went to Moscow to the funeral of Vassiliok, our family physician, who had outlived Dima but a short time. His health had been badly shaken at the beginning of the revolution. His lifelong dreams had taken a hideous shape and disillusion had been exceedingly painful to him. Dima's death had been the last blow. After that, one might say Vassiliok did not live, he only existed – silently, gloomily, he did his work until one morning he was found dead by his servant.

At the end of the second week my husband was assigned to the Black Sea fleet; I accompanied him to Sebastopol.[19] It had been

---

[19] Sevastopol. I have a certificate written in Kislovodsk and dated 27 March 1917 which reads, "Lieutenant Pavel Alexeyevich Voronov has been under my medical observation during spring this year. He is suffering from: weakened functioning of the upper parts of the lungs, anaemia, and neural exhaustion. Therefore, I regard it necessary for the health of Lieutenant Voronov to have a change in climate conditions and a service transfer to the Black Sea fleet, to a stress-free coast-based position, if possible. I certify the above-written by my signature and my personal seal."

There is also a certificate from 28 July 1917 which states, "By referral No 64964 of the Medical Inspector of the Black Sea Fleet dated 13 July, and by order No 518 of the Medical Inspector of the Port of Sevastopol dated 9 April this year, we the undersigned, assessed on today's date the health condition of Lieutenant Voronov for consideration of his transfer from active duty to the reserves due to illness, and have found the following: the assessed is of average height, underweight, of correct build; the skin and mucous membranes are pale; the heart beat is clear, the outlines are normal, the rhythm is accelerated to 90 impossible for us to get in touch with the Imperial prisoners at Tsarskoe Selo, and we left Petrograd with heavy hearts. We took with us only our summer clothes, as I intended to return in the autumn; but my husband persuaded me to take my diamond earrings, besides the few little pins and the string of pearls I had always with me, thinking it would be safer to have something to sell in case the banks had to close on account of disorder. I flatly refused to take most of my jewels with me, as we were going to stay at a hotel and I was afraid they might be lost or stolen. If I only had known what awaited us I would have taken all I had, and we would have been saved from the very hard times we had to go through.

Sebastopol seemed quiet after the excitement of Petrograd; but this serenity lasted for only a couple of months. Propaganda was converting the sailors to revolutionary ideas, and it was becoming difficult for the officers to keep them in hand. In the city itself everything was upside down. The rebels had taken hold of the city hall. Prison doors were opened and all the papers regarding criminal cases burned in a public place. Meetings of a very violent nature took place more and more frequently in the streets, and I often heard such exclamations as, "Death to the bourgeois! Why are we waiting to exterminate them?"

Many officers had been imprisoned, and one day my husband was told at the staff that they had heard that he would be arrested the same night. He was given a leave of absence with the advice

---

beats a minute. From the lungs' aspect there is a muffling on the upper right side; the muscles are flaccid; the knees reflexes are exaggerated; it is noted that the eyelids are trembling when the eyes are shut and the fingers are trembling when the hands are extended. The assessed complaints on becoming tired quickly, being depressed, having worsened memory, becoming easily irritated, insomnia, palpitations and constriction in the left part of the chest, strong headaches and weight loss. Based on the aforementioned, we conclude that Lieutenant Voronov is suffering from anaemia with reduced eating and a severe form of nervous exhaustion, and therefore he definitely requires systematic long-term treatment. Therefore, it is recommended that he is transferred from active service to the fleet reserves."

to leave Sebastopol at once. So we went to visit some friends of ours who were staying at their estate near Kharkov.[20]

At the end of a very restful month spent with them, we began to hope that the danger had blown over and we returned to Sebastopol. A few days later, after our arrival there, I fell desperately ill with diphtheria. The hotel manager told us that we would have to move out at once, so my husband, begging him to have a little patience, went out to find me a place in a hospital. I should here explain that the centre and particularly the south of Russia had for a long while refrained from joining in the revolutionary upheaval. While Lenin was already successful in Petrograd, communists were still being expelled from the cities of the south. Therefore, many people moved southward, fleeing the disturbed north, and thus the southern cities became overpopulated. Added to a slackening of sanitary measures, on account of the general disorganisation, this overcrowding produced epidemics of all kinds. And, also, a persistent communist propaganda was secretly being spread, sapping order at its root. Lenin's agents, dressed as sailors, soldiers or workmen, did their destructive work and every day gained converts to their ideas.

At the Navy hospital, the chief physician met my husband with a despair equal to Paul's own. "They make me take in people whether I have a place for them or not!" he said. "The hospital is jammed. There are three sick people for each two beds. Try the city hospital."

There it was even worse. People were crowded together without regard to the character of their illness – typhus, scarlet fever, diphtheria – not only in the same ward, but in the same bed! The orderlies (men who previously had done such humble work as sweep the floors) ruled the place and ordered the doctors about. Two or three physicians who had opposed them had been

---

[20] Now Kharkiv in Ukraine.

arrested and shot. To segregate people according to their diseases was a "bourgeois prejudice" unworthy of a proletarian.

Sebastopol is a small place and my husband had soon been in every hospital, with the same result. He was coming home in perfect despair, wondering what he could do next, when he met a fellow officer in the street. He told Paul that he was on his way to take the submarine he commanded out for a twelve-day cruise and learning of our predicament insisted that we should move to his apartment, the key of which he turned over to Paul then and there.

I am sorry we could never return his kindness. The poor fellow was shot later by the Bolsheviks. We moved into the tiny apartment. There was no ambulance to take me there, so my husband carried me to a cab. In the apartment he gave me the only bed, and he slept on the rug alongside of it, while my maid had the davenport in the next room.

We had wired to my sisters of my illness, and Tata came down two or three days later. She was just in time for both Paul and my maid, Katia, were taken by a violent form of the influenza. Tata, to whom we had forbidden the entrance of our apartment, passed us food and medicine through the window. A doctor came twice a day and very kindly did what he could for us. It was out of the question to get a nurse, of course. Eventually, however, we all recovered and moved back to the hotel.

The first time that I was able, after this illness, to take a walk, I went to the public gardens by the sea, and this is what I saw: On an open stage, the audience yelling their approval, stood the famous bass, Chaliapin, dressed as a sailor and embracing a sailor on either side of him, while he sang a revolutionary song.[21] Chaliapin, who had sung on his knees the Russian anthem in the

---

[21] In July 1917, Chaliapin organised a charity open-air concert in Sevastopol for injured seamen and soldiers and the disabled. He did sing "The Song of the Revolution" at this concert.

presence of the Emperor at a performance of the opera *Boris Godunov* was now playing the part of a revolutionary enthusiast!

Church was a great comfort to us, and I went to Mass nearly every day. The priests openly and fearlessly condemned the crimes that were daily being perpetrated, and they strove to awaken the conscience of the people. I admired their courage, for they were certainly exposing themselves to great danger.

Things were getting worse. Officers were disarmed and many of them arrested. When a group of sailors came onto the Admiral's ship to disarm Admiral Kolchak, the commander of the fleet, he refused to give them his sword; unclasping it from his belt, he flung it out into the sea. The Temporary Government was absolutely lacking ability and power to do anything to prevent slaughter. Worse, Kerensky had awarded the Cross of St. George, the highest award for courage, to the first soldier who had killed his officer. The soldiers and inhabitants of cities had quite lost their heads. People were robbed of their clothes in the streets at night, and it was not safe even to go out in the daytime for fear of being shot down by a stray bullet.

At the front, a complete dismemberment of the army was rapidly progressing. Kerensky and two or three others went to the front and harangued the soldiers, trying to persuade them to continue the war; but can words have any power when a machine goes to pieces? Soldiers in crowds were leaving for their homes after killing the officers who tried to keep them back. Regiments formed only of officers continued to fight; but what was that against the huge German army?

EIGHT
# FACING DANGER

Finally, there was no use any longer in trying to struggle against the tremendous madness. My husband's resignation from the Navy was accorded him, and we decided to go to some small and quiet place where nobody would know us and where we could think over the situation and decide what we would do next.[1] As I was still weak from my illness, and Paul had not gone through a real treatment, we chose a small seaside resort on the Black Sea and arranged for rooms in a sanatorium there.

Tata, my husband in civilian clothes, and I, accompanied by Ida and Katia, our two maids, arrived one morning at the sunny beach of N.[2] We took rooms for our maids in a nearby villa, as there was no place for them with us in the sanatorium. That very

---

[1] Certificate, numbered 163, states, "The holder of this document, the former service member of division 184 of the light artillery battalion Pavel Alexeyevich Voronov is completely discharged from service due to shell-shock sustained in combat. This is certified by the signature and seal on 27 January 1918 in Tiraspol by the Acting Commander of division 184 of the light artillery battalion Colonel Mordovskiy." This certificate is signed by Colonel Mordovskiy and aide-de-camp Lieutenant Solovyev.

[2] N is most likely Evpatoria in western Crimea, north of Sevastopol. Originally Olga refrained from naming this place in case any of the people she mentioned were still there.

night I had a most vivid and terrifying dream. I dreamed that Paul and I were at a railroad station crowded with sailors and soldiers. We had a horrible feeling of being tracked and were hoping against hope to leave the place undetected. Then I saw a group of sailors at a distance. Talking to them was a short but strongly built man. He, too, was wearing a sailor's uniform and was armed from head to foot with revolvers, bombs, and so forth. As I looked at him, he turned on his heel, pointed at us and with a leisurely, swinging gait, walked up to where we stood. His cap was tilted back and he was smoking a cigarette. The man's features impressed themselves upon my mind.

"We know who you are," he said to my husband. "You will have to come with us."

I knew what that meant and flung myself against Paul, encircling him with my arms, while the rest of the men were closing in upon us. With a jerk I sat up in bed, trembling all over, cold perspiration on my forehead. Was this dream a result of overstrung nerves or a premonition of what might come true? The sailor's face seemed to peer at me through the darkness, I felt that if this man really existed, I would know him in a million.

The sanatorium was full to overflowing. There were very ill persons who never appeared at the *table d'hôte*, there were convalescents, and also those who were staying there just for a rest and a refuge. Among these was a young soldier, just recovered from typhus contracted at the front. He was only seventeen and very proud of his uniform. He was taken care of by his beautiful sister, a divorcee, who worshipped him and was more of a mother to him than a sister. And there was an elderly couple of the *nouveau riche* type, their fingers bedecked with jewels. From breakfast till night they would walk, arm in arm, solemnly and silently, on the beach and in the garden, diamond rings on at least three fingers of each of their hands glittering gaily in the sun. We also made friends with a newspaper reporter, who was a very agreeable companion and who had always the latest news.

In the evenings, my husband usually played billiards with the manager of the sanatorium. This man, Mr T, a simple but very able man, was a socialist; he believed thoroughly in the revolution, and he and my husband, each night, had endless political disputes, in spite of which, they grew very fond of each other. Mr T was such a good and straightforward man, and so glad to help anybody he could, that we had great esteem for him.

One of my cousins, Count Nicholas Kleinmichel, had also come with his family to live in N, where he had bought some land and planned to build a villa.[3] In the meantime, he had rented a house on the beach, a few houses away from our sanatorium.

Everything was calm at N; but the news from Petrograd and all of northern Russia grew steadily worse. General Korniloff, now Commander-in-Chief of the Armies, (and who, by the way, came from a peasant family and during the old regime had become a General) advised Kerensky to take severe measures against the communists and to send troops to Petrograd.

Kerensky at first consented and even discussed with Korniloff the ways and means of obliterating the communist propaganda; then, most suddenly and without consulting the other members of the government, he proclaimed Korniloff a traitor to the revolution and ordered his arrest. General Korniloff was freed on presentation of false papers ordering his release and procured for him by his friends and left Headquarters under the guard of the *Tekinsky* regiment, which accompanied him halfway to the Don. It was here that general Korniloff began the formation of the Volunteer Army.

Soon after this treachery of Kerensky's came the downfall of the Temporary Government; Kerensky locked himself up in the Winter Palace where he was defended from the mob by a battalion of women soldiers. At the last moment, finding a means of escape, he fled, without even warning his valiant defenders,

[3] Count Nikolai Vladimirovich Kleinmichel, son of Olga's uncle Count Vladimir Petrovich Kleinmichel.

who continued to fight until they were exterminated after a most odious mistreatment. Kerensky was said to have crossed the border into Finland dressed as a Red Cross nurse. He was the last frail and untrustworthy obstacle to anarchy, and with his fall from power Russia became one bloody sea of hatred, death and despair.

Tata, in spite of our warnings, shortly before this had gone to Petrograd to store our furniture and to put her jewels in a safe. I was terribly worried about her when we learned from the papers what had happened, especially as no mail was arriving and we could not learn where she was or what had happened to the rest of my family. Two weeks later, however, she arrived safe and sound. The new upheavals had surprised her in Moscow, where she had stopped for a couple of days on her return from Petrograd, to see my mother. She was with my mother and was about to leave when sounds of shooting were heard in the street. My mother begged Tata to remain with her overnight but Tata would not listen; she said goodbye and went out. On her way, however, she stopped to pray before a miraculous image of the Holy Virgin that had been brought that morning to a church across the street. The crowd was so dense that by the time she got out of church it was already dark, and Tata decided that after all it would be better to stay with my mother, which she did. This delay in church saved her life. For in the morning, the doorbell rang faintly and Ida, Tata's maid, entered shaking and almost collapsing. She said that a shell had broken down a wall of the house where Tata would have spent the night, and bullets had come through the windows. One of them struck the wall just above the pillow of Tata's bed! (Tata brought the bullet to me as a present!) Later in the evening some Bolsheviks entered the house and carried away all they could, including Tata's clothes and all of her jewels. Poor Ida, in the meantime, was trembling for her life in the cellar.

Scarcely had Ida finished telling my mother and Tata this tale when there was a knocking on the door and several armed men trooped in, a small boy, who looked about ten but said he was fourteen, bringing up the rear of the procession. He was wearing a soldier's coat, which was much too long for him; it was fastened across his chest with a safety pin and its folds lay on the ground about his feet; every once in a while he tripped over it, frightening everybody because he carried a loaded gun. The men posted him in the kitchen and started to search the rooms for weapons. Suddenly there was the loud report of a rifle in the apartment. In horror Tata ran to see what had happened, afraid to think what it meant. The boy, bored by waiting, had started to sing a revolutionary song, beating time on the floor with the butt of his rifle. Carried away by his own singing, he struck the floor too hard and the gun had gone off – happily into the ceiling.

We were glad to have Tata back with us again at N, where time dragged on with no diversions – only the horrible news of the slaughtering of officers that reached us daily from everywhere. There were terrific killings at Yalta, where hundreds were thrown from the mole alive into the sea, with a stone tied to their feet. Captain Doumbadse, one of my ex-partners at dances in Yalta, was lowered alive in a cauldron of boiling oil on board one of the warships.[4]

In N there was the quiet that precedes a storm. Christmas and the New Year of 1918 passed sadly but safely enough. I was depressed, and yet happy, at the time, to receive a long letter from the Grand Duchess Tatiana from Tobolsk in Siberia, where the Imperial family had been deported. In it she told me how glad they all had been to hear from us (I had written from Sebastopol); that in thought and prayers they were always with us; that our photograph was hanging on the wall at her bedside among those of her dearest friends and relatives. She also told me how, accustomed from their childhood to sports, they suffered from lack of exercise, as they had a courtyard only twenty by forty feet to walk in. She warned me that a commissaire read all the letters they received before giving them to them, and asked me also if I had received her sister Olga's letter. I had not; but even today I

---

[4] Possibly Captain Alexander Ivanovich Doumbadse.

still have a faint hope of finding it at the address to which I know it was sent. It will be my only relic of the past, besides the little icon, for everything else has been lost.

One day we were taking tea at my cousin Nicholas Kleinmichel's. Nicholas was in very good spirits. He joked and made us laugh very much; but at last the conversation came unhappily to the subject of the dreadful slaughter of officers at Yalta. Nicks's wife and mother-in-law immediately began to beg him to leave N, which they felt was becoming unsafe. They assured him that nothing could happen to them or the children, and they were perfectly right, for at that time, the worst ruffians took pride in showing themselves respectful and even gallant to women. It took about two years of Bolshevik regime to re-educate the Russian people in that way. My cousin, however, would not hear of leaving his family without a man to protect them. "Besides," he said, "I don't see why I should hide – I am no criminal and haven't done harm to anyone."

"But Nicks!" I exclaimed. "Can't you understand that it is the class they are after and not any particular person? It is foolish to expose yourself to an unnecessary and terrible end." I did not know then how soon my words would come true.

But there was no arguing with him. He said he would not leave his family and hoped we did not really expect him to act in such an unmanly way. This ended the discussion, and we left, Nicks accompanying us through the little garden in front of his villa. We had walked but a few steps along the quay when he called us back and pointed to the sea. There were several little lines of smoke on the horizon. "What do you think that can be?" he asked.

"They are too far away yet to be able to tell what kind of ships they are," my husband answered. "But as trade or passenger boats do not travel in fleets, I would not be surprised if by night we had a visit from some of the battleships from Sebastopol. The visit could prove to be an unpleasant one." My cousin silently waved his hand to us and turned into the house.

"I have an idea that those ships mean mischief," my husband said to me. "They may start bombarding the town, and the first thing for us is to find a place where we can be safe in case of such a thing."

So when we had reached the sanatorium, we walked through the garden behind the building. At some fifty yards from it there was a slit in the earth with narrow steps leading to a closed door. It was the place where the water turbines were located. "Here is what we need," said my husband. "At the first shot, run to this refuge." Night came and all was calm, though there was no more doubt that the far away silhouettes were those of battleships. By this time, the inhabitants of N had noticed the approaching ships; people were standing in groups all along the shore, watching them and discussing the matter in low tones. There was nothing to do for the present, however, but go to bed so that is what we did and were soon sound asleep.

A terrible noise, as though a bomb had exploded in our room woke us up the next morning. "Here they are!" said my husband. "I told you so." The windows shook and I heard the sound of broken glass clattering onto the stone porch, while we were dressing as quickly as we could. In the corridor exclamations and hurried footsteps were to be heard, and above all the calm voice of the manager ordering stretchers to be brought to some of the rooms to carry away the sickest people.

My maid, Katia, burst into our room, forgetting to knock at the door. Her face was as white as a sheet. "Run!" she cried. "Why are you still here?"

"My dear girl," I said, "don't you see I have to lace my shoes first, and…"

"Shoes!" she interrupted indignantly. "Will you care if they are laced or not when you are killed?" Her exasperation was so comical that I could not help laughing.

Then Ida, my sister's maid, walked through the open door. She looked even ghastlier than Katia. Her lips were twitching and tears were running down her cheeks. "The Countess is sure to get killed!" she gasped. "She is in her bathtub and refuses to come out until she is through with her bath!"

I dismissed both girls, sending them down to the cellar, and then I ran to Tata's bathroom. "For goodness sake, leave me in peace!" cried my sister as I rapped on the door. "I will have finished in a minute."

"Don't be foolish," I told her. "Dress anyhow and come out."

"I know where to go," she answered. "Run along. I will be with you in no time."

After some more useless arguing, my husband decided to see me safely to the hole in the garden and then return for my sister.

By that time the sanatorium was nearly empty and as we hurried down the stairs and along the corridor to the door leading to the garden, we saw two men bearing an old man on a stretcher. His face was deathly pale and wore an expression of surprise and fright. A nurse was walking beside him. My husband took me by the hand and made me run with him across the garden. As we arrived in the open, a shell came flying over our heads. It flew with a sort of whistling sound and exploded with a terrific bang. I involuntarily bent down as if I had been aimed at. The next moment I felt ashamed of myself. My husband was smiling down at me. And when two more came, one after the other, before we reached our "trench" I did my best to keep my head up and look very brave. As we hurried down the steps and Paul made me crouch in the hole, I heard the singing of another shell coming from afar. It seemed an eternity before the terrible crash came –

some earth fell into our hiding place. "Oho!" my husband said, "that was close. I am going back now and will bring Tata. Stay right here and do not try to look out of the hole."

There was a lull in the firing after that last shell and my husband got out and hurried back into the house. Then the shooting began again. It seemed to me that a long – a very long – time had elapsed since Paul had left. Several times, in spite of his request, I peeped over the edge of my "trench." There was no sign of a person. Dreadful pictures came to my terrified imagination. Crouching where I was, I lifted my eyes to the little bit of blue sky I could see and prayed more fervently than I had ever done before. I was just on the point of getting out to look for them and was halfway up the steps when my husband came running down. He had not reached the last step when there was a loud crash and more earth came raining on our heads and shoulders.

"Tata is in one of the cellars," he said. "There are eight cellars and it took me some time to find her; she is perfectly safe and wants to stay there." The shooting did not unnerve me now, and Paul and I began to discuss matters calmly. "The next thing," he said, "will be those men coming to search us. They want to sow panic in the town so that they can plunder and arrest before the people have recovered from their fright."

After about three quarters of an hour the shooting suddenly ceased; a few minutes later we decided it was safe to emerge from our "trench." A heap of fresh earth lay close to the steps. Paul poked in it with a stick and soon found what he had expected – a large piece of shell: judging by this morsel, the shell had been a six-inch one. As we walked to the house, we found eight other pieces. The inmates of the sanatorium were all now returning to their rooms. Strange to say the building had only a few shattered windows; it had not suffered otherwise, though the roof of a neighbouring house had been torn off. The first excitement was not over and we, with several groups of people, were still talking in the hall when it was abruptly invaded by sailors and soldiers, holding revolvers in their outstretched hands. Bombs and hand grenades dangled at their belts, and across their uniforms they wore two rows of machinegun bullets. Leading them was a sailor, his face completely black, besmeared with coal. We learned later that he was a friend of one of the maid-servants in the sanatorium and he was afraid of being recognised later, in case reaction came.

Most of the patients flew to their rooms. The armed men scattered all over the place and stood in groups at each end of the long corridors, a sentry being left at every door; only a squad of seven or eight, led by the blackened man, entered the rooms. We had stayed in the hall, thinking it best not to go back to our rooms. I heard Mr T, the manager, ask the men what they had come for and their answer that they were here to arrest the officers if there were any in the place. Mr T told them there was not an officer at the sanatorium; but they were determined to look for themselves, and all he could do was to insist upon their letting him at least inform those of the patients who were seriously ill of the coming visit.

The manager was the only one who knew that my husband was an officer of the navy, for ever since his arrival at N Paul had worn only civilian clothes.

"I think a walk would do your husband good," Mr T whispered to me, smiling cheerfully. "Tell him I will take care of you and your sister. If he keeps to the adjacent streets you will easily find him when it is safe for him to come back."

After I had delivered the message and begged Paul to do as he was told, my husband got his hat and strolled through the back garden and out into the street. I heaved a sigh of relief when he was gone.

About an hour later the armed men departed, leading away with them one of the inmates of the sanatorium, a very wealthy businessman who was staying there with his wife and his three children. There was no reason for his arrest because he had never been in the army, but in spite of his wife's pleading and the manager's protests, he was put in jail. (Two or three days later he was released, after his wife had paid down a large sum of money, about 50,000 roubles.) Then I went out to look for Paul and found him impatiently pacing one of the side streets. We spent a rather nervous and excited day. My cousin, Nicholas, sent one of his servants to inquire about us, and tell us that a shell had blown off a corner of his villa so now one could admire the stars at night through the ceiling of one of the bedrooms upstairs. Luckily, nobody was hurt.

That night we heard some shooting in the town and early the next morning the sanatorium was full of sailors again. This time they did not deign to explain why they had come. They went into every room, turned the cupboards inside out, shook the clothes, read any letters they found, and helped themselves to any photographs of men they saw. Thanks to photographs they got hold of in this way, they identified and arrested many officers.

Another perquisition took place in the afternoon. One of the men left downstairs, as a sentry, talked to Tata. "We are no wild beasts," he said. "We do not want to harm anybody; but we have to exterminate officers and most of the 'dirty bourgeois.' Only last night I myself helped to drown forty of them. We took them to our ships and then made them slide overboard from a plank, hands and feet tied, a big stone fixed to each man's ankles. Splash! they went down, while the others watched them, waiting for their own turns. But tell me," he went on, "what is it you so-called nobles know that makes you die without a sign of fear? We would have crawled on our knees imploring mercy; but you never say a word. There was only one who went mad, suddenly laughing uproariously while we were tying another man. We had to throw him in before his turn had come."

Tata and I had made a package of our most important papers and sent them by Ida to a poor woman in the neighbourhood whom Tata had befriended, moved by sympathy for her. We thought our compromising things would be safe if she kept them for us, as surely nobody would think of searching her miserable room. I had put into the package the Grand Duchess Tatiana's letter and my passport as Maid of Honour. Ida took them safely to the woman, who hid the papers beneath the ashes of her stove. We therefore survived this first one of the sailors' searchings and were unmolested. The young seventeen-year-old boy soldier was arrested, however, accused of "hiding under a soldier's uniform!" The sailors took him away and he would certainly have been shot if it had not been for his sister. I watched them walking away, the prisoner between two armed men; the sister, flushed and furious, immediately following them. Sometime later they were back; she had bribed the men and released her brother.

Several days followed in which our anxiety grew more and more acute. We were searched two or three times a day by new groups of soldiers who behaved more roughly each time. The nervous strain of it was getting unbearable. I sat at the window by the hour, unable to do a thing, watching feverishly for the disorderly crowd of sailors and soldiers to appear at any moment from around the corner. The minute I saw them, I made my husband leave the house.

All the doors being guarded, our friend the reporter had urged my husband to use the French window of his room on the ground floor. My husband was getting tired of his forced walks, and he grumbled at me now and then for asking him to go; but all the men had to show their passports every time there was a perquisition, and he would have been arrested at once. It was not by any means safe in the streets, either. Several persons had been stopped in the street and taken to jail "for identification" and had then been shot.

One day my husband was walking past our sanatorium when two soldiers stopped him, holding revolvers close to his temple. "Officer?" they asked briefly. The janitor of an empty villa next to the sanatorium was peacefully smoking his pipe at the garden wicket. Before Paul could say a word, the watchman spoke. He told the soldiers that he had seen Paul every day for the past three months and knew he was no officer. So they let Paul go and passed on.

Soon the sailors began confiscating all the jewels they could lay their hands upon. The elderly couple of whom I have spoken were talking that day at one end of the corridor, when they suddenly realised what was happening. Silently they turned on their heels and disappeared in their room. Five minutes later they themselves and all their belongings were searched; but there was not a single jewel found! It was like a conjurer's trick. Where the sly old couple had hidden them was something we never learned; but it made us gasp in admiration.

My maid Katia had asked me to give her all my things (of which, alas, I had very few with me). She wore them in a little package pinned under her dress. I had made up two pairs of earrings as buttons. Rolling them in cotton I had covered them with some material and had sewn them on a blouse which I now wore continually. Our money was already running low, as all that we had deposited in the banks had been confiscated and there was, of course, no means of getting any from our estates. I had sold my string of pearls to one of the patients in the sanatorium, and we clung carefully to that fund of cash. Then one day the rumour reached us that my cousin Nicholas had been arrested. My first impulse was to run over to his villa and find out what had happened. On the other hand, I was terrified to leave my husband, not being sure to find him there when I came back.

We passed a dreadful night, and, when next day by noon news came that Nicks had been shot, my sister and I decided we must go.[5] I prevailed on my husband not to accompany us, for I was afraid that the house would be watched and any man who visited it might be arrested. As Tata and I drew near to the villa we noticed a man leaning against the wicket, pretending to read a newspaper. I said "pretending," because his whole attitude struck me as being unnatural. He did not even lift his eyes when, in

---

[5] He was shot in January 1918.

passing very near him, I happened to brush his sleeve with my coat. On the steps of the house, I turned around and saw him peeping cautiously at us through the fence.

The house was silent. In the hall, leaning against the wall, Nicks's mother-in-law stood crying. She told us that Nicks had been arrested on charge of being a monarchist. Nina, his wife, had been assured as he was led away that he would be released in a day or two and that she could bring him food and a change of clothes every day while he was in prison. The following day when she took him a little bundle of underwear and some food, she had been told that all was well and that she would see her husband very soon. The next morning she went again and was at once shown into the "chief's" study. He was sprawling in an armchair, his hands in his pockets, his sailor's cap tilted on one ear, a sullen expression on his unshaven face. "You will see your husband no more," he told the poor woman as soon as he caught sight of her. "You can have his clothes."

"What?" Nina stammered, fearing to understand the meaning of his words.

"I am telling you that your husband has been shot!" he yelled at her. "You can take his things." He tossed a bundle toward her. "And get out of here now. I have some work to do!"

As one in a nightmare she staggered out of the room, clutching unconsciously the package to her. As she stepped out into the yard a sailor came up to her and murmured, "Wait for me in the street. I have something to tell you." He joined her a few paces away from the prison and thrusting a small package into her hand, he whispered, "This has been entrusted to me by your husband. When he was told that he was going to die, he wrote this note and asked me to give it to you. He died very courageously. He told them that he had always been a monarchist and would die as one." The next moment the man was gone. Nina unfolded the paper and as she did so, her husband's wedding ring rolled out of it. In the note, a short one, scribbled in pencil on a tiny scrap of paper and signed "Nicks," he bade her farewell and asked her to kiss and bless the children for him. Realising fully now that Nicks was really dead, she returned to the prison in the hope that his body would be delivered to her and that she would at least be able to give him a Christian burial. But this last consolation was denied to her. She was told that the bodies of the executed were never given back to their families. So she walked home feeling fainter at every step, all life gone out of her.

When the sad tale had been told, we sat speechless for a few moments; then, gathering up our courage, we knocked at Nina's door. Inside we heard her voice, but so changed: she was teaching her two little girls to pray for their dead father. She said, "Come in!" and got up to greet us. Even her lips were absolutely white; but she seemed perfectly composed. She told us her story again, and she urgently advised me to think quickly of some means of getting Paul out of N. Terrible anxiety for my husband seized me with renewed strength, and I got up to hurry back to him.

Outside we saw the strange man still reading his paper by the wicket; so when we had passed him we deliberately walked in the direction away from the sanatorium. At the corner of the first street we came to, we glanced back – the man was following us! My heart gave one leap and then went on hammering wildly. I was afraid that if he tracked us to the sanatorium, there would be no escape for Paul. My sister suggested that we should continue walking to the centre of the town and that I then should take the first tram home and she would try to make the man lose sight of her in the greater traffic. Increasing our pace as much as we could, without seeming to run away, we soon reached the main street, the man following us closely. Just at that moment a tram was stopping on the opposite side. I squeezed my sister's hand and started running across the street, arriving just in time to jump in before the car moved away. Through the window I saw our pursuer standing helplessly at the corner, looking first at the car that was carrying me safely out of his reach, then in the direction where my sister was hurrying away. Involuntarily I laughed, to the amazement of my neighbours, but just as we swung around a corner, I saw that the man had made up his mind and was starting almost at a run after Tata.

As I reached the sanatorium, I saw two large trucks standing in front of the gate and armed soldiers and sailors busily running to and fro between the house and the cars. Another raid! Could we not have peace for one day! I hurried into the house and found the manager. He was watching the men empty the storeroom. They were filling their pockets with cans of food and carrying away sacks of flour and everything they could lay hands on. "There is enough here to feed all the poor of N," they were saying, "and all this is to be wasted on the dirty bourgeois!"

When the storeroom was empty, they strode triumphantly to their trucks, handed two or three cans to each of the several women that were standing gaping at them near the gate, then, driving to the jetty-head, threw the rest into the sea! I am afraid that the poor of N were not much better off after that. Just as they were leaving, Tata arrived. She had gone into a church, and then slipped out of a side entrance, thus escaping the man.

That night the sailor who had been at the head of the squad announced that he would stay for dinner at our sanatorium. He was wearing an officer's sword at his belt with the decoration of St. Anne. I could not help imagining by what means this sword had come into this man's possession. Mr T invited him to his table and kept talking to him all the time so that he had not much chance to see who was in the dining room. But the next day Mr T spoke very seriously to me and told me that I would have to persuade my husband to leave the town as he could not answer for his safety any longer. The servants had been reading the sanatorium registry book and had found out that my husband was an officer.

Mr T said that he had arranged with a young man named Nikitin who belonged to his own socialist party to help my husband get out of town. I remembered the man from seeing him once or twice at the sanatorium. He was young and somewhat effeminate, though rather good-looking. I had been told that he had had a good education, having been a student at the Kharkov University, at the time the war was declared. Nikitin was a soldier, Mr T said, and since the revolution he had been elected president of the soldier soviet of the southwestern front. Therefore, he had some influence and being very ambitious he tried to be friendly with the Bolsheviks so as not to lose his title and perhaps get a bigger one. Mr T advised my husband to pretend to be ill, to go to bed and have his meals brought up to him so that in this way the servants would not hurry to denounce him. And the next night Nikitin would take my husband to his home and from there would accompany him on his journey by train to Kharkov in central Russia.

It took us some time, Tata and me, to persuade Paul to leave us. But I implored him not to repeat my cousin Nicholas's fatal mistake. We knew that we two women could get out much more easily alone. We promised to join him as soon as possible. At last all our plans were made and my husband went to bed before dinner. We told everybody that he had fever and he would have to stay in bed for some time. In the meantime, the manager procured for Paul a passport according to which my husband was a soldier of some obscure regiment and of course bore a name not his own. Late in the night, when everybody was asleep, we said goodbye to each other, not knowing when we would ever meet again, and my husband stole out of the house. It was pitch dark. At the gate, the watchman called out "Who is there?" for he had heard the steps but could not see who was coming. "It is I," replied Nikitin, who had joined my husband in the hall, and he called the watchman aside, asking him to hold up his lantern as he wanted to get out some money to give him for opening the wicket at such a late hour. Under the cover of this diversion, and of the absolute darkness, Paul slipped through the gate undetected.

NINE
# HUNTED

I could not sleep that night. I was going over and over in my mind what Paul would have to accomplish. There was a whole night before his train would leave, and then after an hour's journey, there were four hours for him to wait at a junction – the most dangerous part of the trip, for here the trains were searched. Many an officer perished at that junction.

Early the next morning our sanatorium was surrounded by about seventy armed men, on foot and on horseback. They arrived with much noise and clatter, and, leaving their horses in the garden, took up their posts, fingers on the triggers of their guns, at each door and window on the ground floor. A few moments later Tata and I heard heavy footsteps in the corridor, then a loud rapping on our door. I said, "Come in!" and started to my feet. As the door opened and a sailor walked in, I caught a glimpse of six or seven soldiers standing in a semicircle around our door. Then the door closed and the sailor turned to the bed. He had certainly been told that there was a sick officer in this room because his face expressed blank amazement at seeing the beds empty and made up for the day. He at once suppressed his astonishment, however, and, turning to us, pulled a slip of paper from his pocket. He was a strongly built fellow, his cap tilted on the back of his head and, following the mode of the revolution, he was covered from head to foot with revolvers, bombs, bullets and what not. He was carrying a rifle under his arm and was smoking a cigarette.

There was something so familiar in his appearance that I stood still, trying to remember where I could have seen him before – and suddenly with a sickening feeling of horror, my nightmare came back to me. I could visualise the whole picture again, the station, the crowds of soldiers and this man coming towards Paul and me. With a quick glance I saw the name Woronoff written on the paper, followed by many other names. The man looked at the slip and then at us. "You have an officer by the name of Woronoff in this room," he said.

I said, "No, you can see for yourself."

He continued, "He is here. I have correct information about it."

I do not know why on earth – but I suddenly blurted out, "He has left N." I regretted it the moment the words were out of my lips, for they could take me as a hostage in order to make Paul come back.

"You are lying," he said. "But, if that is so, he was lucky to get away. He would have gone for a swim."

I knew what that meant, and a nervous tremor was shaking me. I dreaded his noticing it.

"I know you're lying," he continued, "because I have had two men watching his every step for some time. Besides, I know him myself. He is in N, and I will find him." Upon this, he touched his cap, and, to our amazement at such politeness, he said, "Excuse me for the trouble," and went out of the room.

I sank into a chair, utterly exhausted by this last experience, and the torturing uncertainty of not knowing where my husband was, or whether he had even succeeded in escaping from N.

When we came down for lunch all our friends surrounded us, anxiously asking us why we were the only ones the sailors had wanted to see this morning. Nobody knew that my husband had gone. We soon learned that the order had been given to the men posted at the doors and windows to shoot Paul down if he attempted to escape from our room. Baffled at his sudden disappearance the sailors had gone into the sanatorium library for a long meeting, after which they had departed without a word.

The same day, Tata's maid, Ida, was warned by neighbours of the poor woman in whose care our documents were that soldiers had been seen noticing her visits. Ida herself had suspected that she had been followed to the sanatorium, and thus a link between the two places had been established and a suspicion had arisen against the unhappy woman who had our papers. We were perfectly horrified at the thought that she might pay for wishing to help us, and we asked Ida if she were willing to run and tell the woman to burn everything belonging to us at once. Ida hurried – and was just in time, for the ashes were still warm in the woman's stove when a group of men broke into the place and searched it thoroughly. Thus perished the sentimental treasures we had hoped to save.

Something had now to be done about my husband's uniforms and sword, and all our remaining letters and photographs. When all were asleep that night, we gathered our letters and papers and crept to the icily cold trunk room. There, by the light of a candle, crouching on the floor behind the trunks, we read the letters through and tore them up into small bits. At midnight soft footsteps stopped at the door, which was then cautiously opened. The manager, followed by the gardener, an Austrian prisoner of war, carried out both trunks and the sword and buried them in the garden. All night long Tata and I stayed in the cold room, tearing up papers and carrying them from time to time to the six different bathrooms on the floor.

We dared not leave them in a waste basket, as some people had done, only to have their letters picked out by one of the servants, pasted together and taken to the revolutionary tribunal. The floor creaked under our steps, and we often paused in the corridor in cold terror and held our breath. By 6 in the morning our work was done. Shortly after 6 we crept back to our rooms and dropped down all dressed on our beds. We felt very tired but happy to have destroyed everything that could serve as a clue to find out who and where all the members of our family were.

I had torn up all the pictures of my friends and relatives, even to the films of amateur snapshots and had kept only photographs of those friends and relatives who were dead – though Katia, my maid, had insisted on keeping for me one of my husband's best photographs, which she sewed up in her pillow. There was not a written line left. I had hidden in the springs of our davenport a diary that I had been writing for some time. On second thought I took it out and tore it up, too. It proved to have been a wise thing to do. My sister and I became idiotically amused at such conscientious and sound work, and an irrepressible laughter was shaking us as we stretched our aching limbs on the bed; but we sobered suddenly on hearing the sound of a horse's hoofs in the garden. Rushing to the window we saw the same sailor who had come the day before to arrest my husband; he was galloping furiously toward the sanatorium, closely followed by his squad.

They came straight to our room. This time it was they who did conscientious work! All the drawers of our desk were turned out, our suitcases opened, the seat of the davenport torn up and the springs searched. One of the men even put his finger in my powder box probably hoping to find a ring or some other small jewel that I might have concealed in it. Tata and I recovered our high spirits, and I must confess that a malicious feeling of joy at having played such a good joke on our persecutors made me rather enjoy this perquisition. But it somewhat faded when, the next day, I received a telegram and later a letter from my husband, signed Paul. I was inexpressibly relieved to have news of him; but we had agreed that he should sign his missives with a woman's name, and I was very much surprised that he had not done so. The telegraph and post-offices were pervaded by sailors and soldiers, and such a lack of precaution might lead to serious consequences for Paul, I feared.

That evening we received the visit of Nikitin, who had returned from Kharkov. He gave me my husband's address and told me that he had money from him to take Tata and me to him at once. I asked Nikitin why he had let my husband sign his own name in the telegram and letter. "Oh, he did not want to. It was I who persuaded him to do it," he answered. "There is no danger in that." And he laughed lightly; but a sudden blush crept up his face. I wondered why.

The idea of leaving N filled me with joy; but my sister refused to go at once. She belongs to those people who hate to make quick decisions. In spite of the terrible strain we had been under for the past weeks, she did not feel like moving, and she pretended that if I left N, things would go perfectly smoothly for her as nobody would think of touching her.

I did not know what to do. On the one hand I did not want to leave my sister; but on the other hand I was afraid of being arrested as a hostage to attract Paul back to N. Torn between these two alternatives, not knowing where my duty was, I spent the worst hours of my life. I wished sincerely, and prayed to God, to be arrested and shot at once, as I could bear the strain no more; but then I thought that such an end would only bring more complications to my husband and sister.

Two or three people living in different hotels in N came to tell me that my husband was being looked for everywhere. The hotels and two other sanatoriums had been searched in the endeavour to find him. Feeling very restless and nervous, I went out that afternoon for a walk and met Nikitin in the street. He told me to hurry up with my decision as he had heard that the Chief of the Revolutionary Tribunal, who was a friend of his, was in town.

"I can go at once and get you the passports while he is here," he said, "but I cannot promise you to get you one tomorrow. Give me three hundred rubles, as I shall have to tip the fellow, and I will do it." There was no time to waste. I decided to take the chance that was offered to me. As I carried all my cash with me, I handed him the money and he walked off. He had gone a few steps when he turned and came back to me. "Do you agree to travel as my wife?" he asked. "Your sister can travel as my sister."

I said yes, and he left me, walking off quickly toward the town.

Back at the sanatorium, I told my sister and the manager all that had taken place. Mr T looked very worried. "I am sorry," he said, "that I did not know you would see that fellow Nikitin today. I have just a few moments ago learned that he is an agent of the Bolsheviks. He will try to get all the money from you that he can and then he will denounce you to the tribunal. You cannot go back on your decision now – it would make him suspicious – but try to get rid of him on the way, and when you have reached your husband you must change your quarters immediately."

In the evening, Nikitin brought the passports with our false names, and said that, Tata having refused to leave at once, he would come for me at six o'clock the next morning. Thinking over the manager's words, I remembered how Nikitin had blushed when telling me that he had advised my husband to sign his own name to his letters. Surely Nikitin had done this on purpose to have Paul compromise himself and place his fate in Nikitin's hands.

I packed my things in a little handbag. Tata gave me one of her coats to wear as it looked somewhat more democratic than my sealskin, being only lined with fur. Early next morning we said our prayers together, Tata promised to follow me soon and we bade each other goodbye. Nikitin was awaiting me in the street. He took my bag and we walked quickly away. I was wearing felt boots up to my knees, as it was bitterly cold, and my sister's coat, much too big for me, was tripping me about the ankles. I must have looked very ridiculous.

The sea was frozen at the edge and a thick fog was hanging low over it. Nikitin stopped now and then to warm his hands; then he would pick up the bag again and we would hurry silently along. The station was over a mile away and, afraid of being late, we had been nearly running, which did not keep us from feeling frozen. There was a crowd of soldiers and workmen on the train and we had some trouble in finding a place; but it was half an hour before our loaded train finally left N. Arrived at the fateful junction we had four hours to wait for our next train.

The waiting room was so dirty and the air so close that I went out; but the cold soon drove me in again. I shared with Nikitin the package of sandwiches that the manager's wife had thoughtfully prepared for me – this food was to be all we would have until the following day. Nikitin tried to keep up a cheerful conversation with me; but he was the only one to speak, and I was in no mood to do so. He told me that his mother and sisters lived in Ekaterinoslav, a city on the way to Kharkov, and that as soon as he had deposited me safely into my husband's hands he would return and take his family some provisions which he had bought for them in N.[1] As president of a soviet he was well paid and could afford to give presents to his relatives.

Suddenly the idea dawned upon me that I could get rid of him in Ekaterinoslav under the plea of letting him visit his mother first and join us afterward in Kharkov. I mentioned it to him in a casual way; but he flared up at me, saying that he would not think of leaving me until we reached Kharkov. Then our train pulled in. It was so crowded that I wondered how we would ever enter it; but my pseudo-husband used his title to make way for us both, and we painfully squeezed into the passage of one of the carriages. There could be no question of sitting down, and I thought we were going to be condemned to stand for twenty-one hours. The place was simply jammed with soldiers and their guns, and peasant women with huge bags of flour, bread and different provisions.

---

[1] Ekaterinoslav is now Dnipro in Ukraine.

When the train was started, Nikitin peeped into a compartment, named himself, and asked if some of the comrades would not make a place for his "wife". One of the men got up willingly enough, and I managed to squeeze into his place. In this compartment, made for four people, there were now eleven. There were two women, besides me – the rest were soldiers and sailors. One sailor attracted my attention at once. He was immensely fat and the expression of his face was at the same time sullen and fierce. All had cigarettes in their mouths and the air was dense with smoke. The conversation was general and dwelt upon the execution of officers in the south. Each in turn told how he had chased and killed his victims, and I remember a particularly vivid tale of a man hiding in a mosque, found there and killed. They spoke with the excitement of hunters who glory in having slain some game. To me this conversation was essentially disagreeable, and I tried not to listen but to urge my thoughts away from these bloody tales.

The night came and we continued to sit in the same position, packed closely together. I was pretending to sleep as I did not want to join the conversation, but all my limbs ached. I was hot with my fur coat and felt boots on, and there was no room to take them off. Some of the men began dozing on each other's shoulders, my pseudo-husband had dropped his head on mine and was vigorously snoring away. The two young women had climbed into the upper berth and were sleeping soundly. Hour after hour passed. From time-to-time new people put their heads in to see if there was any place for them. By 2 in the morning I felt my strength giving away. I had sat for fourteen hours in the same attitude without a single movement. The cramps in my legs and back were unbearable.

I woke up Nikitin and told him I could not stand it a minute longer and would he ask the young women to let me lie down in their place for a while. He did and they at once got down. At the moment when I was struggling, with joy, to my feet, the fat sailor who had watched the scene with his sullen eyes, got up and turned to me.

"If you are tired," he said, "so am I, and I do not mean to give you that place to which I have the same right as you! It is I who am going to lie down."

I sank back helplessly into my seat, feeling like a child that gets a rough deal from a grownup person; tears came to my eyes and the pain in all my limbs grew a hundred times stronger and more acute. My tormentor probably saw my despair, for he added, "If you want to come up with me, I can make a little place for you. You won't take much room."

"But I am afraid that you will," I thought to myself. Impossible as this offer may appear to me now, I remember how gladly I accepted it. He even went so far as to let me choose the place I wanted – either near the wall or on the opposite side. "Oh! Near the wall, if I may!" I cried out involuntarily, as the idea of hanging on the edge of a precipice in danger of being hurled down by the least of his movements did not attract me at all.

Swaddled as I was in my long coat and clumsy felt boots, I somehow managed to climb up on the berth and I made myself as small as I could against the wall. A few moments later my fat companion was peacefully snoring by my side. He had kept his cap on his head and the hilt of his sword was digging into my side; but I was at last lying down, and oh, what a bliss it was! Then the absurdity of my adventure struck me and I lay laughing silently to myself, wishing that my family could see me. I could not sleep but was soon praying to God to help me to get rid of Nikitin. As the train was slowing down at Ekaterinoslav, I cautiously climbed over my friend the sailor and jumped to the floor. I shook Nikitin by the shoulder, and, telling him that we were at Ekaterinoslav, I said that I insisted upon his getting out there and then, so as to visit his mother. "To-morrow," I said, "you will join us in Kharkov."

Half asleep, he tried to protest; but I did not give him the time to wake up entirely; I gently pushed him out of the compartment, handing him his parcels. He actually did get out – and our train went on. Gladly indeed I retook my seat between slumbering traveling companions.

At last I arrived at Kharkov. One of the sailors very amiably carried out my bag and shook hands with me, wishing me good luck. And within a few minutes I was with Paul again.

TEN
# A TURN OF EVENTS

My husband occupied a room in the apartment of a certain Mr G, manufacturer, a most amusing and peculiar being. He had lost much of his money in the revolution, but not his very cheerful disposition. He was a short and wiry man, very alert and alive, speaking in curt sentences and saying the funniest things without as much as a smile. He was married to a German – a tall and rather fat woman. She worshipped her own country and her husband. Never, she assured us, could a revolution occur in Germany. The Kaiser would see to that.

As for Mr G, there was a man for you. He did not lose his head and went on working just as before. As a matter of fact, Mr G spent all day sipping his coffee or port in a cafe in the company of other businessmen, he explained to my husband with a wink. He said he had to stay away from home and play up to his wife's belief that he had still some work to do. Her orderly mind, he asserted, could not grasp the situation, and to realise that normal life had stopped in the country would simply kill her. Upon my arrival at the apartment, I had to go through the ordeal of a long and tedious breakfast with Mrs G insisting that I should taste of all the dishes, all the while burning to have a talk with my husband in private and tell him of all my recent experiences and anxiety for the future.

At last we were left alone. First of all, I told Paul of my distrust of Nikitin and how I had escaped from him. I felt sure he would soon be on our trail again – since he knew Paul's address – and that he would be doubly dangerous to us, on account of the trick I had played on him in forcing him off the train at Ekaterinoslav. Paul believed we could trust the people who had found him the room he now occupied, so we set out immediately to see them and ask them to recommend to us a new refuge. On the way there we exchanged the tales of our respective journeys from N to Kharkov; Paul's had been extremely precarious, for before the train had left N it had been searched and thirteen officers had been arrested and taken away to be shot. Nikitin's protection, even if it was that of one who wished to despoil us before betraying us, had been useful; and that this had truly been his gentle role we learned with certainty from Paul's landlord a short time later. Nikitin arrived at Paul's lodgings the day after my arrival there, and, upon hearing that we had vanished, he had exclaimed in a rage, "Don't let them think they can get away from me! I know all about them, and have their fate in my hands. Sooner or later, I will reach them!"

After some deliberation, the kind people to whom Paul and I went in our dilemma and our anxiety to elude Nikitin, decided to take us to the home of a Mr Z, a student of the Kharkov University. "He is a peasant," they said, "and lives in his village about ten miles outside the city. He is a kind-hearted fellow and, we are sure, will ask no questions if we tell him you are all right and that you have to disappear for some time." So we took a train, got off at a small station, and were led by our new friends to a wooden house in the middle of the village. Mr Z very willingly accepted us as boarders, and not once in the three months that we stayed with him did he or any other member of his family ask our names or who we were.

Mr Z had a wife and two children; his sister also lived with them. In the morning all three adults left for the city; our host to go to his university, his wife to a musical institute, and his sister to college, the children being left at home in the charge of a servant.

The house was not large; the sister gave up her room to us and moved into Mrs Z's room, while our host had to sleep on a camp bed in the hall. In addition to the sum that we paid for our board, and which we had insisted upon making quite high, we helped our hosts as best we could: we sawed and chopped wood for them, fed their pigs and chickens, and made ourselves as useful as we were able. We never went out into the street, but stayed always either in the house or the back yard. I washed all of our linen in a small basin in our tiny room.

We had kept up a correspondence with Tata through Paul's friends in Kharkov, and the tone of her infrequent letters showed more and more anxiety. Then, one day, a month after we had parted, she appeared at our village, followed by our two maids. We gave Katia and Ida enough money to enable them to live comfortably in the city and we asked Mr Z to take my sister in. We said that Tata was my husband's sister, so that her name, Kleinmichel, a name well known in Kharkov, should by no means be revealed. Tata had left N just as she was about to be arrested as one of our cousin Nicholas Kleinmichel's relatives. She was being searched for in N and the manager, Mr T, and his wife, hid her for some time in their apartment; but she realised that staying there was compromising for them, so she made up her mind to go. That day, as she was reflecting upon her decision, the door burst open and a woman of our acquaintance came panting into the room. Seeing my sister, she sank into a chair. "Thank goodness!" she exclaimed. "You are still alive! I was told that you had been taken to prison – even that you had already been shot. I am so glad to be still in time to embrace you." And she fell on my sister's neck. After that, our leisurely Tata left!

My husband moved to the dining room, where, from that day on, he slept on the floor, and Tata came in with me. In spite of the privation and lack of comfort, we were all in very good spirits; indeed, I think we never laughed so much in our lives. My hair had been shaved after the diphtheria and I looked like a boy. Paul, on the contrary, had not had a haircut for quite a while and he had let his beard grow. He was the picture of a cave man. My sister joined us in our work in the yard and barn and we really had a wonderful time. When Mr Z and his family came home in the afternoon, we spent the rest of the day helping our host's sister in her studies or wiping dishes in the kitchen to the accompaniment of endless scales played by our hostess on her piano. In the evening, my sister and I retired to our room, where we read the New Testament together, or sometimes books that Mr Z brought to us from the university library, while our host and Paul played their inevitable game of chess in the next room.

Mr Z was a socialist and we often had very heated political discussions with him. Trying to prove the justice of his convictions, he often brought his fist upon the table and gesticulated in a terrible manner; but at the end he usually agreed with us in the meekest way. We had a genuine liking for him and will ever be grateful to him for his kindness in giving us a shelter.

Sometimes his friends came to see him. They were few – an old, retired actor and a young post office employee were our most frequent visitors. Life was quiet in the village. The Bolsheviks that came to the village from Kharkov did not stop long in so small a place where there was not much to be got out of the inhabitants. A revolutionary committee was organised by communists in our village, but as yet we had not been annoyed by them – although Mr Z, a socialist but not a communist, had often told them frankly what he thought of them and they had threatened him many a time in retaliation.

One night we were awakened by the booming of cannons and, hurrying to our windows, we saw a sullen red light on the horizon. The cannonading lasted for several hours. The next day our friend the post-office employee, who always had the latest news, told us that the peasants of a village a few miles away had refused to give up their grain to the government and, as a consequence, their village had been wiped from the face of the earth. More than a hundred families perished in the flames occasioned by the bombing. The rest, stripped of all their belongings, were now seeking shelter in other villages.

Bread was getting scarce. The peasants did not want to sell their grain and flour to the cities that were supporting the Bolsheviks. Our host rationed our food and we had one loaf of bread a day for the whole houseful. Then came a day when we had no bread at all. In the meantime, the papers brought us news of the advancement of the Germans into that part of Russia now called Ukraine.[1] Every day they came nearer and the Bolsheviks were fleeing before their army. Although the approach of the Germans meant the reestablishment of normal conditions of life, the idea of having our enemies rule our country lay as a heavy weight upon our hearts.

In Kharkov and its suburbs, the Bolsheviks were getting nervous and therefore cruelty followed upon cruelty. Houses were ransacked and all that could be appropriated hastily loaded into trains and sent off to the north. The post-office employee told us that the Germans had taken hold of an important railroad junction about seventy miles away from us, and the next evening we heard the faraway booming of the German cannons.

That night, when my sister and I retired as usual to our room, we had left Mr Z in an agitated state. It looked as if he had only now realised how far into our country the enemy had penetrated, and this without meeting with any serious resistance. Amidst sobs our host burst forth with a series of imprecations against the Germans and the present situation. My husband remarked that it was Mr Z's own party and the so-called "advanced" parties that had brought this shame on our country; upon which Mr Z let out a bloodcurdling howl that sent me trembling to my knees, praying to God that bloodshed should be prevented, while Tata succumbed to a violent and what I thought untimely fit of laughter, which she tried to choke in her pillow. On the other side of the partition after the outburst, there was a silence of death.

I struggled to my feet, shaking all over. I had never seen a man hysterical and felt sure that something terrible had happened. Just

---

[1] 1918.

then Mr Z moaned and, to my intense relief, Paul's voice said, "Come, calm yourself – we can't help it now, can we?" Mr. Z heaved a deep sigh, then he got up – and brought the chessboard.

The following evening we saw Bolshevik troops retreating hastily along the railroad track. The Germans were following at their heels, so to speak; by the next morning German troops were in our village. It was lucky for us, for among the papers left behind after the hurried departure of the communist committee of our village, there was a list of those who were to be murdered on that very night. At the head of the list was the name of our host, Z, followed by the words, "and all the inmates of his house."

Free now to go where we pleased, we were at last at liberty to take a long walk. Just on the edge of our village we saw the vanguard of the German artillery. The soldiers were talking and joking, sometimes addressing as they passed along the road the sullen little crowd that had gathered on their way. In the automobiles were the officers, two or three in each car. They sat up rigidly, monocle in the eye, freshly shaven, and as neatly dressed as if they were going to a ball. A few moments later the order was given to halt and bombard Kharkov. We stood a few steps distant from the cannons and watched the bombardment for a while. It was not aimed at the city itself, but only at the northeast station, by which the Bolshevik troops were leaving the town.

Back at our home, Mr Z said that he had heard German troops were to be quartered in our village; but he announced that he would not permit a German soldier to enter his house. A short time later we saw the men marching through the streets and entering all the houses.

There was a knock at our front door. A German officer was waiting outside with his squad. He told us that he had received orders to quarter his men in the village and that Z would have to give shelter to fourteen men. Z protested warmly, saying that he would let nobody in. It was in vain. The officer silently brushed him aside.

There was a large, unfurnished room next to ours in which they all settled down. The Sergeant in command of the squad told me that every two hours his men would have to relieve the guard at the station, and he expressed the hope that this would not disturb us too much in the night. My husband bolted the doors separating our room from the soldiers' quarters, and we prepared to be greatly annoyed by the presence of these men. In the evening, the partition being very thin, we heard their conversation. They belonged to a regiment of the reserve and had come from different parts of the German Empire. Each man was praising his own state and asserting that it should have the supremacy in Germany. They were suddenly interrupted by their Sergeant. "When it is a question of the German Empire," he said, "put your private sympathies into your pocket." Upon which, there was silence.

We slept very well that night, and I asked one of the men next morning why we had not heard them go in and out of the house to their guard duty. "We wore our boots only outside of the house," he answered. I thought that was rather nice, especially from conquerors, so to speak. When Kharkov was entirely occupied by the Germans, we left the family Z, thanking them warmly for what they had done for us. We told them who we were, and invited them to come to see us at Kharkov, where we were going to stay at a hotel. It was nice to be ourselves again, to sleep in good beds and to be able to walk freely in the streets.

During all this time, practically since the start of the Bolshevik revolution, we had been out of touch with our families; we had no idea where they were or how they fared, nor were we able now to find out. One day, however, soon after our return to Kharkov, Tata was walking through a garden in the city and she saw a child playing in the sand, a little girl who she thought looked like Ella's little girl. At first Tata believed she was mistaken because the child was terribly thin, but there, sitting on a bench, was her nurse, a faithful soul who had stayed on with Ella through many hardships. Intensely glad, Tata hurried with the child and nurse to the little hotel where my sister was staying, and soon we were all with Ella, hearing her story and telling ours.

Not long after our departure from Petrograd, Ella had found herself in financial straits. Her income in rents from the apartment house that belonged to her in Petrograd never came into her hands, as the house was now ruled by a so-called house committee headed by the janitor. We had all left Petrograd and Moscow by that time, and she did not know where we were, nor where any of the rest of our family might be. So she decided to move south where food was cheaper than elsewhere and life seemed easier. While we were in N, she had a most terrible experience in Novocherkassk, one of the cities in the Cossack district of the Don.[2] This town had passed three times from the Cossacks to the Bolsheviks and back. Each time there were many killed in the bombardments and the battles in the streets. Thousands of young Cossacks, the best men, were killed. Awful scenes of murder happened under Ella's very eyes. She got out of this place as soon as she could and moved again toward the north, the amount of money she dared to spend on the trip bringing her as far as Kharkov.

Here she had taken a short course in typewriting, and in a fortnight, having brilliantly passed her examinations for speed, she took the first position she could find. As it was her first job, it was for a very poor salary; but her wages paid for the room in her little hotel and she could afford one meal a day for her little girl. She and the nurse had nothing to eat but a cup of coffee and a piece of bread a day. Now, however, with peace in Kharkov – though it was a German peace – circumstances became easier for us all. Ella and her little girl and the devoted nurse went to stay with friends, and Paul, Tata and I accepted the invitation of an old

---

[2] Novocherkassk is not far from Rostov on Don.

friend of ours, Madame Charitonenko, to spend the summer with her on her estate near the little town of Soumy.[3]

My father had been a devoted friend of her father-in-law John G Charitonenko, a most remarkable man.[4] A simple peasant, John G Charitonenko, through his work, his sound brains and fine character, had not only made his way in life but also built an immense fortune. He was universally respected and loved for his loyalty, his straightforward character and his kindness, and for the generous charity work that he did. He never concealed his birth but often spoke of it himself. He was widely known and had many foreigners among his friends; his son was given the title of nobleman by the Tsar.[5] The Charitonenko family had escaped arrest by remaining on one of their country estates, where their loyal peasants took good care that the Bolsheviks should not reach them. It was a beautiful place; there were three houses on its park, so that a number of guests could be accommodated, and the hospitable Charitonenkos always had friends spending the summer with them. This time, besides us, there were several friends of our hostess's son and two or three other people.

It was so blissful to live the old country life again; but the calm was not so great as to let us quite forget the revolution even temporarily. The Germans had occupied Soumy; but they kept only the town in order. Gangs of Bolshevik bandits roamed in the country. It was dangerous to go far from the house and if we went out for a drive, it was always with loaded rifles. Madame Charitonenko had a bodyguard of several men formed to guard the house and park, and, especially at night, the place looked like a camp. Several times, indeed, there was shooting in the night and some of the guards were wounded. All the men in the house

---

[3] Now Sumy in Ukraine.

[4] Ivan Gerasimovich Kharitonenko, who became one of the largest owners of sugar beet factories in Russia. Constantin Petrovich Kleinmichel also owned sugar beet factories which is most likely how they knew each other.

[5] Pavel Ivanovich Kharitonenko was also well known for his charitable donations and work.

were armed, and a post was assigned to each one in case of alarm. We slept with a loaded gun at our bedside. One night the signal of alarm was given; the men jumped to their posts, while the women and children gathered in the hall, and the children's nurses prepared bottles of milk for the babies in case we should have to hide in the woods. Happily, however, the gangsters were chased away before they reached the house.

At the end of July, we received news of the Emperor's murder in Siberia.[6] The Bolsheviks did not yet dare announce the monstrosity of the whole family's massacre. We felt stunned by this awful, unexpected blow. Somehow we had believed that they were safer there, away from the capital – the centre of all revolutionary activities, all the struggle and changes – where the manifestations of hatred, cruelty and vengeance were at their worst. Large sums of money had been collected among those who had remained devoted to the Imperial Family and had been sent to Siberia at different periods through trustworthy men; and the prisoners' rescue had been carefully planned. But each time both men and money had vanished. It was only much later that I learned about the treacherous organisation that had made its nest at Tioumen, not far from Tobolsk.[7] These people posed as monarchists and, intercepting the messengers who brought the money, they persuaded them that a powerful organisation had made everything ready for the Imperial Family's escape; that every possibility had been studied and that individual attempts might only ruin everything and put the prisoners into a critical situation; that it was far more reasonable to join this group and not try to do anything on the side of it.

Those men who believed this story, gave the money over and joined the organisation to disappear forever shortly after. Others refused to join or give up the money. These were immediately shot.

---

[6] 17 July 1918.

[7] Now Tyumen in Siberia.

In the marvellous little church – a perfect gem of antiquity into which year by year the Charitonenko family had gathered lovely, antique icons – a funeral service for our Tsar was held. All of the employees on the premises came in throngs to the church. Most of them, even the men, were crying bitterly.

Twenty-four hours after the Emperor and his family were murdered, the Grand Duchess Elisabeth, the Empress's sister, and several younger members of the Imperial Family were thrown into a mine-pit near Alopaevsk.[8] It is unhappily supposed that they had been thrown in alive to die of broken limbs and starvation, for bullets were found in only one of the bodies. When the retreat of the Bolsheviks permitted the exhumation of the bodies, that of the Grand Duchess Elizabeth was unchanged. According to the instructions she had given during her life, her body was taken to Jerusalem, and there it was put to eternal rest. Thus ended tragically another chapter of our life.

---

[8] North-east of Ekaterinburg.

ELEVEN
# IN THE ARMY

In the meantime, the small group of men who had gathered around General Korniloff was growing into an imposing force – soon to be called the Volunteer Army.[1] General Korniloff had succeeded in keeping this kernel of brave men from extermination, and more and more men willing to fight the murderers of their country were coming from all over Russia to join the little army that was now forming on the land of the Kouban Cossacks. My husband determined to enlist in it and so, in the early autumn of 1918, we left the Charitonenkos, directing our steps towards the southeast. Most of the young men who had spent that summer with us were also going to enrol in the White Army.

I accompanied my husband as far as Rostoff on the Don – Tata, faithful to her peculiarity in hating to move, had decided to stay where she was! – and then Paul went on to Ekaterinodar, where the new army's staff was quartered.[2] Rostoff was still occupied by the Germans, and the German staff was at the hotel where I stayed alone with my maid, Katia. There was a sentry at the

---

[1] Known abroad as "The White Army".

[2] Rostov on Don in southern Russia. Ekaterinodar lies south of Rostov on Don, now called Krasnodar.

entrance and machine guns on every landing. These did not long remain, however, for by this time the revolution was breaking out in Germany, shaking the German army to its roots. Moved by Bolshevik propaganda, the troops in Ukraine were losing their discipline and marvellously drilled military appearance. There came a day when the officers disappeared from the hotels, the restaurants and theatres.[3] The Kaiser had fled from Germany.

I had hoped to join Paul in Ekaterinodar as soon as he could find a place for me there; but before this happened, he was given a special mission in the Crimea. He did not want to take me, in the first place because he did not think he would have to stay long and secondly because to reach it he had to cross a dangerous zone. The Bolsheviks were again advancing on Kharkov, where he had to change trains, and it was not certain that he would not fall into their hands. Also, between Kharkov and the Crimea trains were robbed nearly every night by a large gang under the lead of a man by the name of Makhno.[4] The bandits, dressed as peaceful bourgeois in good fur coats, got in at different stations. When the train was speeding through uninhabited stretches of land, they pulled out revolvers and robbed the passengers. If they showed any resistance, they were shot or thrown out of the train.

In Rostoff I received tidings from Tata that my sister Clair and her family had turned up, coming from the Caucasus where Clair's husband had escaped death by a miracle.

The motive for his arrest had been his protest against the "confiscation" of all of his shoes except the one pair he was wearing. Immediately he was led away to be shot. Clair followed, entreating the head of the squad – who, I might here add, was intoxicated – to let her husband go, but this made matters only worse. The man announced that if she did not stop talking, he would shoot him there and then. My brother-in-law was then

---

[3] November 1918.

[4] Most likely Nestor Makhno, a guerrilla leader of the Insurgent Revolutionary Army, which fought against both the Red and White Armies.

placed against a post. Seeking to gain time, he expressed the desire to smoke a last cigarette. And as he lit one with apparent calm and composure, the drunken man suddenly changed his mind and, expressing admiration for his courage, let him go.

My husband got safely through to the Crimea, passing through Kharkov on the very night that the Bolsheviks took it back. The Charitonenkos, as well as Clair and Tata, had also gone to the Crimea, which was still occupied by the Germans, and Ella was in Odessa. I did not know where my mother was, or even if she were alive, and I began to feel most desolate and lost. I now spent most of every day in church, my great and only comfort throughout those blank and dreary months.

The Bishop Arsenii of Rostoff had organised daily gatherings of the congregation at which Father Vostokoff, an outstanding preacher, spoke on various religious themes.[5] These gatherings took place in the vaults of the Cathedral and were a source of great consolation to many. Great crowds, forever increasing, attended these meetings. Anybody could ask questions of Father Vostokoff or bring his life's problems to him. He would take them as a theme for his talk and deliver a sermon that would make a deep impression on the audience.

One day, in the middle of a sermon, a man's voice in the crowd cried out a blasphemous insult to the priest. In the immediate silence that followed I could almost hear my heart beat as I stood there sick with horror. Then a woman shrieked and as if this had been a signal, a wave of indignation suddenly swept the crowd. It seemed as if hundreds of hands stretched out towards the man, furious faces glared at him, and if it had not been for the priest's imperious interference it looked as if the fellow would not get out alive. As it was, Father Vostokoff called out to leave the man in peace and let him speak. He was, the priest said, probably one of those misled human beings who needed help the most. The

---

[5] Possibly Father Vladimir Ignatievich Vostokov who was well-known in southern Russia for his call to restore the absolute monarchy, as well as his anti-Semitic, anti-Freemason views.

fellow stood red and panting in the middle of a close circle. "You, priests..." he started to say, shaking his fist. He never finished – in the twinkling of an eye, he was forced out of the church.

One day, as I was returning to my hotel, I saw German troops marching down the street, they were going toward the station, ordered back to Germany. Immediately after their departure the Bolsheviks began their work again, although Rostoff was still in the hands of the Cossacks. It became dangerous on the streets; people were robbed and the sound of shots was not unusual. One day I saw through my window a man lynched in the street. A furious crowd was striking and hammering him as he stumbled forward. His clothes were torn, and blood was streaming down his face from a wound in his head. I cannot forget his eyes – they stood out from his head in an expression of untold horror. He was killed a few moments later; but I did not see that. I never knew who he was and just had not the courage to investigate.

From this time, I began to have attacks of terrible suffocation during which I could neither sit nor lie down, but had to stand, bent over, holding on to the back of a chair. The first one lasted thirty-six hours. Frightened, Katia fetched a doctor; when he came, he said I had nothing but nervous asthma caused by a shock. From that day on, for years, whenever I was acutely worried I would have one of these attacks.

At last, I got a letter from my husband telling me that he would have to stay much longer than he had planned and that I might join him in the Crimea if I would come by sea. So Katia and I set out. We reached Ekaterinodar, where we had to change trains, without trouble; but there we had to wait in the station from 9 in the evening until 3 in the morning. The waiting-room was so crowded that Katia and I could only sit in turn. There were clouds of smoke in the room. Outside there was a heavy fog and I was having one of my worst attacks of asthma. When the longed-for train finally came it was immediately taken by assault by the masses of people. Carrying our heavy suitcases Katia and I ran from one carriage to another – there was no hope of our getting in! Suddenly I felt myself being lifted into a carriage outside of which there was a guard. "Get in quickly, so that nobody will see you," said a voice. "This is the carriage where we transport the exchequer of the regiment, and I really have no right to take you, but you looked so unhappy that I decided I would." Already Katia was pushed in after me. In the dimly lighted car we saw that the windows had iron bars. Two or three men were seated on wooden benches and were discussing in low voices a paper that they had been reading together. Our rescuer pointed to two wide wooden shelves high up under the ceiling and separated from the rest of the car by a thin partition. "If you can manage to get up there and keep quiet it will be all right," he whispered. The shelves looked pretty high and there was nothing to step on to get up there; but I suppose when it is needed, the instinct of the primitive man suddenly awakens in one. At any rate, we both swung up onto our shelves with the ease of monkeys. To my tired limbs this wooden bed was like a bed of down.

In this way we arrived safely at Novorossisk, a Caucasian port on the Black Sea.[6] We slipped out of our carriage unobserved and were met by my cousin Peter Kleinmichel, an older brother of Nicholas who had been murdered in N. Paul had asked him to meet us and escort us on the boat to Yalta. Then, after twenty-four hours on the sea, there was Yalta and my husband on the pier – the same pier that had harboured the Emperor's yacht so many times, and that, bathed in blood, had seen so many people die!

Yalta seemed to have changed its aspect entirely, though the scenery was the same. Where was the joy that had filled the air? Where were the Tartars, in their beautifully embroidered costumes, who used to do their lazy and happy loafing on the quay? Instead there was a tenseness and worry in all of the pale, preoccupied faces of the inelegant, hurrying crowd.

The Germans by now had left the Crimea, too; it was occupied mainly by detachments of the White Army. They had tried to get

---

[6] To the west of Krasnodar.

the bodies of the murdered men out of the sea, in order to bury them; but the first diver who had gone down near the pier had been brought up insane. He had seen a forest of corpses, all standing up and swaying to and fro! They had been thrown in with a stone at their feet and had ever since stood up in the water. The idea of getting them out was abandoned.

The winter passed slowly in a monotonous way. It was good to have it monotonous, in one way; but I was continually tormented by lack of news about my family. Clair and Tata were safe; but we had lost touch with Ella and the last news of my mother was in a letter to Clair received a year earlier. My mother and stepfather – for my mother had married again – had narrowly escaped death in the Caucasus.[7] They had left there just in time, fleeing in a truck, for all the trains were stopped. Sitting on empty kerosene cans, they had travelled 500 miles through steppes and swamps in their truck. At night they stopped at villages where they slept, all dressed, on the floor of an *isba* or even camped in the swamps.[8] My mother had written of this terrible trip while she was still *en route* and we could not find out whether or not she had reached Petrograd in safety – for the south, where we were, was completely cut off from the other parts of Russia.

---

[7] Olga's mother's second marriage was to Dr Vassiliy Leonidovich Yakovtsoff, an obstetrician/gynaecologist. It was also his second marriage.

[8] An *isba*, or *izba*, is a traditional peasant log hut.

In the spring of 1919, Paul was ordered to Ekaterinodar again.[9] Katia and I went with him only as far as Novorossisk, and there we passed three months – alone again – living as economically as we could in the room we had found in a peasant's house on the outskirts of the town.[10] Again I was spending all of the time I could in church – at services or in the silence, lost in thought or in prayer. The tragic murder of the Imperial Family was always present in my mind. I knew none of the details, then, but was not able to avoid imagining what they must have gone through before and during their martyrdom. (Much later I learned the truth, and it surpassed in suffering all that I could imagine.) What had befallen – or could befall – us was less than nothing compared to their fate. Thus I would meditate until the daylight faded, the gold on the icons grew dim and the tiny flames in the coloured lamps threw flickering lights on the darkened faces of the saints.

On the Saturday before Easter, I went in the afternoon to the Cathedral; but that day I was not alone in the church. Some women were decorating it for the Easter night service and I joined them in their task. They were attaching garlands of artificial flowers above the icons and tying white muslin bows

[9] On 5 April 1919 Paul wrote to Olga, possibly in relation to her joining him in Ekaterinodar. In part, the letter reads, "My dearest, I have just returned from confession and received your first telegram. I have already sent you two letters and this is the third one. Please forgive me if I sometimes send them without a stamp and you are asked to pay. They say that this way they are treated as registered mail and are more likely to be delivered. I ask you to forgive me for all my outbursts of anger, because tomorrow I'm going to have communion. At (illegible) they were asking about us, he is happy to take me but when he was told there would also be a lady, he apparently said that he could not imagine such a crazy woman would exist, because clearly travel is extremely difficult and dangerous. We would have to ride nearly 100 miles, all on horseback. This is clearly not an option. Tomorrow I will report in and will try to stay here. I'm looking for a dwelling." Pavel continues the letter the next day when he writes, "The Christ has risen, my precious happiness. I'm constantly with you with all my thoughts and my soul. Don't be sad that we are apart. We are not far away from each other and this is only temporary. Your Pavlik."

[10] On 4 (17 new calendar) April 1919, Olga again began to write a diary. For ease of reading, diary excerpts will be found in Appendix 1. Dates are in the old calendar style. Additional annotations to diary excerpts will be footnoted.

around the tall silver candlesticks. As I worked with them, pictures of other Easter preparations before the war and revolution crowded in upon my mind.

Easter, I think, is the greatest holiday in Russia, even more so than Christmas, for Easter means the accomplishment of our Lord's promise when the gates to Heaven are open. There is a general feeling among all Russians of union in brotherly love and forgiveness.

Easter with us was preceded by seven weeks of a very rigorous fast. The church services during Lent are particularly moving; the prayers are sung to sad and grave melodies, and the priests wear black velvet robes with silver trimmings and silver crosses embroidered on them.

My family used always to take Holy Communion on Thursday of the seventh week; and Dima, my brother, even when he lived in Tsarskoe Selo always joined us on that day and took the Holy Sacrament with us. He would come straight to church, and, although we were not allowed to turn our heads in church, I remember how we could not help looking out of the corners of our eyes to see his tall and handsome figure in full dress uniform.

On Good Friday, an image representing our Saviour in the grave is placed in the middle of the church, where, surrounded by masses of flowers and hundreds of burning candles, it remains until Saturday night. All day Saturday preparations for Easter are made, both in church and at home. At home, the traditional *koulitch* (a high and round cake with raisins) and *paskha* (a sweet dish made of fresh cheese-curds, eggs, raisins and finely cut candied fruit) are being made, and great numbers of eggs are being painted. It is also a custom to send flowers to friends at Easter, and quantities of them are brought to the house all through the day. They are sweet and plentiful in every room. One *koulitch* and a *paskha* and a dozen or so of painted eggs are taken to church in the evening to be blessed, for it is with them that one is supposed to break the fast at the midnight supper. In Moscow, where we were so many, this supper was always served in our ballroom at a huge table which was set as for an ogre's feast – for, though at the Easter supper usually only relatives and close friends were present, it was the custom that in the next three days anyone could come to the Easter table. The servants always had their own supper table, also laden and decorated with flowers.

As children we were put to bed and supposed to take a nap before going to the midnight service; but the excitement invariably kept us awake. At last the moment came when we were allowed to get up and put our white dresses on. At eleven-thirty we would go to our church. I can picture it even now. It is in semi-obscurity, candles burning here and there in front of the icons. The representation of Jesus Christ in His grave has been removed, but the priests are still wearing their black and silver robes. A short service is said. Then, silently, a procession is formed. Preceded by a cross, icons and banners, the priests – now clad in silver and gold chasubles – walk slowly out from the church; the doors are closed behind them, and the congregation remains in the semi-darkness and the silence full of expectancy.

The procession, representing the women who went to the grave and there learned of Christ's resurrection, streams round the church, stopping before the door. The priest pronounces the words of the angels announcing the resurrection of Jesus Christ. The doors are opened and the joyous sounds of the anthem *Christos voscresse* (Christ is resurrected) burst into the church, which all of a sudden is ablaze with light. There is such a flood of joy that it sweeps even those who do not quite understand the service. I once heard a foreigner, tears of emotion gathering in his eyes, say to his companion, "It seems to me that I am in Heaven!"

The church bells begin to ring. In Moscow, the signal was always given from the tallest steeple in the Kremlin, where the largest bell struck out its grave note, followed by the booming of a cannon, and then a pealing of bells from the more than a thousand churches of the city. In spite of their number the churches cannot hold all the people, and there are large crowds standing outside with lighted candles.

At the end of the service the priests turn to the congregation with the words: *Christos voscresse*! and the people respond: *Voistinou voscresse*! (In truth He is resurrected!). It is with these words that we greet each other this night and the following days and kiss each other three times. We give and receive Easter presents, too – usually little golden, silver or enamelled eggs, that we wear over our dresses on a golden string or chain.

On Easter Sunday all the members and employees of the Ministry of the Imperial Court and of the different departments gathered at the Alexandrovsky Palace to present their congratulations to Their Majesties. The Emperor and the Empress, surrounded by their children, received them in one of the drawing rooms of the Palace. Men of all ranks and situations advanced in endless file. First came the clergy of the Imperial Chapel, followed by the Commandant of the Palace and his assistants and all those who were in the service of the Palace, down to the cooks and dishwashers. Each person was greeted by the Emperor with a *Christos voscresse* and kissed three times. Then they kissed the Empress's hand and received a present from her. After the representatives of the Ministry of the Court, came the Emperor's bodyguard in their picturesque *Tcherkess* uniforms, and the whole of the *Svodny* regiment, more than 2000 people every Easter.

In 1919 in the Cathedral in Novorossisk it was hard to believe in the reality of those other Easters. However, whatever the circumstances, I knew Easter would always be Easter to me, wherever I might be, as the joy and hope it invariably brings are of a nature that no sorrow of this world can tarnish. Having hung the last modest little paper flower, I hurried home and lay down to rest before the midnight service, feeling rather weak as I had not had much to eat in the last few days. Food was very scarce in the city – too scarce even to supply a fast-day meal. I dropped off to sleep and did not awake until the loud ringing of the church bells startled me. The Cathedral being too far, I decided to go to the nearest church. I practically ran all the way.

It was a dark, southern starry night; the lights of the city glowed in the distance and reflected themselves in the sea. It reminded me of Yalta, and a wave of happy memories rushed to my mind as I made my way up the hill where I could already hear the singing of Easter anthems. There was a large crowd in the garden that surrounded the church, for there was no place left inside.

Bordering the path that ran around the church there sat on the ground a row of peasant women and men. In front of each of them, on an outspread clean towel or cloth, was a tall *koulitch* with a lighted candle stuck in it, and surrounded by a heap of dyed eggs. They made a bright edging to the grass and gave the impression almost of an illumination. These people had come to have their *koulitches* blessed. Although I had to remain outside the church, I could follow the service very well as the prayers and the singing were distinctly heard outside. Alone in that crowd of peasants who were praying fervently around me, I did not feel lonely or lost. Far from it. In that unforgettable night, I realised fully that distance and death do not mean separation. I felt a heavenly conviction that although all my dear ones were so far from me, some I knew not where, and although some had left this world, we could not fail to meet in thought and prayer on this holy night.

TWELVE
# BEFORE THE END

At last, the long wished-for letter from my husband came, and I could join him. A few days later, Katia, Paul and I were established in another new home – two small rooms in the house of an old Cossack woman in Ekaterinodar. The heat was stifling, and epidemics of cholera and typhus were devastating the country. Both Paul and I had cholera inoculations given to us and we forced Katia to follow our example. A friend of mine, who had laughed at me when I told her of this precaution, lost her mother and her son a week later; they were carried away by cholera in the space of a few hours. During that summer of pestilence, the White Army was advancing rapidly and victoriously, though suffering great losses. All but one of the young boys who had spent the summer with us at Madame Charitonenko's had been killed before the summer was over. In the autumn, the staff of the White Army moved north to the little town of Taganrog on the sea, and, as Paul was on the naval staff, we moved there also.

In Taganrog we were soon joined by my sister, Tata; she came escorted by Clair's husband, who had enlisted in the White Army. Tata, Paul, Katia and I – Tata's maid, Ida, had left to try and find her mother in Petrograd – then took an apartment where, for a short time, we were happy and comfortable. This apartment happened to be opposite the palace where the Emperor Alexander I had died. It had remained just as it had been at the time of his death and was open to the public. I took a sorrowful joy in going there and seeking to forget for moments the present state Russia was in.

As time passed, things were going worse and worse at our front; our valiant little army was retreating under the pressure of the Bolsheviks, who outnumbered us, in some places, ten to one. Makhno's bandits, too, were a force, and they were operating more and more actively in the vicinity of Taganrog; finally, the pillage of the town was feared. In December, as a result of another retreat of the army, the order was given to evacuate Taganrog, and we all moved over to Novorossisk. There was no room to be found for us here, so we were quartered on board an old passenger boat. It was full of rats, and I kept a light burning all night so they did not dare walk over me. At night, a rat – I think it was the same one – would sit on the edge of the empty berth opposite mine and watch me with shining eyes, hoping that I would put my light out. I was happy when we at last got a room, though it was anything but large, and Tata, Katia, Paul and I had to share it.

Another gang had formed in the vicinity of Novorossisk. They were known as the "Greens", perhaps because they dwelt in the woods that covered the mountains.[1] They claimed to be against both the Bolsheviks and the White Army; but in truth were only a robber gang. They attacked the peasants who were bringing their country products for sale to the town and frightened them so that they stopped coming altogether. As soon as it was dark, the Greens robbed in the very streets of Novorossisk and quite often we heard bullets whistling under our very windows. The price of food naturally became extremely high – we paid forty rubles for a slice of sausage. This was more than we could afford

---

[1] The "Greens" were a collective force mostly made up of landed peasants who disagreed with the Soviet policy of confiscating their harvests and livestock in order to feed the Red Army. They also defended themselves against the White Army who often raided farms for food.

for a meal! There were days when we had only a cup of condensed coffee a day and no bread because there was none to buy.

We were selling our last belongings now. Numbers of second-hand shops had opened everywhere; most of the customers were peasants who were investing their money in the clothes and jewels of the stranded "aristocrats". I remember how once I sold a dress for quite a good price and was rejoicing, when on my way home I suddenly remembered that I had left in the dress a ruby and diamond pin! There was no way of finding my fortunate customer – and this expensive absentmindedness of mine was the cause of a strangely dubious merriment among the inhabitants of our room!

One day the bell rang at our door and a little boy, dressed as a soldier, asked for us. He was the carrier of a letter from my brother-in-law, Clair's husband, who was at the front. I will call this little boy Peter – to give his full name might injure him, for, if alive, he is still in Russia. Peter and his two younger sisters had been living with their mother on their estate in one of the southern governments. One day the mother was called away to the deathbed of her sister in a place at some distance away from her home, and two or three days later she was cut off from return by the Bolshevik advance. Not hearing from their mother, the children thought something terrible had happened to her. They put their heads together and it was decided that the boy should go to look for her. In secret from the housekeeper and servants of the household, the eleven-year-old child, Peter, thus set off on his journey. Arrived at the front lines of the army, he had to turn back – but by that time his home was already in the Bolshevik zone.

From that day he wandered along the railroad track, without money, without food, away from his family. It was at that stage of his adventure that my brother-in-law caught sight of the forlorn little figure, trudging along in the rain, and, by one of the coincidences that the war and revolution seem to make almost commonplace, he recognised his own nephew!

He and his comrades fixed a soldier's overcoat for little Peter, gave him money and put him on a train for Novorossisk. In his letter, my brother-in-law asked Paul to put the boy on a boat going to Sochi, a place on the Black Sea where a sister was living, who would give shelter to the little fellow until he could get back home.

There was no boat for four or five days, so young Peter joined our company and there were now five to share our room, our troubles and joys and our condensed coffee. I must admit that my maid was the only one to take everything tragically. We always somehow managed to see the funny side of every new complication; but Katia cried from morning till night.

Sometimes her despair would turn to indignation at the sight of our merriment, and she would reproach me bitterly for seeming to enjoy such uncomfortable conditions. She would not hear of leaving us, however; the very idea of that brought new floods of tears to her eyes.

At last we found a boat going to Sochi and my husband took Peter to it, asking the captain to take care of him. Just after this, a typhus epidemic – which was sweeping away new victims every day – struck our dwelling. Our landlord's daughter, a very pretty girl, who had been married only two weeks, fell seriously ill. She became so violent in her fever that she had to be held down in her bed. At last she was wrapped up in a blanket and tied up with cords and in this way taken to the hospital. It was such a pathetic sight when the young husband carried this human bundle down the stairs. She died the next day. That same day there was news of a tremendous Bolshevik advance, and my husband decided that he must put Tata and me on a boat that would take us out of Russia. In vain had I begged him to have my sister go alone and to let me stay with him. He would not hear of it.

Being certain that we would have to work for our living abroad, I was afraid to take my maid along. I did not know if I would be able to provide her with food and lodging, and, as she knew no language but Russian, she would have difficulty in finding work for herself.

I was brooding over this question when it was resolved in an unexpected and satisfactory way. Madame Charitonenko, who had also come to Novorossisk, asked me if I could do without my maid, and if so, would I ask her if she would enter her service. I talked it over with my Katia, who, although reconciled to leaving me, wept bitterly when the time came to part.

All these things happened quickly – in three or four days – and I was just coming home after having accompanied Katia to her new quarters, when, standing at our door, who should I see but our little friend, Peter, who had a new adventure to relate to us in his very businesslike manner. His boat had entered a harbour after a day or two of peaceful sailing in the direction of Sochi, and no sooner was it at anchor than the Greens boarded it, robbed all the passengers, and led the captain of the ship away into the woods. Peter, seeing what was going on, destroyed his papers and threw them overboard; then he hid. He stayed in his hiding place for a whole day and night while the robbers pillaged. Eventually they left the boat and set the captain free.

Fearing a similar raid in the next port, the captain had set back in to Novorossisk, determined to sail again only with a squad of soldiers on board. A few days later, he did so, again taking Peter with him. This time they travelled safely and the little fellow reached his aunt's home.

In the meantime, my husband had secured places for us on the English steamer *HMT Hanover*, which was taking refugees to Constantinople. The situation of the White Army was terrible and I could not imagine being sent away from my husband, with the conviction that things were coming to the worst. I prayed with all my heart for "something to happen," and I had firmly decided that if nothing did, I would stay with him anyway; but of course I kept this decision to myself. Two days before our planned departure, without a hint of warning, Paul was ordered on a mission to Paris – and furthermore he was given a mission to fulfill in Constantinople first. He would be free to travel with us – by a miracle![2] All the money we had made by selling our things we gave to Katia as we bade her farewell. With this money she could live comfortably for several months even if misfortune should befall Madame Charitonenko and Katia should thus lose her place.[3]

---

[2] In one of Olga's memories, she wrote: "This was in January 1920. The Reds were coming closer to Novorossiysk. Terrible anguish oppressed the hearts. There was no hope left to save Russia from the horrid godless power that had it in its grip. Unexpectedly, my husband was ordered to go to France in the capacity of the liaison officer. My sister and I were allowed to go with him. At that time the English military transport Hanover came to Novorossiysk to collect refugees and we managed to board it. As it turned out later, it was the last ship on which the Russians who were in the city at the time, and were fleeing Bolsheviks, could leave Russia because in three days Novorossiysk was taken over by the Reds. The ship boarding happened on a sunny, frosty and windy day. Snow was lying on the streets. A long queue of refugees was moving extremely slowly towards the ship. It's hard to describe what a heavy stone of a thought leaving Russia was, oppressing the hearts. There was no hope of coming back soon, and we were thinking that maybe it would never be possible to return to the Motherland, visit the places of our origin, venerate the sacred Russian places and things.

With these thoughts I kept glancing back to the Russian shores that we were leaving. Suddenly, in the far end of the street running along the harbor, I saw a small procession. At the front two people without hats were carrying an icon which I immediately recognised even from that distance, by the pale blue backdrop surrounding the image of the Holy Mistress. That was the Kurskaya Icon of the Holy Mother of God. It was followed by a group of five or six people. I abandoned my spot in the queue and ran as fast as I could towards the icon, fearing that the procession would turn to a side street and I would lose the sight of it. Luckily, I reached it at the very moment when they started turning into another street. I managed to persuade them to stop momentarily and let me venerate the miraculous image which, as I found, they were carrying to a sick person. As if having received a blessing from Our Lady Herself for the long journey and a new life afar from the Motherland, I returned to the ship feeling calm."

[3] On 28th February 1920 Olga wrote in her diary, "In the beginning of the month Admiral Khomenko arrived in Novorossiysk and took Pavlik in, temporarily posting him here. The Naval Department very reluctantly let Pavlik

It was a very cold and frosty morning when Tata, Paul and I arrived on the pier, which was crowded with refugees. We took our place in the long line of people waiting to be admitted onto the ship. They sat or stood in groups in silence beside carts loaded with their belongings. There was no joy in their faces. A heavy weight was on my heart, too. I was going to leave my country – not for a pleasure trip, but maybe forever.

As in a procession, there passed through my mind pictures of my happy childhood and youth; of those places that were dear to me, almost like human beings; the image of those whom I had loved and cherished, of graves that I was leaving behind...

I felt that never, in spite of all the anguish that I had been through, and whatever might be the circumstances of my life now, never would I be able to forget or cease to love Russia.

go. I have let my Katia go and gave her 12,000 roubles as a reward for her good service and all the rudeness I have endured from her in the last three years. With God's help, on 12 January, we were able to board the English steamer Hanover, which was completely full with refugees being taken to the Princes' Islands. How much anxiety, tears and praying have preceded this!"

# EPILOGUE

We stayed on deck until the Russian coast had been replaced on the horizon by an endlessness of tossing grey water. Danger was left behind on that vanished coast for us – and yet, for me, this strange new security was constantly to be invaded by the ghosts of the dangers we had survived. For long months, the noise of an automobile stopping in front of the house would set my pulse to hammering and I would have to conquer an impulse to rush to the window and see who approached so that I might prepare for the worst!

While the danger had been present, I had usually succeeded in holding to my self-possession and calm; but my nerves had all the time been storing up an alarm that had eventually to be released. Not until we finally were within the hospitable boundaries of the United States of America did I find myself able to think back over the years of my youth and the following years when I had to see so much suffering and cruelty around me.[1] Then I thought that I would try to write of my experiences – they would interest my daughter, Tatiana, who was born in exile while Paul and I were still in France.

---

[1] After leaving Russia, Olga and Paul went first to Constantinople, where they stayed for a short time before sailing for France. They lived in France for several years and then, in 1928, made the decision to migrate to the USA

Tatiana will never see Russia as it was. I hope that my story will help to give her a more complete and familiar picture of Russia than perhaps she could get by general reading – since most of the recent books on Russia seem to me to be very one sided. I have been many times shocked by the false parallels often drawn between the Tsarist regime and the Bolshevik tyranny. It seems to me that most such books are written by individuals who seek to bulwark preconceived social or political theories or who do not know the country, and I have thought that the story of a woman who offers no viewpoint but the personal and human one might perhaps give a more complete and truthful picture of Russia to others as well as to my daughter, Tatiana.

I am one of the most fortunate of all the fugitive victims – I think we may be called that – of the Russian revolution, for not only did my husband miraculously survive it but so did my mother and all three of my sisters, though I have my brother to mourn. Clair, my eldest sister, escaped to Bulgaria, though her children caught the influenza on the way there from the Crimea, and died. Clair's husband did not learn of this cruel misfortune until much later; he joined Clair safely in Bulgaria after the Crimea had been left by the Army, and several years later he followed his children into the grave. Ella and my mother and stepfather were safely with us in Paris before we sailed to America.

My mother contrived to bring with her a few photographs, and these are the only tangible reminders of the old days that I possess. Tata is still living in Paris. She has not changed at all in her character; she is as cheerful and reliable in a crisis as ever and as stubbornly tied to whatever place she may be in. She very sweetly but firmly refused to come and live with us here, giving as her reason the mere fact that she did not feel like leaving Paris yet.

Before we left Paris, we learned the fates of many of our friends. Madame Charitonenko got successfully to France, though she died a few years ago. My maid, Katia, did not come with her, but sent me a touching letter telling me how much she missed us.

Unfortunately, Katia gave no address so I could not answer her letter and have now, I am sorry to say, lost track of her. Mr T, the manager of our sanatorium in N, had left his place while we were still in Russia; he and his wife escaped to France a few months later. In Paris I met the pretty young divorcee of the sanatorium in N. Her brother, who she so courageously saved from the Bolsheviks, had died from typhoid fever while in the White Army.

I had also the surprise – a rather disagreeable one – of meeting the brother of our treacherous escort, Nikitin. He told us that Nikitin, with whom he corresponded, was occupying a high position in Soviet Russia, which made us wonder what he was doing abroad. My cousin, Peter Kleinmichel, brother of the Nicholas who was killed at N, had met his death at the hands of the Greens; they took him from his farm in the Caucasus and killed him in the woods. A neighbour found his body – it had only one large wound, a deep cross cut in his breast.

The last we heard of our socialist friend, Mr Z, who had sheltered us so loyally in his home, was that he had enlisted in the White Army and had been wounded in one of the battles. What happened to him or to his family after that we never have learned; nor have we heard anything further of Peter, the adventurous little boy who spent several days with us in Novorossisk, except that he did succeed in joining his family.

It was not until some time after we had left Russia that we heard the details of the Tsar's and his family's life in captivity and of the circumstances of their death. We met the coroner, Mr Sokoloff, who, upon the occupation of Ekaterinburg, was appointed by Admiral Kolchak to hold an inquest into the circumstances of the murder. And later I met Mr Gilliard, the Tsarevitch's tutor, who had remained with the Imperial Family through all the tragic days until a forced parting shortly before the massacre. The dignity, the Christian humility and the deep faith with which all the members of the Imperial Family bore their crosses had impressed every soul near them. After the first midnight Easter service following the arrest in Tsarskoe Selo, the Emperor gave the kisses of brotherhood to all the men present, including his jailers, causing them an emotion they were unable to hide. The kindly interest and attention, as well as the simplicity and sincerity in their relations with every person who came into contact with them awed their guards, so that even they were won over. In Tobolsk the guards tried to show the family their sympathy and respect in many ways; they brought flowers to the young girls and played games with the Tsarevitch. As soon as this friendliness of attitude was noticed by the Bolshevik chiefs, however, these guards were replaced by others – but these in their turn were changed from insulting brutes into respectful and devoted men.

Each day of captivity, alas, brought new restrictions and severities upon the unhappy family. After their removal to Ekaterinburg, the vilest kind of men were assigned to them as jailers. The doors leading to their rooms were taken off the hinges so that the prisoners could be watched incessantly, day and night; they were forbidden to go near the windows, and, later, the windowpanes were covered with paint, so that they were deprived even of the sunlight. One day the little golden chain and cross that the Tsarevitch kept attached to the head of his bed was taken from him. The faithful sailor, Nagorny, and the footman Sednieff, both formerly of the Navy Guards, who had followed the family into prison, having been unable to repress their indignation over this unnecessary act of brigandage toward a child, were taken away at once and shot.

Two days before the murder of the Imperial family, and after a long period during which they had been deprived of such consolation, a priest was allowed to hold a service for them in their prison. He told later how deeply he had been impressed by the spiritual height the family had reached. He said that he felt they already did not belong to this world.

It is upon the image of those who I lost in those tragic years, and who have shown me how to live, suffer and die with unwavering faith in God, courage and forgiveness, that my thoughts are dwelling as I close my story. Their memory will forever help me along the path that I still have to tread.

# AFTERWORD
BY ALEX DE FIRCKS

My grandmother minimised the horrors and atrocities she bore witness to. Both the Revolution and the Civil War were unspeakably brutal and many Russian people lived in terror for years. She also left a huge chunk of her life story out of her book. The reader might imagine that, once they sailed from Russia, they only spent a short space of time in both Constantinople and France. That is not true. Several years and many adventures passed before they sailed to America, where they yet again began new lives. My grandmother penned notes for a sequel to *Upheaval* and I hope to gather these together in order to publish the sequel my grandmother never finished.

After over forty years in America, my grandmother once again faced tragedy when my grandfather died in 1969. My grandmother was seventy-six years old and the death of the man who had been not only her one true love, but also her rock, was a blow from which she would never recover. From that time she seemed to shrink, both physically and as a person. Shortly afterward my father decided we should immigrate to Australia. Was my grandmother given the option of remaining in America? I do not know the answer to that. But I doubt she would have wanted to be separated from my mother, her only child. My mother was incredibly close to both of her parents, and it was only natural for her to assume the care of her mother. So, at the age of seventy-seven my grandmother once again boarded a ship, this time to be taken to what would be the last country she was to live in. My grandmother and I shared a cabin, and I can imagine that would have been difficult for her.

From that time on, my grandmother lived with us. Every day she mourned her beloved husband, and lamented the fact she could not even visit his grave. Over the years my grandmother fell into a depression that never lifted. She insisted on wearing clothes that were too big for her, adamant that she was fat. In reality, a strong wind would have blown her over. Her mental capacity began to wane and she spent most of her time sitting in her bedroom, either gazing out of the window, reading religious books or napping. Her sister Ella, with whom my mother maintained a correspondence, became increasingly frustrated with this situation, writing to my mother, "What's the good of such one sided correspondence, if nothing happens to cure Olga of this terrible indifference?" Later she suggested finding vitamins to "improve her brain capacity". My grandmother was indeed suffering from the beginnings of Alzheimer's. She became forgetful and less able to cope with everyday life.

Needless to say, my mother became more and more worried about my grandmother. With a full-time job my mother had no way of providing twenty-four-hour care for my grandmother. Eventually she made the difficult decision to move my grandmother to a local nursing home, which specialised in looking after patients with Alzheimer's. My grandmother declined rapidly and no longer knew where she was or who we were. My mother was devastated, blaming herself for the decline in my grandmother's health. Whenever I visited, my grandmother knew that she knew me but did not know who I was. She thought my mother was one of her sisters. She was always very polite to us, but the familiarity of family was gone.

One day my grandmother escaped from the nursing home. The police were called and, together with the nursing home staff, they spent several hours searching the nearby streets. She was eventually found sitting in a stranger's living room, "waiting for the train to Paris."

In 1982, aged eighty-nine years, my grandmother became ill. She seemed to give up on life and, on 29 October, she died peacefully. It was not until years later I discovered she had also been battling a chronic kidney disease. After a traditional Russian Orthodox funeral service, my grandmother was buried in the Russian Orthodox section of Karrakatta Cemetery in Perth, Western Australia, and is listed on the cemetery's Historical Walk Trail.

# ACKNOWLEDGEMENTS
## BY ALEX DE FIRCKS

As is often the case, I have many people to thank for their assistance in putting together this new edition of my grandmother's memoir.

I am grateful to Helen Azar, translator, scholar and author, not only for agreeing to write the foreword and reading the first drafts of this manuscript, but also for her friendship and assistance over the last few years. Helen's knowledge of the Romanovs and the connection between my grandfather and the Grand Duchess Olga has been invaluable and her translations of the Grand Duchesses' diaries can be found on Amazon.

I could not have pieced together the history of my grandparents, their families and the times they lived in without the aid of Svetlana Starkova, researcher and genealogist. She has made tireless efforts to find and transcribe information from the archives of St. Petersburg and Moscow and I am very grateful to her.

My thanks also to Claire Jounievy, translator and writer, for the information she discovered about my grandmother and her family.

I could not have updated my grandmother's memoir without Anna Panarina's translations of my Russian documents. I am constantly impressed by her ability to read a wide variety of handwriting and ancient script.

My appreciation goes to the State Archive of the Russian Federation (GARF) for giving their permission to include the letters between my grandmother and the Grand Duchesses.

I am grateful to both George Hawkins and Marilyn Swezey, who was one of my grandmother's students, for sending me their copies of the letters. George's books on the Romanovs can be found on Amazon.

Thanks go to my editor Kathryn Tafra, and to designer Sophie White, for converting my idea into an incredible book cover.

Over the years I have been fortunate to have worked with various writing mentors and I especially thank Ella Carey and Lee Kofman for their advice with this manuscript.

To everyone who has sent me photographs and information about my grandparents via email, or one of my social media platforms – thank you. I appreciate each and every one of your messages.

Thank you to everyone I have corresponded with over the years and who have been generous with their advice and assistance. Many of whom pointed me in the right direction with my research, including Professor Lynne Hartnett, Associate Professor of History at Villanova University, and Clare Scott – whose website "From Dublin to South Russia & Return Journey" has interesting information on the evacuation from Novorossiysk – as well as the many others whose names have slipped my mind.

I am also very grateful to Mitchell Cheng-Mader at Downingfield Press for making this project a reality.

I appreciate and thank all of my friends who have offered their encouragement and their feedback.

Finally, thank you to my family, especially my three sons, who continue to be interested in their family history and the stories of their ancestors.

APPENDIX I
# OLGA WORONOFF'S 1919 DIARY

Dates are in Russia's old-style calendar. The notes are from my translator and my own research.[1]

4 April 1919. Novorossiysk.

Yesterday Pavlik went to Ekaterinodar.[2] I'm anxiously waiting to hear from him. Our near future will be settled.

Today is the first sunny day after a long while, and quite hot. After waking up I saw a small spider on the wall and thought that it was a harbinger of some bad news. And so it was. Just before officers came to requisition our room. They didn't enter the room, and the landlady put them off for now by saying that it has already been requisitioned. But considering there is no proof of that, I'm worried that they might evict me, un de ces quatre matins.[3] I will try to press all buttons and stay. But God willing, I will leave this place soon to join Pavlik.

---

[1] Until 31 January 1918 the Julian calendar was used in Russia. On 1 February 1918 Russia changed to the Gregorian calendar which was already being used by Western Europe.

[2] Pavlik is an endearing version of the name Pavel.

[3] French for 'one of these four mornings'.

5 April.

The weather is very hot. It seems I have made a blunder with the flat. I visited the commandant, etc. This is my new headache now. I quickly went to Trukhachevs regarding this but he was not at home.[4] She somewhat reassured me though. God willing, this [problem] will be settled. Went to the railway station to post a letter to Pavlik.

I'm still worried about the flat and missing Pavlik very much.

7 April. Christ's Easter.

On Thursday I attended the Twelve Gospels. Was walking back in the darkness. The whole Novorossiysk was sparkling with lights that were reflecting in water. It reminded me of Yalta. Yesterday morning I venerated the Holy Shroud, then had breakfast with friends in the Europe.[5] I was thinking to cheer myself up a little being with people. Met another friend, he had heard somewhere that those who fled to Constantinople were not allowed to come ashore there and the poor refugees are still stuck on the ship sailing from the Sea of Marmara to the Black Sea and back. Apparently, they will be allowed to disembark on the Princes' Islands.[6]

From the Europe I went to the Cathedral to pray. They were tidying up there, preparing everything for the Easter Matins, decorating the icons with flowers, etc. A local old lady asked me to help her. I have worked 2 hours and, as I happened to be the tallest of all working there (!) I was climbing the ladders and securing festoons of flowers.

I was a little late for the Matins, but I have never before felt such a joyful excitement, when yesterday I was almost running to the church, as if it is precisely here Christ has risen and everyone is

---

[4] Possibly Major General S Trukhachev.

[5] Hotel Europe.

[6] The islands were called Adalar in Turkish, they are an archipelago in the Sea of Marmara.

running to witness this joy. Circling the whole church on the ground were sitting people who came to bless their kulichi, which are called paskha here. In each kulich there was a burning candle. The service had already started. They were singing "The Christ has risen". Both the clergy and the people were standing outside the church holding gonfalons.[7] By the local custom, the whole Matins, except for the first few intonements, is conducted on the church porch. I met Lika and Dima Golitsyn there.[8] We stood together. Unfortunately, the most beautiful prayer ("Death, Where is your Sting?") was read by a Greek priest and we could not understand anything. I stayed for the whole Mass of the first Easter day for the first time in my life. When we came out of the church, there was a thick fog outside, and we went around the church with gonfalons again. So different from our northern customs.

Today, unlike previous summer-like sunny days, the weather is overcast.

I'm hoping to hear from Pavlik today or tomorrow. I promised him not to feel too sad without him, but it's hard.

8 April. Easter.

I found out that Sasha has arrived and is living on the transport Anatoliy Molchanov and I rushed to see him.[9] Luckily, I met an officer from the regiment of chasseurs who brought me onboard, otherwise they would not have let me in. Found Sasha. He looked much older and skinnier. We sat together on the deck on two boxes. How much he has endured! Has gone through the fire and water. When it became dark, I went home. Sasha walked with me half the way, despite my protestations (his leg hurts).

Today he came to me in the morning and stayed several hours. It was so nice. We had a good heart-to-heart talk. Today I thought

---

[7] A banner or pennant, especially one with streamers.

[8] Prince Vladimir Golitsyn.

[9] Probably Pavel's brother.

he looked fresher and younger. I would like Pavlik to see him. I have just sent him a telegram saying that Sasha cannot come to Ekaterinodar and will spend several days here. Maybe Pavlusha will come. Yesterday I received two letters from him from the 3rd, but there is still no news for us. The weather is marvellous.

11 April.

Yesterday morning Pavlik arrived. He had enrolled in the Navy department. And I think we'll have a room in Ekaterinodar. Today Pavlik is going back to make arrangements for this room for me. He is in a hurry because our landlord here became sick with relapsing typhoid.

Yesterday was the wedding of Sophochka Ivanenko with Bobka Trepov. I didn't go.[10] I was not invited, possibly because they didn't know our address. I feel very sad about it. I prayed at home for her. Sasha stayed with us yesterday and today. We had breakfast together in the Europe today. I'm very much looking forward to going to Ekaterinodar.

14 April. Ekaterinodar.

I arrived this morning. Despite all precautions something has been biting me. Last days in Novorossiysk I spent in a scurry. Yesterday I went to Europa hotel to say good-bye to everyone. They are all so nice, there are still many good people in the world. On the way to the station I met two seamen – friends of Pavlik. They offered to help me embark onto the train.

Yesterday morning Sasha came to say good-bye. They are embarking on a ship to go to Taganrog[11] and from there to Mariupol,[12] to fight again. Today Pavlik rushed to work at 9am

---

[10] Sophockka is an endearing form of Sophia – Olga was referring to her childhood friend.

[11] A port city in south-west Russia and the birthplace of Anton Chekov.

[12] Now in Ukraine.

and I'm gradually settling in the room. It's small but nice and full of light. There is almost no furniture yet.

18 April.

We have settled in very cosily. Our lovely landlady gave us rugs and put flowers everywhere. It has become really nice now. For now I live with Katia, and Pavlik is in the study. Today my roommates moved out so maybe we will have this room. Or maybe the people who are now in the living room will take it, and Pavlik and I will move there. Pavlik is busy almost the whole day – from 9am to 1pm and from 3pm to 6pm, so we even have lunch separately because here everyone has lunch at 4pm. But he is very happy with his job, and I'm happy that it takes his mind away from all the grim thoughts.

There is a very nice little garden here with a fountain. There are many lilacs, apricots and cherries. My window looks into the yard where chickens, geese, a piglet, etc. are walking around the whole day. A lot of dogs and cats. Sasha came here while on his way, visited us.

25 April.

Life stills goes on quietly and peacefully. Pavlik is busy for the whole day and is very tired. Yesterday afternoon he and I made our last will and testament.

Today I made the acquaintance of Fr. Vostokov. He promised to give me an interesting book as a gift.

Pavlik met today Matvey Ivanovich Skarzhinskiy and invited him to visit us. It turns out, he works in the court here. I'm looking forward to seeing him. It brings memories of the old Moscow of Papa's days.

My birthday, 21 April we spent quietly. Went to the Mass to the Ekaterininsky cathedral. Two bishops were conducting the service – one local and another from Chelyabinsk.

The dogs developed a great affection for me. Druzhok, the black dachshund, licks my hands and feet, a little menace!

I have resumed embroidering my lilac shroud for the altar stand.

30 April.

No changes. Yesterday our 'lovely' baroness brought a gossip that the Headquarters is moving to Rostoff. Will we really have to move again?! We think that this is not true. Recently Pavlik met Matvey Ivanovich Skarzhinskiy on the street. He visited me the day before yesterday. He works here in the Ministry of agriculture on developing the agricultural law. He said, the land will be compulsorily acquisitioned for a payment, leaving a certain maximum to the owner. Some really unexpected encounters happen here. Recently we went to the revue theatre called Chat Noir.

The other day we wrote to Tata trying to convince her to come to us. I would like to see her and feel so sorry for her. Yesterday I received long letters from her and Clair. They settled in fine but don't have any money because Tata's money has long been spent on everyday living! This is just terrible! The food supply is bad there. Though this letter was not the response to ours, Tata writes that she intends to stay there till Autumn because the air is wonderful and overall, it is very nice there. I'm writing to her again today. She can stay there or come here if she wants.

Clair is asking us, at the request of Georgiy,[13] to find out if it is feasible to do some financial operation here because they are completely à sec.[14] They have not mentioned anything at all about what they can use to secure a loan.

My hair started falling out badly again. Today I started Kharkov's treatment.

---

[13] George Martinov, Clair's husband.

[14] French for 'dried up'.

3 May.

I wrote letters to my sisters and in a rush spilled ink on my favourite blouse and skirt. What a misfortune! Spent the whole day trying to get it off with our mixture but some small spots are still visible.

The day before yesterday a friend visited us, she was saying they have a lot of work unpicking sacks and making pillowcases from them. Yesterday I took 50 sacks from them to unpick. Planning to finish and bring them back today.

Yesterday evening Fr Vostokov came for a cup of tea. Pavlik didn't like him very much. He was telling how he was fleeing Sovdepia.[15]

10 May.

The other day Matvey Ivanovich came by, spent an evening with us. Yesterday Pavlik and I went to a slapstick comedy (from Petrograd, they say). It was better than we expected. We heard that friends left for Italy on the French steamship Navarra. But in Constantinople the French made them disembark, refused to give back the luggage and left for Toulon. Such scoundrels!!!

They are saying, the Cossack chieftain Grigoriev has seized Odessa and finished off several tens of thousands of Jews! It is a shame though that the bigger fish must have escaped, of course.

Yesterday I've listened to two beautiful sermons. One of Fr Vostokov (a little like a rally speech) but brave and true. And another of the Archbishop Dmitry of Tavria.[16] Such a wonderful old man! His sermon was witty, measured and full of dignity. He so well ridiculed the pathetic spirit of the denial of the God, I really enjoyed it. Dima would have loved it.

---

[15] A derogatory reference to the Soviet regime.

[16] Possibly Archbishop Dmitry Abashidze.

12 May.

Yesterday evening we went to Chat Noir. They were showing plays of the writer Teffi and she herself was reading her works.[17] She is younger than I thought, a plain dark blonde, rather plump. Her reading was not great.

I have been to church, Fr Vladimir Vostokov delivered another short speech.

18 May.

On 12th evening Fr Vostokov visited us. We spoke about many things. He brought me the book; I'm reading it now.

From yesterday we are having cherries straight from the tree. The trees are all covered with them.

Today we are going to the lecture "The future of Russia and the Jewish question". It promises to be interesting.

Today I finished unpicking all the sacks that I received, which were then being made into pillowcases for the officers' dormitory.

Tomorrow is the Ascension of Christ.

25 May.

The lecture was interesting not as much itself as an illumination of the crowd's sentiment. The lecturer was a courageous man, he called things as they are, and openly accused judo-masons in the destruction of Russia. Among other things, he exposed the pseudo names of many activists of the revolution. In the first place, the great provocateur Kerensky. In reality, he is Aron Kirbis, an adopted son of a teacher of the Simbirsk (or Saratov, I

---

[17] Russian humourist author and playwright.

forgot) gymnasium[18] by the name Kerensky.[19] Savinkov, as the lecturer said, is also a pseudo name. The Jews, quite a large number of whom were among the lecture attendees, started shouting: "Lies, nonsense!". At that moment everyone jumped off their seats and started shouting to them: "Out! We've had enough of the Jews!". I thought that there would a punch-up, but fortunately impudent Jewish cowards left and everyone continued listening to the lecture with great attention. The League of Nations is a judo-masonic organisation, which I always thought was the case.[20] The lecturer kept stressing the detriment of a backlash and pogroms against them and called for an organised fight against the masons. A funny incident happened during the lecture. The lecturer said: "Those people who under the soviet regime were chummy with the Jewish commissars, are now shouting: 'Bash the Jews!'". At this moment from the upper gallery, where there were many Cossacks, in a silent moment a loud voice said: "That's right!". Obviously, he liked the last words "Bash the Jews" but the meaning of the whole phrase escaped him. After the lecture the Kuban military choir gave their performance. All male voices, it was magnificent!

A few days ago I listened to Fr Vostokov's sermon again. He suggested that people of Ekaterinodar appeal to the Church Council, that is being held in Stavropol, for help with the pastoral word in the battle against the Bolsheviks and declare the universal repentance for the innocent blood that has been spilled by the murderers-Bolsheviks. He also invited those who are interested to become members of the Christian brotherhood whose aim is self-improvement and comprehensive help to others.

---

[18] Gymnasiums were prestigious grammar schools.

[19] Orlando Figes, along with other historians, claims this is untrue.

[20] This appears to be a conspiracy theory.

27 May.

Yesterday there were public festivities in the city gardens, the proceeds of which will be donated to Kornilov's committee. There were various entertainments and a lottery for which I helped to sell tickets. There were a lot of people. Saw Denikin with his wife. He seemed to me full of self-grandeur, but I've heard that he is terribly shy.

It has been raining today from the morning and the second day of festivities didn't proceed and will be postponed.

Yesterday evening Botkin, the son of Evg. Serg visited us.[21] He hasn't had any news about his father from March last year, but doesn't believe, or rather doesn't want to believe that he and others are dead.

Recently Genishta visited us.[22] Not long ago he had two types of typhoid consecutively – typhoid fever and typhus. It is amazing that he has survived!

Pavlik now has lunch at the Directory so I don't see him from 8.30am until at least 6.30pm – for 10 hours.

I'm making a hat from my petticoat. It seems to be coming out not badly.

We have recently disinvited the barons from our dinners and since then they are being incredibly rude.


30 May.

The day before yesterday in the evening Pavlik went to Novorossiysk with the English, he is tasked to show them something there and is due to come back today. The English are ingratiatingly polite.

---

[21] Dr Evgeniy Sergeyevich Botkin, physician to the Imperial Family, who died alongside them.

[22] Possibly Lieutenant General Genishta.

A few days ago a whole Bolshevik organisation was captured here. They had a printing works, machine guns and what not. Twenty-five people were arrested.

On the 28th I was helping again with selling the lottery tickets in the city gardens. They say, on Sunday there will be a festival again, in lieu of the one that was cancelled because of the deluge.

31 May.

Yesterday evening Pavlik came back. I feel happy again. The day before yesterday Genishta paid me a long visit. He said that he had recently met in Novorossiysk officer Koptev who had been in Luga at the same time as Dima. They spoke about him, what a good serviceman he was and that he needed to go away from there because he was not liked for his strictness. And the memories rushed back again, and vivid pictures of the past stood alive in front of my eyes. All the past, dear to the heart. Ah! ...

5 June.

On 1st of June I went to Vespers and Matins, at our small chapel, as usual. Pavlik brought the news that Denikin declared by his order that he serves under Kolchak's command. This was completely unexpected for everyone. What a beautiful gesture! I'm ashamed for suspecting that he was ambitious. Motherland is above all for this honourable man. Truly an exception in our days. The figure that deserves utmost respect. On the 2nd after the Mass there was a military parade to honour this act.

I attended the Mass at the seminary (very lovely church), then walked to the Cathedral Square. The regiments were already lining up there. I didn't stay for the start of the parade and rushed home to make sure that the lunch was ready early because we were going to the opening of the races. Pavlik came home at 4pm and we went to the races. There was a big crowd there and the horses were not bad, so Pavlik even betted on one and won. All the generals (except Denikin) and the Cossack military chieftain Philimonov were there, as well as the French and many English.

We also saw Golitsyn Protophis who told us about the horrible things that are happening now in Kharkov.[23]

Generally, it was quite nice at the races and the best was the pleasure to breathe the wonderful steppe air. There was no dust because it was the grass track.

Pavlik and I are dreaming of going one day to the pine grove outside the town. They say it's lovely there.

There has been no news from Sochi for a long time. We are very worried about Pavlik's family because Ufa is seized by the Reds again.

9 June.

Last night someone stole all the linen that was washed and hung to dry overnight in the shed. The locks were broken and everything was taken. A lot of linen was lost, primarily dining linen.

10 June.

Pavlik came from work earlier than usual and we decided to go for a walk and on Krasnaya. We walked into a cheburek café to have some chebureks.[24] They were very tasty and the small courtyard there was very nicely set up. From there we went to the city garden and then to the theatre. The Priestess of the Fire operetta was on. It turned out to be much better than we expected.

---

[23] Alexander Dmitrievich Golitsyn.

[24] A kind of mutton pie, popular in the Crimea and the Caucasus.

11 June.

In the evening Pavlik and I went to Badurov's Caucasus restaurant and in its tiny garden we had yabbies and a beautiful shashlik. Came back home by the evening tea. Today, if it doesn't start raining and if Pavlik doesn't have to stay back at work, we want to go to the pine grove outside the town. It's still very hot. I have been sitting in the garden now baking in the sun.

Today our cook – Varya the Armenian – has left. Another one has been hired but I'm not sure for how long.


13 June.

Yesterday Pavlik and I (he came back from work earlier than usual) took a tram to Chistyakovskaya grove outside the town. The grove itself is dense and shady, a mixture of spruce and deciduous trees, but it is being very badly maintained. It's dirty and bleak. We had a disgusting clabber there.[25] Then we watched airplanes taking off from a nearby field which was very beautiful.

The progress at the front is fantastic, thanks God. Kharkov, Belgorod and Astrakhan are taken over.

Pavlik is going to take three days leave in the next few days and we will travel on a steamer along the Kuban river up to Temryuk. For several days now it has been quite hot.

The new cook refused to start. What are we going to do!?!!!


17 June.

On Saturday the 15th Pavlik's colleague First lieutenant Ilvov invited us for lunch.[26] He lives outside the town, right next to the Kuban River. We went there together with him. They live in a small house, like a hut, with one room and a kitchen. There is a small garden there with cherries and huge light-pink poppies. His

---

[25] A fermented dairy drink.

[26] Possibly Boris Yakovlevich Ilvov.

wife was a Sister of Mercy in the Kuban campaign, and they have a 6 year-old-son, a very sweet boy. They are both very nice, especially he, a very likeable person. With his eyes he slightly reminds me of Greve[27] and a little of my brother Sasha.[28] The table was taken out to the garden under the trees and we had lunch in open air which was very pleasant. Lieutenant Molchanov with wife also came for lunch. They are very young and seem very nice too. Everything was prepared by the hostess and was very tasty, and the atmosphere was warm. Later we sat on the bank of the river and went home when it became almost completely dark.

There are big developments today – the funeral of the Kuban Rada's Chairman Ryabovol.[29] An unknown assassin shot him dead in the Palace Hotel in Rostov. Rada is making a huge noise about it. The shops and entertainment venues are closing for three days. Also, there will be also no electricity and no trams. Proclamations from the Rada to the residents and Cossacks are displayed everywhere in town stating that "the people's representative" was murdered by the "treacherous monarchists", and similar nonsense and disgusting lies. An absolutely unacceptable and outrageous proclamation. And by the way, it has not even been found yet who murdered him. A fierce agitation is going on in town against the Volunteer Army and Denikin is being accused of instigating the murder and paying somebody to carry it out.[30]

The Rada issued a decree that all newspapers that have ever written anything against Ryabovol, are to be closed and their editors deported out of the Kuban area, and all branches of Osvag are to be closed too.[31] This is a direct attack on the Volunteer

---

[27] Possibly Archbishop Greve.

[28] My grandmother's brother-in-law.

[29] Chairman Nikolai Stepanovich Ryabovol, shot on 14 June 1919.

[30] There was some evidence that Ryabovol had been shot by officers of the Volunteer Army, although the perpetrator was never found.

[31] The official PR agency of the Volunteer Army.

Army and I would love to know how Denikin will find a way out of this situation. Apparently, a large number of agitators and a huge volume of these proclamations have been dispatched to the front. At the time when things are going so brilliantly at the front, they must stir trouble at home. What a vile act! God willing, everything will be resolved well! Denikin is not here now – he went to Sochi for 2–3 days.

18 June.

This morning Pavlik took me to the town's outpatient clinic to have anti-cholera vaccination (he is already vaccinated) but, luckily, the vaccination didn't go ahead. I still cannot stand any injections. This is some sort of idiosyncrasy. An incision is fine, but not injections! After this huge willpower effort (sounds funny) I feel really awful. Can hardly drag my feet. As a reward and consolation, Pavlik takes me today to Silva,[32] starring Piontkovskaya[33] and Koshevskiy.[34] We had to queue at the theatre for about an hour and a half, and still only managed to buy seats at the very end of the second row.

Pavlik is looking after me like after a baby and is worried about me more than I am. May God reward him for everything that he does for me. I often wonder why the God blessed me with such an immense happiness??

They say, Ryabovol was shot dead by a woman in a restaurant. Cherche la femme![35] And the proclamation said that he was shot on duty by the "traitors – monarchists". A nice duty indeed. Apparently, at his funeral very many passionate speeches were made in the spirit of the proclamation.

---

[32] An operetta by Hungarian composer Emmerich Kálmán.

[33] Valentina Pointkovskaya, a prominent Russian soprano.

[34] Possibly Aleksandr Dmitrievich Koshevskiy, Russian comic actor and star of operetta.

[35] French for 'look for a woman'.

Great news came today – Tsaritsyn is taken over![36]

On the 14th I went to see Natalia Mkhailovna and was told that she had gone to the cemetery for the burial of the daughter of Dmitry and Vera. She was only 3 months old! What a tragedy!

23 June.

Silva was lovely and Piontkovskaya was charming in it. We so much enjoyed it that we want to see it again. We saw it in the Parnassus theatre.

Yesterday we came back from a two-days boat trip by Kuban river. We went on a small steamer to Temryuk and back.[37] The first half of the trip is very boring (in terms of the shoreline), so we even started thinking of going back from half the way. The terrifying thought of sitting for hours in some stanitsa's inn waiting for a steamer going back (this was in the evening), made us continue the trip.[38] A very nice sailor was travelling on the same steamer to Taman, so we spent the whole day together. On the way back the weather was excellent, unlike the previous day with a nasty wind. We were sitting on the deck for the whole time. The places that we were passing in the night on the way to Temryuk, turned out to be very picturesque and we didn't regret that we went there. Kuban is an incredibly winding river and you don't know what to expect behind the bend, which adds a special charm to the trip. We passed under the bridge that was blown up by the local Bolsheviks not long ago. It looks as if someone's giant hand twisted the iron rails with which it was constructed.

In one of the stanitsas Bolsheviks took all crosses off the church. This is in Troitskaya stanitsa. We made several photos and among others a photo of Kornilov's grave.[39]

---

[36] Approximately six months later it was retaken by the Red Army and later renamed Stalingrad.

[37] Approximately 150km east of Ekaterinodar (Krasnodar).

[38] A stanitsa is a Cossack village.

[39] Possibly Lavr Georgiyevich Kornilov, Supreme Commander of the Russian Army during Kerensky's rule, later Military Commander of the Volunteer Army, killed in April 1918.

Tomorrow Pavlik takes me and Katia to the cholera vaccination after all. The pandemic is spreading rapidly in the town, and the disease develops at a lightning speed. In 4–5 hours the person is gone.

Yesterday after the church service I stayed for the prayer service for Elenochka.[40] She is 6 years old now. There is absolutely no news from Ella or other sisters.

For the last two days I have been having lunch in my room. Our neighbour is cooking for us and Katia brings it in.

25 June.

In the evening I had the first cholera vaccination. Contrary to expectation, it didn't hurt at all. The nurse makes injections perfectly. This morning I went shopping and met a friend, we went for a walk around the town together. We visited the French mission – a sleepy kingdom, a tiny house on the outskirts with no-one there. Two or three officers, looking bored, were lazily going through some papers on the table.

29 June.

I saw a friend who told me that Tata was in Batum, and Georgiy went to Tiflis. I'm desperately hoping that he will finally manage to secure some money and Tata would be able to come to us.

On 26th there was a military parade in honour of the victories at the front and the seizure of Tsaritsyn. Denikin said several words and then Filimonov gave a speech. The whole Rada was present there. Such criminal types!

Apparently, it has been decided that we are moving to Taganrog. I'm happy that it's not to Rostov (there was such a suggestion). They say, Taganrog is like a great big garden and there is an excellent baths establishment there. This is very important! Pavlik asked our billeting officers to find a good flat for us, not at

---

[40] My grandmother's niece.

the Jews. This probably will be difficult, the latter condition, because the town seems to be full of them. It is rumoured that the President Wilson is from there too.[41]

1 July.

Yesterday evening Pavlik went as a billeting officer to Taganrog. There is terrible emptiness without him. This evening I had the second cholera vaccination and thank God it's over now.

I found an old book in the table's drawer – Letters of Svyatogorets to his friends.[42] They start from 1843. There are many interesting things there about the Old Afon.

5 July.

This morning I received a telegram from Pavlik saying that he is in good health. It was sent on the 2nd. There are rumours in the town that the headquarters are staying in Ekaterinodar. Why then were the billeting officers dispatched, and so on, which will incur a big expense?

I received a letter from Tata. She is going to come to us soon. We need to think where to accommodate her. A friend visited me, her hair was cut short after the typhoid. She was talking about the dreadful conditions in which the wounded and the sick are in Armavir's small hospitals. There is shortage of space, linen, medical supplies. This is so sad!

I have been doing much embroidering in recent days and hoping to finish this work here. Then I will start the second one. I'm feeling depressed.

---

[41] This must have been another conspiracy theory. President Woodrow Wilson was born in Staunton, Virginia. His ancestors were Scottish, Irish and English.

[42] Written by the monk-priest Sergiy Vesnin about the holy mountain Afon.

5 July, 7.30pm.

I visited friends and then went to the church. I lit candles and went around to look at all icons.

Yesterday I saw the end of the night service there. On the way home I went to see Fr. Vostokov. I like Father and feel sorry for him. There were some unpleasant incidents involving him at the church council in Stavropol and he was telling about this with such an agony of embarrassment and pain, that I can't help feeling terribly sad for him when recalling this. Since then I feel a kind of a motherly-tender sympathy for him. It would be good to cheer up the poor old man. He has no money, even the cassock he is wearing is not his, such a pity.

Recently Pavlik's relative Mikhail Mikhailovich Voronov, the brother of Nikolay Mikhailovich, visited us for the first time, A petite, dapper, fresh and still quite young general. He made a pleasant impression. He was telling us about his trip to Palestine and mentioned that the begging and hustling for money from everyone who comes there by the local monks was really off-putting. Literally everybody has been saying this. This is terribly sad.

8 July.

The day before yesterday Pavlik came back. He is delighted by Taganrog. He says that the town is just like a small Odessa. It's a shame though that they don't have a water pipeline there. Here we have bathrooms in our flat. Oh well, what can you do.

Yesterday we went to the operetta Pink Domino.[43] I have never seen such a rubbish before. I felt embarrassed for the actors, how could they play in such a nonsense. And the music was made up of pieces borrowed from everywhere.

---

[43] Possibly based on the play Les Dominos Roses by Alfred Delacour and Alfred Hennequin.

Pavlik came home earlier than usual today. He feels unwell. Something with the throat. I'm hoping it's nothing serious. I put him to bed.

14 July. Taganrog.

In the evening of the 10th we were suddenly told that on the 11th we are going to Taganrog. Pavlik was sent to prepare the premises there. Thank God, he had completely recovered from acute tonsillitis. In the evening we went to the operetta, The Polish Blood - Piontkovskaya's benefit performance.[44] At about 6pm Pavlik and I went to the church for the prayer service.

The journey here was excellent, we travelled in the officers' carriage. It was terribly dirty, the seat covers (the 2nd class) were ripped off, the upholstery must have been taken away by the Bolsheviks. Having arrived here, I caught a l–se on myself.[45]

We could not find a cabby at the train station (there are generally only few of them here during the day, everyone is going out in the evening), so we had to walk almost all the way, it was terribly hot, and probably because of all this, the town didn't impress me very much in the beginning. But now I'm starting to like it more and more. At first, we arrived at 21 Grecheskaya Street where a two-bedroom flat was allocated to us. The rooms looked completely ravaged. The landlady took out all the nice furniture and substituted it, rather scarcely, with something terrible. She greeted us very coldly and then came to me and said many disgusting things about the Volunteer Army. In the same evening we moved to the neighbouring house because the first landlady made only one room available instead of two and we had nowhere to live.[46] Here it is very nice and perfectly clean. The landlords are lovely people and it feels as if we have known each other for a long time. Pavlik is very busy with the Department's tasks and I see him only at dinner. There are some quite good restaurants here. The town is charming – very green.

[44] A famous and popular Czech operetta written by Oskar Nedbal.

[45] It appears my grandmother could not bring herself to write the word 'louse'.

[46] Katia was with them so they would have needed two rooms.

Today I have been to the cathedral which I liked very much. It has old magnificent icons in rich settings. After the Mass I served the litany for the dead for Dimusha.[47]

Today we swam in the sea for the first time. The water was marvellouslyy warm, about 22 degrees. There were very many people there. The water is very shallow, it's still only up to the neck for as far as you can go.

15 July.

Our house is directly opposite the palace where the Tsar Alexander I died. It is a single storey building painted in yellow (ochre), with white eaves, very similar to Ivnya. There are guards at the entrance. We will go there in the next few days to see inside.

23 July.

Recently we visited the palace. All the furnishings are very simple. The original handmade wallpaper was preserved there. Small flower garlands are hand-painted on the grey background. Also the original carpets remained. A carpet hand-embroidered by the Empress Elizaveta Alexeyevna is displayed.[48] The room where the Tsar died is turned into a church. The wall to the next room is demolished and the Tsar Alexander I ambulatory church is set up. In the next room there is a clock with the hands stopped at the moment of the Tsar's death. For almost 100 years now it has been showing 10:47. He died in the morning of the 19th November, 1825. Under the church, on the underground floor, there is a kind of a monument, inside of which the Tsar's internal organs are said to be buried, which were taken out during the embalming of his body. On the front of this stone monument a small copper bas-relief is installed displaying the moment of Alexander Pavlovich's death.

---

[47] My grandmother's brother Dima.

[48] Wife of Tsar Alexander I.

The Department has arrived the day before yesterday but has not completely settled in yet. Tata has not come yet. Yesterday I went to a friend's birthday party.

I swam in the sea today and went very far away. Today the water was higher – up to my neck.

Denikin has arrived. He lives on the same street, two blocks away from us.

26 July.

Today a service for the dead was conducted by Fr Shavelskiy in the headquarters' church.[49] Denikin and almost all headquarters' ranks were there. I attended.

Yesterday the sea was below the knee, and to submerge yourself you needed to lie on the bottom. Today it's the opposite, the water is high. I saw someone who arrived today with the family from Anapa.[50] He said that Ella has not come yet. Could it be that Tata is also still in Batum and, God forbid, something has happened there!?

28 July.

Yesterday friends came to us for tea. Katia, with some guidance, made a delicious apricot tart.

I had a dream last night where Elenochka with flowers in her hands was standing before the communion cup, she wanted to have a communion. I woke up in the night and said to Pavlik that I was afraid that she, God forbid, might die. It's so heavy on the heart.

---

[49] Possibly Protobesbyter George Shavelskiy.

[50] North-west of Novorossiysk.

30 July.

The weather already resembles Autumn. It's fresh and clear in the morning, raining in the evening.

There is no news from Sochi. Is it really so hard to write a couple of words to spare us worrying?!

1 August.

Recently we went for a day to Rostov for shopping. We have not bought much because we could not find everything and the prices were insane. An example: one bottle of Guerlain perfume – 2000 roubles!!!

I received a letter from Clair. Georgiy left for the regiment. Tata is still in Batum and doesn't show any signs of life. I received a letter from Vera Uspenskaya today.

A friend suddenly arrived in the company of an English officer and invited us to the dancing evening at the English mission tomorrow. It's quite funny. Pavlik went for a walk. I will surprise him.

8 August.

We didn't go to the English. We have decided there might be some ladies there whom the English could have met here only in the city garden or on the street. Instead, Lieutenant Mashukov visited us. This is the kind of man that Motherland needs. He is full of energy and desire to apply it for the good of Russia. An honest and noble person. He has already done very much and is being offered high ranks, almost admiral positions but he modestly declines.

9 August.

Yesterday friends visited us for one day, and stayed until evening. Because Pavlik was busy, I was entertaining them, took them for a walk, and though they were very nice, I became quite tired of the strenuous affability.

12 August.

Yesterday I discovered the English were quite upset that we had not come to their evening. As I understood, everyone was waiting for us and for some reason we were meant to be the highlight of the evening.

We are reading Hadji Murat and other novels now.[51] Tolstoy's biased tone irritates me. In all his works. The elevation of the common people almost to the saints' status and the merciless vilification of the higher classes, starting with the Tsar's family. We can see now, who the God-bearing people have revealed themselves to really be and how the so called 'unworthy aristocrats' are meeting their death! Did Tolstoy see everything upside down in his sick imagination? The baseless criticism of the Orthodox faith and even (!) the Holy New Testament is also outrageous.

18 August.

A few days ago Georgy came to us and stayed overnight. On the next day we went together to Rostov where the estate manager from Ivnya should have come. The latter has not come, of course, and G. and P.[52] were settling only financial matters. We stayed overnight at Georgiy's because we were late for the train which departed half an hour earlier than expected without any notification to the passengers about the change of schedule.

Georgiy visited us again the day before yesterday, in the next few days he is going to the front to the 2nd cavalry regiment.

---

[51] By Leo Tolstoy.

[52] Georgiy and Pavel.

22 August.

Georgiy telegraphed us that he was going to Sochi for 3 days and would bring Tata to us from there. We are expecting her by the end of the month.

26 August.

The day before yesterday we went to the English for dances. It was very nice. They are all so cordial and hospitable, it is rather surprising. They organised a separate motorcar to take Pavlik and me home. The people we like most were Captain Cass and the seaman Lieutenant Peploe. The mission's directors Hollman and Kiss was there, as well as Commodore Norris, Captain Fremantle who arrived from the Caspian Sea, Pavlik's mate and many others. The doctor livened the party by dancing the Irish jig for 15 minutes.

There is no news from Tata – I'm expecting her to arrive in the next few days. Yesterday Admiral Gerasimov held a dinner for the English seamen.[53]

11 September

On 28 August Tata and Georgiy arrived unexpectedly. We were out, came back by 8pm and found them already at home. The next day Georgiy left for Rostov and Kharkov and from there to the front. Tata has settled quite nicely with us. We have already danced twice with her at the English. Once it was a proper evening party and the next time we had tea with them at 5pm and then were dancing. At the evening party I danced the Russian to show them.[54] Apparently, I did well.

Today Tata and I are going to the theatre, there will be dancing and singing. Recently we held a Bridge party at our place.

---

[53] Probably Vice Admiral A.M. Gerasimov, head of the Naval Directorate.

[54] This must be a specific dance.

Several days ago Pavlik went to Rostov regarding financial matters but so far nothing could be done.

About two weeks ago, Peploe and Davis organised yacht sailing and breakfast in the yacht-club.

A good job opportunity for Georgiy is coming up at our Department. I so much hope that they agree to take him in! Then Clair would be able to come here too.

24 November.

So many things have happened in the last 2 and a half months, I don't know where to start.

On 21 September Pavlik went with Denikin to visit the Black Sea ports. Two days before that, we were invited to visit a really nice old couple with a daughter. There we were introduced to their son. He has a terrible appearance. Short, with a huge, elongated head shaped as a cucumber or an egg (Peploe calls him 'The Egg'). His eyes are unnaturally sunken, cloudy and vague. For the whole evening he spoke in a muffled voice on religious and mystical topics. The next day he visited us and for 4 hours was talking complete rubbish.

On the day of Pavlik's departure Tata and I went to a dancing evening at the English and – o horror! – we saw 'The Cucumber' there. In the middle of the evening, he suddenly formally asked my permission to let him reveal his feelings to Tata and ask for her hand and asked me to pass a letter to Tata to this effect. I firmly declined, anticipating Tata's dread. The next day we went to visit our friend, K, who had been sick for several days. She told us that she was overwhelmed by the dark forces as the result of the hypnosis conducted on her by 'The Cucumber' who was making spells over her and made her say various spells too. She was in a desperate state and scared us so much that we nearly lost our mind. As it turned out, he is practicing black sorcery or something similar. We already had a negative view of him after his visit to us when he preached the Khlystov's heresy to us and we felt as if he tried to hypnotise us with his cloudy eyes and vague speech.⁵⁵ We started praying passionately for protection from him. On the same day, we were going to an evening party given by a rich family from Kharkov. Tata and I have decided that if he dances with us there, we will be doing a silent prayer all the time. And so we did, and afterwards exchanged our similar impressions. He could not make even a tour of Waltz with us, his hands started shaking, he apologised and sat us down. From that moment, we felt that with God's mercy we were relieved from him and his harmful and scary influence.

The next morning at 7am, K knocked on our door and when I opened, clad just in my night dress, she fell on her knees in front of me, asking to cross her and told me, in tears and all disheveled, that she herself was no longer able to cross herself because evil spirits possessed her. Tata immediately took her to the church for the sacred communion and, because Pavlik was away, we took her to live with us, because she was afraid to come back to her place. She lived with us for a week, completely insane. Her delusions were sometimes so dreadful that I felt chill in my bones. God gave Tata strength, and she was able to calmly sit with her, while I sometimes felt that I was also losing my mind. One episode frightened me most, when in the church she backed away from the cross offered to her by the priest. I thought she would start behaving like a possessed. Luckily, all this was a mental and nervous breakdown, and by the end of the week she appeared completely normal.⁵⁶ By the time of Pavlik's return Tata moved with her to Rostov and stayed with her there for two weeks, and then K went to Crimea to her mother.

During the trip on the ship, Pavlik pulled ligaments on his leg which is still swollen and hurts.

The English very frequently hold evening parties and are getting ever more courteous. Sometimes on Sunday the Denikin's symphony orchestra plays there which is very nice.

---

[55] Most likely refers to the secret religious sect Khlysty.

[56] At the bottom of the page my grandmother wrote 'The Cucumber proposed to Tata in writing'.

The newspapers reported in passing that the English made a deal with Bolsheviks, and we told them about this. They assured, of course, that this was a lie and started behaving even more ingratiatingly.

Makhno came very close to here (in September, I think) and was apparently only 15 miles away from Taganrog.[57] After that the campaign was going excellently. We advanced so far that we even seized Orel.[58] Now though things again are not going very well at all. We are on the brink of surrendering Kharkov.

A few days ago the Icon of Our Lady of the Sign was brought from Kursk to save it from desecration. We went to greet it at the railway station and walked it with the cross procession to the church. Denikin was in the cathedral; in my view, he should have met such a sacred relic at the station, considering that the Holy Mother of God herself is visiting the headquarters. God willing, there will be a breakthrough for the better!

Georgiy has long been in the cavalry regiment now. He is managing the regiment's workshops at the base. Before recently he had been stationed in Sumy and when Sumy fell, he must have moved somewhere else. Clair settled with children in Yalta. Ella and Kolushka are in Odessa.[59]

Yesterday someone was going to Petrograd and we wrote a couple of words to Mama on a small piece of paper. The people who went there promised to bring back a response if they have a chance.

We heard that the Loan Treasury has been definitely and irreversibly plundered and is lost. I am truly devastated! Why did I, a fool, take everything to Moscow, despite Pavlik's dissuasion. All my diamonds, letters of Pavlik and children are lost!

---

[57] Nestor Makhno, an anarchist who worked with the Red Army to defeat the White Army.

[58] North of Kharkiv (Kharkov).

[59] Kolushka is a diminutive form of the name Nikolay. After the death of her first husband, Ella married Prince Nicholas Troubetzkoi in February 1919. They divorced in 1928.

Basically, we are totally destitute!! We have to assess what we have left after the blaze that has engulfed the whole of Russia. Currently, the pound is traded 1,300 roubles!!! instead of 10 roubles in the past (oh, madness!), the Franc – 30 roubles!!!!

The English are planning a huge ball for 400 people for their Christmas with Denikin as the main VIP. The events at the front are likely to disrupt these plans. I would have much preferred not to go, I'm so disgusted with them and their double game.[60]

1 December.

Last week Tata and I were fasting and preparing for the holy communion. Andryusha often visits us.[61] Pavlik and I have noticed long ago that Tata gives him very sweet looks. I think she is very much in love with him. This afternoon at her request we visited Vera (he also lives there) but she was not home. Tata is going there alone in the evening to catch up with her, despite all my persuasion not to walk alone in the dark. I can't go with her because I have a headache and feel tired. When we were at Vera's, we were told that she was in the cinema, and Tata immediately wanted us to go there, but I dissuaded her – in such a crowd it would be easy to catch a typhus.

I would like to know how he feels about Tata, because personally, I would be very happy if she marries him eventually, because he is a very good and loyal man: in the beginning I thought that he was also interested in her, in any case, he very much respects her and holds her in high regard.

11 December.

Yesterday evening we visited Vera where it was announced that the evacuation of Taganrog has been decided upon and should be

---

[60] Here Olga is possibly referring to the withdrawal of the Allied forces from Russia.

[61] An endearing version of the name Andrey.

executed very quickly. Only Denikin and the operational part of the Headquarters will stay. In the Naval Directorate only Gerasimov and the operational staff will remain. We might have to leave as early as tomorrow. The packing is in full swing. They say, we are going in heated freight wagons straight to Novorossiysk. All missions are heading there today. Andryusha has left for Rostov today and from there will go to the front. Vera is going abroad and has offered Tata to go with her. We are also dreaming of breaking free and going abroad. We are waiting for the arrival of (Admiral) Khomenko, hopefully we will be able to join him.

Recently the Our Lady of the Sign icon was brought here. It is as if Our Lady has taken us under her protection.

20 December.

Novorossiysk. We arrived here on the 14th. We travelled on the train in the third class, but it was very spacious and everything has been washed up with carbolic acid. We spent the first night on the steamer Grand Duke Alexander Mikhailovich. It was clean, but there were lots of rats. The majority of the people who travelled with us stayed there, and we moved to two very clean and warm rooms in a flat at 7 Gorny. Lovely people. But yesterday the wife of Admiral Gerasimov has arrived and moved us out of one of the rooms, so now the three of us are sleeping in one room – and Katia in the room of the local maid. It is still unknown if we are going to Sevastopol as it was previously planned or are staying here.

We have been dreaming for a long time of going abroad and having a rest in human conditions, we are sick and tired of living like cattle. It is a shame that recklessness and obnoxiousness have reached their peak in Russia.

The international passports for me and Tata are almost ready, but how many hurdles we had to jump, this was just awful! We had to see once again with our own eyes the unbearable backwardness of our whole state bureaucracy apparatus. The red tape is bewildering. You are made to come with the same business many times and every time wait at reception for hours while the bureaucrats are having a relaxed conversation with their acquaintances, and when you finally get to see them, they put spokes in your wheels, assume this incredible self-importance and pick at every comma at a wrong place. The things that can be done in 5–10 minutes, take days and weeks. When visiting the counterintelligence, Pavlik found one of the clerks lying on the table drunk. What a disgrace! And this is the counterintelligence! Now everything depends on whether P. becomes posted overseas. We have asked Vera to speak about this with Lukomsky, who is now almost all-mighty.[62] We are looking forward to the arrival of the Admiral Khomenko. He might take us with him.

The dirt here is epic, the whole Russia has sunk into it. In the last few days I found to my horror three or four lice on myself!!! It seems there is nowhere further to fall.


21 December.

Pavlik has just told me that in Novorossiysk there will be only Admirals Ger[asimov], Tikhmenev and two or three officers, and he was offered the choice to either stay here or sail to Sevastopol. We have decided to stay here. The Englishman commander Luker has just dropped by. He has exchanged roubles for the English pounds for us and is promising to organise our departure abroad on the English ship in about three weeks. We invited him for tea tomorrow at 4pm.


3 January 1920.

We celebrated the New Year with our landlords, lovely people. Gerasimov with his wife also came. In the evening of the 31st of December there was a heavy thunderstorm. Everything is upside down, even in the nature. The New Year prayer service was held

---

[62] General Alexander Sergeyevich Lukomsky.

at our place. In our flat, the wife of our landlord's nephew became ill with the typhus. Yesterday she was taken to hospital. The husband of the landlady's niece is also ill. Possibly, also typhus. By chance we met here Smirnov with whom we became acquainted also by chance in Taganrog. He is the Secretary of the Serbian mission and spent time in prison in Ekaterinburg[63] together with the Countess Elena Petrovna Serbskaya[64] and Nastenka Gendrikova [65] He turned out to be an exceptionally nice and kind person and has taken upon himself, hardly knowing us, to help us move abroad. His family is also lovely. An opportunity is coming up for Pavlik to become the representative of the Russian command in Varna in charge of disembarking of the refugees.[66]

The decision about the evacuation has been made, and apparently, the families of the high command are leaving on the first ship. God willing, all of us will be able to leave as well.

---

[63] I have only been able to find references to the two women being imprisoned in Perm and not Ekaterinburg.

[64] Possibly the wife of Prince John Constantinovich, eldest son of Grand Duke Constantin Constantinovich. Her husband was arrested and murdered by the Bolsheviks in July 1918. She was arrested but later released.

[65] Anastasia Gendrikova (Hendrikova), lady-in-waiting at the court of Tsar Nicholas II. She followed the Imperial Family into captivity but was forcibly separated from them by the Bolsheviks who shot her in September 1918.

[66] A Bulgarian port city on the Black Sea.

**A NOTE ON DATES AND FORMATTING**

These letters have been transcribed with minimal editorial intervention. Inconsistencies in formatting, spelling, and especially date notation have been retained to preserve the authenticity of the originals. Minor adjustments have been made only where necessary to prevent confusion.

APPENDIX II
# CORRESPONDENCE FROM THE RUSSIAN STATE ARCHIVES

## CORRESPONDENCE BETWEEN OLGA NIKOLAEVNA AND O.K. VORONOV

**Fund 673, inventory 1, file 253, pages 1–2**

Envelope: To Olga Konstantinovna Voronov

54 Fontanka St, Petrograd

Tsarskoye Selo

25 August 1914

Dear Olga!

I'm sending these small icons to you both. May God protect your husband and you, my dear. I'm kissing you warmly.

Yours

Olga

**Fund 673, inventory 1, file 253, pages 3–5**

Envelope: To Olga Konstantinovna Voronov. 46 Liteyniy Prospekt, Petrograd.

Tsarskoye Selo

22 September 1914

Thank you very much for the dear card, my sweet Olga! I'm very happy that you have good news from your husband. Send him my regards when you write to him. Yesterday a train came with more wounded. There were badly injured [soldiers] there too. But for some reason, only the more lightly injured ones were taken to our hospital. We have attended surgical operations several times but it was not at all scary – and I very much like applying dressings for the wounded.

Maria and Dmitry had lunch with us twice, they are gone now. Good news is coming from Papa, thanks God.

Till next time, my dear Olga, warmly kissing you.

May God keep you safe.

Your Olga


**Fund 673, inventory 1, file 253, pages 10–12**

Envelope: To Olga Konstantinovna Voronov.

46 Liteyniy Prospekt, Petrograd.

Tsarskoye Selo

3 November 1914

Dear Olga!

I thank you kindly for your lovely letter and also your husband for remembering me. I'm happy for you that you have seen him. We have seen many wounded in Grodno and Dvinsk.[1] Many are very badly injured, but they are all so patient and upbeat. Angels, really.

We held exams at home and will receive the cross together with others. We have attended many operations now and help passing the instruments and so on.

So long dear Olga, kissing you warmly.

May God give you all the best.

Your Olga


**Fund 673, inventory 1, file 253, pages 13 and 13 reverse side**

Moscow

10 December 1914.

My dear Olga!

---

[1] Now Daugavpils in Latvia.

Thank you for your lovely letter. I was very happy to unexpectedly meet your husband in Vilna.[2] When you write to him, please pass my heartfelt regards. We have seen so much during this trip, that it is all mixed up in my head and I can't remember where and what we have seen. We were stopping twice a day in different townships, visited the cathedral first, where the bishop would give a boring long speech, and then hospitals. Everywhere it was very nice but incredibly hot. In Oryol and Kharkov we also visited warehouses. This was really boring, I must say, and of course we had to have our photos taken with the flash which was very unpleasant. There were very many people there, so sometimes our automobile could hardly move. We met Papa in Voronezh and travelled back together. He was extremely happy with his trip to Caucasus. He told us so many interesting things and has seen so much. He went right up to the Turkish border in the auto and saw the soldiers who briefly came from the front line. The meetings were most touching, there was a huge boost of morale. Yesterday we met Mama's medical train. Among the wounded there was an officer from Yerevan. He was saying that his regiment had huge casualties, many of our best officers had been killed, including one of those who was with us in Livadia. It's terribly sad. This afternoon we visited the Petrovsky Palace. There are more than 200 wounded there, but it will be possible to accommodate up to 500. In the Amusement Palace there are 50 officers. It is set up quite nicely there. On Friday we are going to Tsarskoye Selo. I'm happy, I miss our wounded, but thank God they are all getting better. One of our officers came back to us after being wounded for the second time. So long, my darling Olga. May God be with you. I'm kissing you warmly and sending my regards to your Mama and sisters.

Sincerely loving you, Olga.

**Fund 673, inventory 1, file 253, pages 8–9**

Tsarskoye Selo

25 December 1914

My dear, sweet Olga!

Thank you very much for your lovely letter and things for the poor which made me very happy.

This Christmas feels so strange, especially when thinking about those who are now at this terrible war. If only it would finish soon. I'm thinking a lot of you these days, dear Olga. May God give you strength to endure this difficult time and reunite with your husband who must also be thinking a lot about you, especially now.

---

[2] Now Vilnius, the capital of Lithuania.

In hospital, every morning we are going to the dressing changes and operations. In the last few days, we didn't go because there was no time, and this evening we are going to the Christmas celebration at ours. So long, dear Olga. I hope we'll see each other one day. I'm kissing you warmly, with love,

Your Olga.

### Fund 673, inventory 1, file 253, page 14 (photo of Olga Nikolaevna with her signature, followed by the text of the greeting)

I'm warmly congratulating my dear Olga with Christmas. May God give you all the very best. Kissing you warmly. I will be thinking of you a lot these days, how hard it must be to be apart for the first time at the Christmas celebration. Please pass my greetings to your husband if you write to him. I wish him too all the best.

God bless you darling,

1914

### Fund 673, inventory 1, file 253, page 6–7

28 December 1914. Tsarskoye Selo.

My darling Olga!

I sincerely congratulate you on the birthday of your husband. May God send him happiness in everything and may He protect him in this difficult time.

I'm with you in my thoughts. Thank you very much for the lovely letter. Yesterday we went to the Christmas celebration in the house for the disabled and afterwards visited the wounded. There is a hospital set up there too. From there we went to the Grand Palace where we go daily at 4pm. There are over 30 wounded officers there. Mama is still feeling unwell and since her return was not able to go anywhere, which is very sad. Papa has recovered but is not going out yet.

So long my darling Olga,

May God be with you. Kissing you warmly,

Yours,

Olga.

**Fund 673, inventory 1, file 253, page 26–27**

To Olga Konstantinovna Voronova

46 Liteyniy Prospekt, Petrograd.

Tsarskoye Selo.

February 1915

I hug you warmly, my dear Olga, and send you my most heartfelt best wishes for tomorrow. May God bless you both.

Your Olga.

**Fund 673, inventory 1, file 253, page 15. A telegram without a date.**

Mama and we all are sincerely congratulating you. Kissing you warmly, regards to your husband, Olga.

**Fund 673, inventory 1, file 253, page 28–29**

Tsarskoye Selo.

19 February 1915.

My dear Olga!

Thank you very much for your lovely letter. I'm happy for you that you managed to see your husband once again. Please pass regards from me when you write to him. We continue working in hospital every morning. These days, there are major operations almost daily, and very urgent ones, because from the last trains the wounded are all very critical. Yesterday one poor man had his thigh amputated, another – a hand, and so on. Tatiana thanks you for the letter and kisses you. She will not have time to write to you today because she is at a class now. In the afternoon we visited a hospital at the Artillery school and Papa was giving medals to the most heavily wounded.

So long, kissing you warmly, my sweet darling Olga. May God protect you.

Yours,

Olga.

I'm hoping very much that we see each other again.

**Fund 673, inventory 1, file 253, page 30–31**

To Olga Konstantinovna Voronova

Odessa. London Hotel (stamp 14.4.15).

Tsarskoye Selo. 13 April 1915

My dear Olga!

I congratulate you warmly with your birthday and wish you all the very best.

The weather is finally very Spring-like and almost all snow has melted. We have started riding the horses again, which is very nice. Otherwise, there is nothing new.

So long my darling Olga,

Kissing you warmly and passing my regards to your husband. Your Olga.

**Fund 673, inventory 1, file 253, page 16**

To Olga Konstantinovna Voronova

Odessa. London Hotel (stamp 7–5–15).

Olga darling!

Thank you very much for the lovely letter. If I had more time I would have written more. Papa has left, otherwise it's all the same. Pass my regards to your husband and to Molokhovets. How is he? Kissing you warmly my darling,

Yours, Olga 6. V. 1915

**Fund 673, inventory 1, file 253, page 17. A greeting card.**

I'm kissing you warmly and sending you my best wishes, my dear Olga. May God protect you.

Your Olga.

1915.

**Fund 673, inventory 1, file 253, page 18.**

To Olga Konstantinovna Voronova

54 Fontanka St. Petrograd. (Stamp 19.7.15)

I congratulate your once again wholeheartedly, my dear Olga, and thank you for the letter. I'm very much hoping that we see each other one day. Here it's all the same. We are working in hospital every morning, and in the afternoon are having walks with Papa or visiting others. I'm kissing you warmly my dear and passing my regards to your husband.

Your Olga

19 VII 15

**Fund 673, inventory 1, file 253, page 19–21.**

To Olga Konstantinovna Voronova

Apt 207, 54 Fontanka St. Petrograd.

Tsarskoye Selo. 5 November 1915.

Dear Olga!

Many thanks to you and your husband for the good memory and wishes that have touched me very much.

It's so good that he is here now and you can be together again. Alexey is writing very happy letters from Headquarters and doesn't want to come back here at all. There he made friends with an old fat Belgian general.

I'm kissing you warmly my dear Olga and thanking you once again. Please pass regards to your husband.

Your Olga.

**Fund 673, inventory 1, file 253, page 22ab**

To Olga Konstantinovna Voronova

Apt 207, 54 Fontanka St. Petrograd.

28 December 1915

Dear Olga!

I warmly congratulate you with tomorrow's date and send my heartfelt wishes to your husband. Thank you for the letter. Midshipman Sekerin is now in our hospital with a dislocated shoulder; he doesn't speak much, so we have learned little new from him.

I'm sending once again my warmest wishes and kissing you warmly, my dear Olga.

May God protect you.

Your Olga.

# CORRESPONDENCE BETWEEN TATIANA NIKOLAEVNA AND O.K. VORONOV

Central State Archive in Moscow
Department of personal fun[ds]
F[und] 651, Storage Unit 102

**Fund 651, inventory 1, file 102**

Petrograd 11 January 1914[3]

My dear Tatiana Nikolaevna,

Please accept the warmest congratulations and best wishes for your Angel's day from my husband and me.[4]

Two hours ago I came back from Warsaw where I spent four days with my husband. I'm hoping to go back there in the next few days. I will be staying in Warsaw, and because my husband and others are stationed 30 miles away, he might be able to drop in for a couple of days once or twice.

I'm desperately hoping that Anna Alexandrovna is feeling better. I was travelling in the same carriage as her brother. Tata told me that she went to hospital to enquire about the health of Anna Alexandrovna and saw you all.

I'm fondly embracing you, my dear, and sending my kind regards to the Grand Duchesses.

Wholeheartedly yours, Olga Voronov

**Fund 651, inventory 1, file 102**

Your Highness,

Dear Tatiana Nikolaevna

I cannot contain myself from writing to you and asking you, if possible, to pass to Their Majesties my most faithful and boundless gratitude for their immensely gracious and kind attitude towards me, which touched me very deeply. I know I breach the rules of etiquette, but cannot help expressing what overwhelms my heart.

---

[3] It appears this letter has been given the wrong year. My grandparents were married in February 1914 and Anna Alexandrovna's accident was in 1915.

[4] Refers to the christening day. In the Orthodox tradition the person being christened is assigned a guardian angel.

The day of our wedding will remain for me the brightest and most joyous memory of my life. Both of us are very often thinking and speaking about you all, and my husband is asking me to pass to Your Highnesses and Tsarevitch his most respectful and heartfelt regards.

We have been staying in Nice for a week now. The weather has been rainy one day, sunny and hot on the next – everybody is walking around without coats. A few days ago we went to Monte Carlo where we played roulette and, to our surprise, did not lose.

We are thinking of staying here for a while longer and before going back to Russia to go for a couple of days to Naples, which I have not seen yet. They say it's remarkably beautiful and there is also a magnificent opera there which we are certainly going to visit.

I'm kindly asking you, dear Tatiana Nikolaevna, to accept and once again pass to Their Highnesses my deepest gratitude for everything and the warmest regards.

Wholeheartedly faithful to Your Highness and very much loving you,

Olga Voronov

17 February 1914. Hotel Negresco, Nice

**Fund 651, inventory 1, file 102**

Petersburg

14 April 1914

Your Highness,

Dear Tatiana Nikolaevna,

Though I have passed through the Grand Duchess Olga Nikolaevna my congratulations to you, I was so touched by your kind, warm letter in response to mine from Nice, that I really want to wish you personally once again all the very best, and tell you how often we are thinking of all of you.

I'm sure you had a very joyful and lovely time during the holidays in Crimea, where it is so warm and beautiful. Here the spring is also felt in the air now – the sun is brighter and warmer, though of course no leaves or grass have appeared yet. Yesterday Tata and I spent the whole day in Tsarskoye Selo. Poor Tata still has not become used to my absence and is missing me very much – previously we had always been together.

She was asking me very much to stay with her in the country in summer, and I think I will do this, while my husband will be in Shkhery.⁵

Let me, dear Tatiana Nikolaevna, fondly kiss you. My husband is asking to pass his respectful regards to you.

Most faithful to your Highness and with heartfelt love,

Olga Voronov

## Fund 651, inventory 1, file 102

Petersburg

21 April 1914

Your Highness,

Dear Tatiana Nikolaevna,

I'm very deeply touched by your kind attention and memory, please accept my most sincere and heartfelt gratitude for your congratulations and a long, interesting letter. I always feel so happy when I receive your letters.

I had a very joyful and lovely day today. In the morning my mama visited us, and in the afternoon my *belle-mère*,⁶ *belle-sœurs*,⁷ Tata and my elder sister with her children came to congratulate me.

The eldest boy (he is 3 years old) came in, ceremoniously carrying a bouquet of carnations in his hands, but could not say the little speech that he was taught to say, having become confused at the sight of unfamiliar faces. He is very cute and speaks very much like an adult.

In the evening we went to the theatre and have just come back. The play was *A Thought* by Andreev. This was the third and the last show for our season ticket to the Arts Theatre. This cast has performed wonderfully and we felt sad that we would not see them anymore this year.

The day after tomorrow my husband is on duty and I'm going with Tata for lunch to the Komstadius in Tsarskoye [Selo].⁸ After lunch, I think, we are going in a big company to Pulkovo for a drive. It probably will be a great fun.

---

⁵ Possibly refers to the Ladoga skerries.

⁶ French for mother-in-law.

⁷ French for sisters-in-law.

⁸ Possibly the family of General Nikolai Komstadius.

We are thinking of going to Peterhof tomorrow morning to make a decision about the *dacha*.⁹ We were given several new addresses and will have to choose something now otherwise it will be too late.

Till next time, dear Tatiana Nikolaevna. Let me very fondly kiss you and ask you pass to Their Majesties mine and my husband's deep appreciation of their gracious regards, and our respectful regards to Their Highnesses.

Tata is sending you her humble regards and thanks for remembering.

My husband is asking you to accept his kindest regards.

Most faithful to your Highness and wholeheartedly yours,

Olga Voronov

**Fund 651, inventory 1, file 102**

Petersburg

20 May 1914

Your Highness,

Dear Tatiana Nikolaevna,

Thank you so much for your lovely letter. It is such a pity that we were not at the bazaar, it was probably a great fun – and you collected so much!¹⁰

I'm sure you will be sad to soon leave the Crimea where you are having such a lovely time.

A few days ago we finally found a *dacha* in Peterhof. An officer of the Ulansky regiment Lieutenant Ilyinsky has rented his flat to us. It's on the Alexandrovskaya street, very close to the train station. It is far away from the sea though, but has all amenities, including electricity.

We are thinking of moving to Peterhof in the end of this week, i.e. 25$^{th}$–26$^{th}$ [of May] – and both are very excited about it because it's already becoming stuffy and dusty in the city.

The day before yesterday the two of us went to Pavlovsk for lunch and later Tata with my *beau-frère* Pushchin came there from Tsarskoye Selo and we all together were listening to the music.¹¹

---

⁹ A dacha is a summer residence.

¹⁰ Possibly a charity event.

¹¹ *Beau-frère* is French for brother-in-law.

A few days ago my husband and I organised a small party for Tata. We invited Musya Komstadius, Daria Gesse, the Urusovs, several hussars and sailors and also the singer Mororessy. She has a very pleasant voice and a huge repertoire of various beautiful lyrical songs.

It was the first time that I hosted an evening party and was very worried that people would be bored but, fortunately, it seems everyone had good time.

Tata will spend about 3 weeks with us in Peterhof. I think it will be more fun for her than spending time together with Madame Girand (her French companion) in the country.

Mother will go abroad in summer for medical treatment.

You were asking about my health – I'm feeling very well and thanking you very much for your consideration.

My husband is asking to pass his most respectful regards to you, and I'm fondly kissing you, my dear Tatiana Nikolaevna, if you allow.

Both of us are kindly asking you to pass our regards to the Grand Duchesses and His Highness Tsarevitch Alexey Nikolayevich.

Most faithful to your Highness and loving you,

Olga Voronov.

**Fund 651, inventory 1, file 102**

26 May 1914

Your Highness,

Please accept my warmest congratulations on your birthday. I'm wholeheartedly wishing you that the new year of your life brings you lots of happiness and joy.

My husband kindly asks you to accept his heartfelt congratulations and best wishes.

We are also kindly asking you to pass our congratulations to Their Highnesses.

The weather is lovely and warm today and we are going to the open-air races. I think it will be great fun, it will be my first visit to the races.

Our departure to Peterhof is delayed for several more days because the owners of our apartment have not moved out yet. It's so boring!

My dear Tatiana Nikolaevna, I thank you from the bottom of my heart. I have just received your photographs and the lovely note.

I'm terribly touched by your consideration, which is very dear to me. I'm fondly embracing you and wholeheartedly thanking you.

I like your photograph very much. My husband and I were looking over it now and noticed a new ring on your hand. I think the photo came out really well and conveyed the great likeness of you all. I'm so happy to have your photographs.

We are thinking of you all very often and reminiscing about the lovely Crimea.

I'd love so much to go back there and travel by the new road to Kozmo-Demyansk. When we were there, the road had not been finished yet.

Till next time, my dear Tatiana Nikolaevna. Warmly embracing you.

Wholeheartedly yours,

Olga Voronov.

P.S. My husband is asking to pass his kindest regards to you.

### Fund 651, inventory 1, file 102

7 June 1914

Your Highness,

Dear Tatiana Nikolaevna,

I'm sending you things for the poor. I'm very ashamed that I'm doing this so late, but I didn't know where to deliver them for you.

Thank you so much for the postcards. I'm so happy that you all have come back now.

I'm embracing you tightly, if you allow, and asking to pass our regards to Their Highnesses. My husband is asking to accept his regards as well.

Yours with all my soul,

Olga Voronov.

### Fund 651, inventory 1, file 102

New Peterhof

23 Aleskandrinskaya St

Your Highness,

My dear Tatiana Nikolaevna,

Thank you so much for your kind and warm letter and congratulations. I cannot express to you how much I'm touched by your kindness towards me. I also was so happy to see you all at *The Dawn*.[12]

In the theatre our box was right above yours, so frustrating.

I also saw you from afar at the parade when we drove past the tribune.

The day after tomorrow I'm going to the country, where I will spend a month, I think. I'll come back to Peterhof or straight to Petersburg at the end of August.

I'm very much hoping that, if you are not bored, you will write to me some time.

Upon arrival at my country estate I will (with your permission) write to you and give you my address.

I'm warmly kissing you my dear lovely Tatiana Nikolaevna.

My husband is asking to pass his regards to you.

Wholeheartedly loving you and faithfully yours,

Olga Voronov.

12 July 1914

**Fund 651, inventory 1, file 102**

Petersburg

15 Troitskaya St

21 July 1914

My dear Tatiana Nikolaevna,

I'm deeply touched by your kind and warm letter and your considerate attitude for which I thank you from the bottom of my heart and soul. You cannot imagine how precious for me are your warm words in this hard for all of us time.

We have not heard anything from Mama and are very worried.

Tomorrow Tata is moving from Tsarskoye Selo to Ella Pushchin (my sister), because Ella's husband marches off already tomorrow.

All three of us want to do a short Sisters of Mercy course and considering doing this at the St George's Sisters of Mercy community.

---

[12] Probably the title of a play.

My husband wholeheartedly thanks you, my dear Tatiana Nikolaevna, for your wishes and regards and asks to pass his regards to you.

I'm warmly embracing you, my dear, and thank you many times for the letter.

Wholeheartedly loving you and faithfully yours

Olga Voronov

### Fund 651, inventory 1, file 48

Thank you dear and sweet Olga for what you and your husband wrote for me in the book. Shura (i.e., Alek. Alek.) just left on vacation today, so when she returns I will give her the letter. I was terribly pleased to see your husband. So tiresome that I forgot to give him the book myself. I got it ready it and forgot it, and then I remembered about it later on. Please, dear Olga, if you have a photograph of you and your husband, I would terribly like to have one. On Sunday, we go to Moscow for 4 or 5 days, and then to Tsarskoe. So terrible that our swimming was ruined and that we could not go to the skerries. Normally we would be in Gangut now, and then we would go to Revel for manoeuvres.

Well, goodbye. Thank your husband too for his autograph. God bless you both. I kiss and hug you tightly and gently my darling. Heartfelt greetings and a bow to your husband.

Your sincerely loving

Tatiana

Peterhof 1914 July 28

### Fund 651, inventory 1, file 102

My dear Tatiana Nikolaevna,

Thank you so very much for your lovely letter and new photographs which I have not yet seen anywhere else and which, I think, are even better than the first ones.

Both of us are very touched that you want to have ours, but unfortunately we don't have any photographs at all at the moment. We made photos after the wedding, but they came out with such a poor likeness that we didn't even bother ordering them. We are going to make a photo tomorrow and I'm hoping that this time it will come out better.

Knowing how much you love Shkhery, I feel terribly sad for you that this year you didn't sail. But what can we do. We should hope that the war will not last long and that upon its end everything will be back as it was.

It's so frustrating – I have got a terrible cold and even spent a day in bed. I'm trying to remedy myself so that I can go out and help my husband in his preparation for the march.

Recently we have finally received news from Mama from London. Poor Mama cannot depart from there now and is terribly anxious. We all are so happy that at least she managed to leave Germany, which must have been very hard.

Till next time, my dear beloved Tatiana Nikolaevna.

I'm tightly and warmly embracing you.

My husband is asking to pass his regards to you.

Wholeheartedly loving you and faithfully yours,

Olga Voronov

29 July 1914

Petersburg

**Fund 651, inventory 1, file 48**

August 27th

My sweet and dear Olga,

I think and pray for you very much. Please send your husband my heartfelt greetings and wishes for all the very best. Do you still go to the community courses?

Mama, Olga and I go every day to the Palace Hospital where we bandage the wounded. We both have 3 people each, whom we must bandage. Mama has the officers.

If it won't be tiresome for you, write to me sometimes about what you do. Where is Tata, that is, is she with you or your sister?

Well, goodbye my dear Olga. God bless you.

I hug you tightly.

Loving you very much,

Your Tatiana

**Fund 651, inventory 1, file 102**

Petrograd

28 August 1914

My dear Tatiana Nikolaevna,

I have just received your letter for which I sincerely thank you.

My husband is deeply touched by your kind wishes and regards and in turn is asking to pass his kindest regards to you.

Our courses will start only on Monday, 1 September.

When my husband departs, I will move to my older sister (Martynova). She is asking me very much for this, and I'm also looking forward to this because it would be too sad to stay alone at home. Her husband has also gone to war.

Tata is staying with Ella.

Our photographs came out rather well. When they are ready, with your permission, I will send one to you, as you have asked.

I'm warmly and tightly embracing you, my dear Tatiana Nikolaevna

Lovingly yours,

Olga Voronov

**Fund 651, inventory 1, file 102**

My dear Tatiana Nikolaevna

I have just returned from the lectures at St Eugenia's community. The three of us went there, my elder sister, Tata and I. For now, it has been the very basics, of course.

I have already received several letters from my husband while he is still on the way. He writes that they all are in good spirits and even elevated mood, and the lower ranks are singing and playing harmonica all the time.

Till next time, my dear Tatiana Nikolaevna.

I'm warmly kissing you and asking you to pass my warm regards to Their Highnesses.

With all my heart loving you,

Olga Voronov

3 September 1914

46 Liteiny Prospect

Martynov's apartment

**Fund 651, inventory 1, file 48**

Tsarskoe Selo

5 September 1914

My dear and sweet Olga,

Thank you very much for your nice letter.

Mama, Olga and I go every day to the palace hospital for dressings, but we don't bandage them in the big house. In the garden, there is a small house, only for officers and 6 of the lower ranks are brought there every day whom Olga and I bandage. Each should be tied three times. And they are changed every day, so that we don't get used to the wounds, but do everything, and then when we are finished, we sit with the officers, and Mama takes turns to bandage them with Anya Vyrubova. On days when a train arrives with new wounded on it, we help at the Big House, because there aren't enough hands. Now Princess Gedroits is letting us in for operations. There still haven't been any big ones, but we were at one where a finger was amputated, then the bullets were pulled out. She cuts, and we take the bullet out with tweezers. Today I pulled one out. At first it's scary as you try not to hurt them, but now the wounds are not nasty. Sometimes though the smell is terrible. This is unpleasant. Then the Princess comes and gives us lectures every other day. Are you bandaging someone or not? Do you have news from your brother and does he write to you?

How hard it must be for your Mama to be abroad at such a time, and not with you. Aunt Olga writes to us from Rovno, where she lives, says that there is so much work there, and a lot of wounded. Well, goodbye my dear darling Olga. The sisters thank you for the bow, and bow to you. God bless you. I kiss your sisters. I hug you firmly and gently, my dear, as I love you.

Sincerely loving you, your

Tatiana


**Fund 651, inventory 1, file 102**

Petrograd

8 September 1914

My dear Tatiana Nikolaevna,

Thank you so much for your lovely, interesting letter.

You are already becoming experienced Sisters of Mercy while we are still only attending the lectures. We will be allowed to tend to the sick only in a week, I think.

We have been receiving good news from my brother so far, thanks God. But he has not received anything from us yet. Such a big quantity of letters is being sent to the filed army now, the delays in deliveries are inevitable.

I must have forgotten to tell you, dear Tatiana Nikolaevna, that Mama had returned long ago. We were so happy for her and for us. Now Mama wants to open a small hospital in Petrograd for 10 beds and is very busy organising it.

Ella went to visit her husband, as some other ladies. She is coming back to Petrograd in the next few days.

Tata thanks you very much for your regards and passes her kindest regards to you.

I'm kissing you very warmly my dear Tatiana Nikolaevna

Wholeheartedly yours,

Olga Voronov

46 Liteiny Prospect, Martynovs apartment

## Fund 651, inventory 1, file 102

Petrograd

Apt 23, 46 Liteiny Prospect

19 September 1914

My dear Tatiana Nikolaevna,

I'm sending you our photograph.

Today there will be a blessing ceremony of Mama's hospital. From there we all will go to St Eugenia's community to say goodbye to Maria Pavlovna who is leaving in the next few days, I think.

Tomorrow Babishchin is leaving and he promised to visit me today to tell me what they are doing there.

I'm warmly kissing you and asking you to pass my warm regards to Their Highnesses.

Very much loving you,

Olga Voronov

**Fund 651, inventory 1, file 48**

Tsarskoe Selo.

20 September 1914

My dear, sweet darling Olga,

Thank you very much my dear for your wonderful photo, which I really like and which will always be with me. Thanks for the nice letter. For whom does your Mama arrange an infirmary, for officers or soldiers? And who will watch over them? Alexei's train should come tomorrow with the wounded, so we will have a lot of work. Today, Papa went to the army, but it seems not for long, just for a week or so. And where exactly we still do not know. First of all to the *Stavka* of the Supreme Commander, but after that is not clear yet. Such a pity that one of them could not go with him. Olga asked me to ask if perhaps you still have some photograph of you and Pavel Alekseevich? If so, then she would very much like you to send it to her. How is your health?

Olga, Mama and Papa and I were in Petrograd for two consecutive Wednesdays, where we visited the wounded, and then from 3–4 Olga sits at the Peasant Bank where she accepts donations for spare families. This Wednesday I will have a committee to provide temporary assistance to victims of military disasters, I already think with horror about this day because I will have to be all alone, not with Mama, then I will probably sit with Olga while she accepts donations, and work, otherwise it's boring. Well, goodbye my darling Olga. God bless you. I think a lot about you. The sisters thank you for your greetings and also bow to you. Kiss yours. I hug you, my dear, as much as I love you.

Your Tatiana

**Fund 651, inventory 1, file 102**

22 September 1914

My dearest Tatiana Nikolaevna,

Your warm letter deeply touched me and I thank you from the bottom of my heart for your kindness and care which I cherish very much.

I'm so happy that you liked our photograph. I'm hoping that Olga Nikolaevna will like the second photo too.

I'm so sorry to hear that you will be by yourself on the committee. I personally find these things so hard.

Mama is opening the hospital for soldiers. Unfortunately, my sisters will not be able to work there because they will be occupied at the St Eugenia community. And I have quit the course because I'm feeling unwell. The doctors are saying that this is all nerves related. I become exhausted after doing just simple things and then I'm good for nothing for the rest of the day. It was very hard for me to make this decision, I really wanted to try myself in this field. But what can I do. I will do something else. I will sew and knit warm things and visit my Mama's small hospital to read to the wounded and write letters for them.

Mama and sisters are thanking you very much for your considerate attention and asking you to accept their most sincere regards.

I'm warmly and fondly embracing you my dear Tatiana Nikolaevna.

Loving you with all my heart

Olga Voronov

**Fund 651, inventory 1, file 102**

Apt 23, 46 Liteiny Prospect

Petrograd

29 November 1914

My dearest Tatiana Nikolaevna,

The day before yesterday I came back from Vilna where I went to see off my brother and visit my husband together with him.

He told me that he met Her Majesty, Olga Nikolaevna and you on the street when you were probably on the way from the railway station. It was the first time that he saw you in the Sisters-of-Mercy outfits. It is such a shame that I was not there with him. I had just arrived and was in the hotel.

Do you have much work now? You are probably being assigned to do more complex things now.

Tata continues attending the St Eugenia community and once a week attends the night shift.

I have been helping until now at the Princess Elena Petrovna's warehouse in the Marble palace, because my sister Ella is working there.

Till next time, my dear Tatiana Nikolaevna. I'm warmly kissing you and sending my warmest regards to Olga Nikolaevna and both younger Grand Duchesses.

Loving you with all my heart,

Olga Voronov.

## Fund 651, inventory 1, file 48

Tsarskoye Selo

30 November 1914

Olga, my darling,

Thank you very much for your lovely letter. I was awfully glad to receive it. I myself was going to write to you, but I didn't know if you had returned. I was terribly glad to meet your husband and terribly regret that I did not see you.

Unfortunately, we did not see all of ours in Kovno, because they were sent on an expedition somewhere. Such a pity. But we saw people – they were at the station. They are difficult to recognise in a different uniform. I also saw your husband for the first time in his land uniform. Tomorrow Mama, Olga and I will go to Moscow for two days, and then to Tula, Oryol, Kursk and Kharkov. We will inspect the infirmaries in all those places. Then in Voronezh on the 6$^{th}$ we will meet with Papa and go back to Moscow, the little ones will come there, and we will probably go back home on the 12$^{th}$. All this will be interesting, but it is terribly sad to leave our infirmary to which we are terribly attached and love. We all have such thoughts and it is terrible when they have to leave us. Now we have two wounded Nizhny Novgorod residents who underwent surgery yesterday. One is very poorly. His whole elbow was crushed and a lot of pieces were pulled out. They are all so patient that you have to wonder sometimes. Please don't talk about where we are going on our journey because Mama does not like it when everyone knows in advance and they are waiting for her, although this almost always happens, because everyone is always gossiping.

How tiresome that we have not seen each other for so long.

How is the infirmary that your Mama arranged? Do you go there often?

Papa telegraphs us that it is wonderful now in Tiflis, warm and everything is awfully good. I must truthfully say that I envy him terribly because I so awfully want to go to the Caucasus, and then he also says that it is that hot in the train, that he sits by the open door and basks in the sun. Unfortunately, it's hard for us to believe this, but I would really like it to be like that.

When we get back from the trip I will certainly write to you.

How are you feeling?

I have a lovely little dog, a French bulldog. She's such a darling. She plays awfully sweetly with Alexei's dog.

Olga and the sisters thank you for your bow and kiss. Please kiss your Mama and sisters from me. If you write to your husband, please give my regards.

Well, goodbye my dear Olga. Christ be with you. I kiss you firmly and tenderly, as I love you.

Loving you very much

Your

Tatiana

**Fund 651, inventory 1, file 102**

Petrograd

9 December 1914

My dear Tatiana Nikolaevna

I thank you wholeheartedly for you your warm long letter. I was so happy to receive it. I also feel very sad that we have not seen each other so long.

Did you have a good trip?

You were asking, dear Tatiana Nikolaevna, where Mama's small hospital is. It is on 18 Zakharyevskaya St. Mama has asked to pass to you that she would be extremely happy and grateful if Her Majesty would allow you and Olga Nikolaevna to visit her small hospital one day. She doesn't dare, of course, to hope for Her Majesty's visit but would be very grateful and happy if Her Majesty would allow you to come. We go there quite often.

Mama wants to organise a Christmas celebration for the soldiers and buy some funny things and surprises. They are such children sometimes and some silly things cheer them up.

Who presented you the dog? These French bull[dogs] are so ugly but so cute, aren't they?

Very warmly kissing you my dear Tatiana Nikolaevna. My Mother and sisters are passing their kindest regards to you.

Loving you very much, wholeheartedly yours

Olga Voronov

**Fund 651, inventory 1, file 48**

Tsarskoe Selo 1914 December 13th.

My dear sweet Olga,

Thank you very much for your dear letter.

Our trip went well. We visited a lot of infirmaries, two or three every day. Mama is very tired of course and has a bad cold. Maria has a bit of a sore throat, terribly tiresome.

I am awfully pleased to be back and to be able to go to our infirmary again.

Does your husband write to you and where is he now? I expect they are somewhere else, but where, I do not know.

You must be quite sad probably, to spend your first Christmas without your husband. In Moscow, we had wonderful sun on the last day, but it was cold. The rest of the days were all damp and foggy.

Unfortunately, Papa did not come back with us and will arrive back on Wednesday, I believe, because he went to Headquarters.

How are you feeling?

Well, goodbye. I kiss you firmly and tenderly, dear Olga, as I love you.

With all my soul yours,

Tatiana

### Fund 651, inventory 1, file 102

Petrograd

16 December 1914

My dearest Tatiana Nikolaevna,

Thank you very much for your lovely letter. My husband is now with his troop in Noviy Dvor.[13] I receive letters from him almost every day. My *beau-père* started his trip to visit both his sons several days ago.[14] My husband's brother is staying on leave somewhere close to there. And they both now went to war without saying good-bye to their parents because they could not come from their country estate. Their estate is in Ufimskaya Gubernia, extremely far away.

I'm very aggrieved by the death of poor Butakov![15] I spent almost the whole day yesterday with his wife. She is in terrible state, they were so happy together. Her boy, he is 6 years old, doesn't understand yet, of course. He says: "Daddy is with the God, but he will come back to us, won't he?". I'm going to the first funeral service now.

I'm terribly touched that you always ask about my health. Recently I have been having strong migraines almost every day.

---

[13] Possibly in Poland.

[14] *Beau-père* is French for father-in-law.

[15] Naval Officer, Senior Lieutenant Aleksandr Ivanovich Butakov.

I had them in the past too, but seldom. Overall, everyone is feeling well. Thank you very much.

I'm warmly kissing you my dearest Tatiana Nikolaevna.

Loving you very much and wholeheartedly yours,

Olga Voronov

## Fund 651, inventory 1, file 102

Petrograd

24 December 1914

My dearest Tatiana Nikolaevna,

Please accept my heartfelt congratulations with the Holiday. I'm sending you my warmest wishes of happiness in the New Year. My husband is joining me in my congratulations and best wishes.

I'm receiving news from him very often. It's terribly sad that we are not going to be together during the Holidays. But what can we do. God willing, it will be possible to see each other someday.

Please accept, dear Tatiana Nikolaevna, these things for your committee for the poor, my yearly contribution.

I'm very warmly kissing you my dearest Tatiana Nikolaevna.

Loving you with all my heart

Olga Voronov

## Fund 651, inventory 1, file 48

My dear Olga,

Thank you very much for your lovely letter and things. I ask you to thank your husband very much for his congratulations.

There will be a Christmas party at our infirmary today at the officers' and we shall go there.

We had our Christmas party yesterday afternoon.

Now we will have many Christmas parties for the wounded and others.

Please congratulate your Mama and sisters from me. Our mother was terribly tired and her heart was not well, because she had to be out of bed all the time (when she needed to lie down) and choose and arrange gifts for everyone when she already felt bad.

Where does Tata live, in Petrograd or here, and where? We are thanking her for her letters, but we don't know where to address them to therefore we are addressing them to you.

Well, goodbye my Olga darling. I wish you all the best for the New Year. I will think about you and congratulate you on the 29th on your husband's birthday.

I firmly and gently kiss you my dear. Kisses.

With all my heart

Tatiana

**Fund 651, inventory 1, file 102**

26 December 1914

My dearest Tatiana Nikolaevna

I thank you from the bottom of my heart for the congratulations and your kind and warm lines which touched me deeply, you remembered about the birthday of my husband.

I'm tightly and fondly embracing you, my dear.

Wholeheartedly yours,

Olga Voronov

Tata lives with my sister Pushchin at 6 Konnogvardeyskiy boulevard.

**Fund 651, inventory 1, file 48**

31 December 1914

Alexander Palace.

Tsarskoe Selo.

My dear, sweet Olga,

May God send you all the best for the New Year. I seem not to have thanked you for the last letter.

It's so heart-breaking that Mama still doesn't feel well and cannot go to the infirmary.

Do you often receive letters from your husband?

Where is your brother now at [illegible]?

I was very glad that I saw you, even if from a distance, at Butakov's funeral.

Every day now we go to different infirmaries to visit everyone. The infirmary is very well arranged at the B[ig] P[alace] where there are many officers.

There is one poor officer from a Cossack regiment who has had his right leg amputated, he plays the guitar and sings amazingly well. They didn't allow him to sing loudly and for a long time, but he can if not so loud and also sad things. I really liked it. I am always so sorry for those unfortunates whose leg or arm is taken away.

The sharpshooters of the 4th regiment were there, but they have all left some time ago. Sorry for such a boring letter. All the best to you. God bless you. I kiss and hug you firmly and tenderly, my dear Olga, as I love you. With all my heart, Tatiana

## Fund 651, inventory 1, file 103

12 at night 2 January 1915

My dear Tatiana Nikolaevna,

I have just learned about the terrible misfortune that happened to poor Anna Alexandrovna. Tomorrow at 1 pm I am leaving to go to my husband in Warsaw and therefore I cannot get to Tsarskoe.

This terrible news struck me terribly and I mourn very much that I can't come to ask after her health at the hospital. Dear Tatiana Nikolaevna, if it's not too difficult for you and if you have a free minute, drop me a line about poor Anna Alexandrovna's health, I love her very much. My address in Warsaw is Polognia Hotel. I'm sure to be there for 3–4 days. Forgive me my dear for my untimely request. We are all terribly saddened by this sad incident.

I hug you tightly.

Your Olga.

But if it makes you a little uncomfortable or you have no time, for God's sake, do not write. I know how you love her. All my soul and thoughts are with you all. My whole heart is transported to you.

## Fund 651, inventory 1, file 103

Varsovie (Polognia Hotel, en face de la garé de Varsovie) Jan 5th 1915

My sweet, dear Tatiana Nikolaevna,

I am endlessly touched by your affectionate telegram and thank you terribly for the detailed information about Anna

Alexandrovna. I am so sorry for her, the poor thing, simply awful! My husband was shocked when I told him about this misfortune and we think about it a lot and with all our souls. We wholeheartedly hope and pray that poor Anna Alexandrovna will recover soon.

My husband asks you to accept his heartfelt bow and sincere gratitude for your attention. He will certainly convey your regards to others. There is such an awful amount of people, all the hospitals are crowded. We have breakfast at the Bristol hotel and catch up with a lot of friends. Incidentally, we saw Polity-Miloslavsky from afar with his wife and stepdaughter, little Yuzia, who, you remember, danced gavotte in Yalta at Princess Baryatinsky's concert.

I really like Warsaw, after breakfast we rode around the city. I'll stay here for another three days. I was so happy that I could see my husband. It is much warmer here than in Petrograd and there is absolutely no snow.

I embrace you tightly and tenderly, my dear, and thank you again sincerely for the telegram.

Loving you with all my heart

Olga Voronova.

**Fund 651, inventory 1, file 48**

Tsarskoe Selo. 12 January 1915

My dear Olga,

I thank you awfully much for your congratulations and for your two sweet letters. I am glad for you that you could see your husband.

Ania's brother told me yesterday that he was traveling with you from Warsaw.

How are you feeling? I hope that the trip did not tire you too much.

I am sending you this photo-postcard, maybe it will be interesting for you to have it, although in my opinion it did not turn out particularly well.

Do you know, or has your husband not yet told you, does he have to be back to business yet or not? Anya is not much better, and at times she suffers quite a lot.

We go to visit her every day when we go to do dressings, sometimes we come back in the afternoon or in the evening. Her parents are there all the time. Her sister came and this morning brought her eldest daughter, my goddaughter, with her. She's a terribly funny and amusing girl.

My sisters thank you very much for your bow and kiss. Well, goodbye, Olga, my dear darling. I kiss you firmly and gently and hug you as I love you.

Yours always, cordially

Tatiana

**Fund 651, inventory 1, file 103**

Petrograd.

13 January 1915

My dear, sweet Tatiana Nikolaevna,

Thank you very much for your sweet letter. The trip did not tire me at all, and tomorrow I am off again. Most of ours in the business have virtually not yet been, that is, the 2nd battalion, but the First is bigger. Today I was told that Filatov was wounded in the leg, but not captured. Thank you very much for the postcard. I really like it. In my opinion, it all turned out well and I would really like to show it to my husband.

I often talk about all of you with him. I am very glad that Anna Alexandrovna is at least a little better. Please bow to her very much from me. It is so terrible that she suffers so much, the poor thing. I wanted to come to find out about her health, but I have quite the cough, and I was worried it could get worse and I'd not be able to go to my husband.

I embrace you firmly and warmly, my dear Tatiana Nikolaevna, and send my regards to the Grand Duchesses. Tata bows to you very much.

Loving you with all my soul,

your Olga Voronova

**Fund 651, inventory 1, file 48**

Tsarskoe Selo. 18 January 1915

My dear Olga, darling,

Thank you very much for your latest sweet letter. I am glad that you again managed to go to see your husband. How long will you stay there? Ania is a little better. Thank God she does not suffer like before, but her temperature is always high. We see her every day when we go to bandage officers in the morning and then we go to see her in the evening.

In order to keep our officers busy somehow, we bring them puzzles and they sit and put them together all day and we sometimes help them. We taught others to knit wristbands, they do it very well, it amuses them and so it's not so boring to be lying in bed.

Well, goodbye my dear Olga, heartfelt greetings to your husband. I hug you firmly and gently. With all my heart

Tatiana

**Fund 651, inventory 1, file 103**

Hotel Bristol. Varsovie

My dear Tatiana Nikolaevna,

My husband was here but has left now, however I do not lose hope of seeing him in a few days.

Ella came here with me one day. Her husband should be here today.

There's an awful lot of people here, a mass of military, commissioners and sisters of mercy. Yesterday, a German airplane flew over the city, and, they say, dropped a bomb. Indeed, they have got so used to it that they did not even pay it any attention.

We were here at the theater, to see an operetta. Bela (sic) Messal, a famous artist.[16] She is very lively, sings well and dances wonderfully.

It's pretty cold here and it is snowing today. How is Anna Alexandrovna's health now? I hug you very, very tightly my dear Tatiana Nikolaevna. My husband asked me to give you and Their Highnesses his deepest bow. I also ask you to pass on my regards to the Grand Duchesses. With all my heart

Your

Olga Voronova

Warsaw

Hotel Bristol

January 19th 1915

**Fund 651, inventory 1, file 103**

Petrograd 27 January 1915

My dear Tatiana Nikolaevna,

Thank you very much for your sweet letter. I received it an hour before leaving Warsaw. So wonderful! They weren't able to find

---

[16] Most likely Lucyna Messal, operetta star – bella meaning beautiful.

me for two days, because this time I stayed at the Bristol, and did not give you my address. I got back from Warsaw yesterday. I managed to see my husband again for several hours. So good!

They are very close to Warsaw, and so far there is almost nothing to do, and I really hope that I can go there again for one or two days to spend our anniversary together on February 7th. Of course, if they don't leave for somewhere before then.

Ella also saw her husband for several days and we came back home together.

Bye for now, my sweet and dear Tatiana Nikolaevna. I very tightly embrace you and bow very much to Their Highnesses. Warmly loving you with all my heart,

Olga Voronova

## Fund 651, inventory 1, file 48

Tsarskoe Selo. 28 January 1915

My dear sweet Olga,

Thank you very much for your two lovely letters, I was terribly glad to receive them. I didn't answer the one from Warsaw because I didn't know when you were leaving and thought you wouldn't receive it, so I decided to wait for your return.

You have probably heard what that nasty 'Breslau' has done in little Yalta.[17] So shameful. I imagine how little Mme Kaubish fusses for her "Russia". We asked Rita Khitrovo to write to us how it all was and what damage. Thank God there were no human casualties. I wonder if they would be so impudent to shoot at Livadia, probably so.

Today I went with Olga again to Petrograd, where she accepted donations. We won't go in the first week of Great Lent because we will be fasting. When will you fast? And where?

Anya, thank God, is getting better little by little. She almost already doesn't suffer. How is your health?

Thank God Mama feels a bit better and has come back to the dressings again, only not at 10 o'clock like us, but at 11, so she doesn't have to get up too early. I am sending you a postcard from us, it was made by Anya while we were working, so we are in our robes.

Well, goodbye. I kiss you very, very firmly my dear, darling Olga. Loving you with all my heart. Your Tatiana

---

[17] The German cruiser *Breslau* bombarded the Crimean port of Yalta, https://trove.nla.gov.au/newspaper/article/238836319/25732287

**Fund 651, inventory 1, file 103**

Petrograd

30 Jan 1915

My dear, sweet Tatiana Nikolaevna,

Thank you very much for your letter and photo, which I really like. It is so good that Anna Alexandrovna is so much better now.

I am terribly touched that you always ask after my health. I have a bad cold at the moment, coughing terribly these days, but I am a little better today.

I'll probably fast during Holy Week, as usual, but I don't know where else. Last year, I fasted at the Naval Cathedral with my husband, but it's an awfully long way to go.

I heard that the hotel *Russia* is quite damaged. From here I can see a commotion in the Kaubish family. But would they dare to touch Livadia? That would be the height of arrogance. And it would be horrifyingly pitiful if a wonderful new palace were to suffer.

I hug you tightly and tenderly, my dear Tatiana Nikolaevna, and ask you to convey my heartfelt greetings to the Grand Duchesses.

Yours with all my soul

Olga Voronova


**Fund 651, inventory 1, file 48**

Tsarskoe Selo. 3 February 1915

My dear, sweet Olga,

Thank you for your letter. Anya was terribly touched by your flowers and letter. She can already sit down for a little bit, but certainly not for long. Are you going to your husband? And when? And where will you be staying? If you see him, please greet him very much from me.

I don't know if you have this picture, maybe it will be interesting for you to have it. It is of your husband taking us.

It is so good that Papa came back yesterday. He was very pleased with his trip and especially Sevastopol, and says that everyone has a wonderful fresh and cheery look. And that the *Diamond* was repainted in grey and became a cruiser the same as in that war. Well, goodbye, my dear Olga, darling.

I kiss you firmly and tenderly as I love you.

With all my heart, Tatiana

## Fund 651, inventory 1, file 103

4 February 1915

My dear sweet Tatiana Nikolaevna,

Thank you very much for your sweet letter and for sending the card. I am very glad to have it, and I am very touched by your dear attention. I am not going to Warsaw, because my husband telegraphed to me that now we won't be able to see each other, and he'll let me know when we get a chance. I don't know when it will be, but I don't think that he will call me for a few days.

My brother was here yesterday. He came from Krechevits and left in the evening to catch up with the regiment. He is so glad that he will finally be with the regiment.

It's so good that Anna Alexandrovna can sit for a little bit! It is very tiring to be in one position always.

Mama left for Moscow yesterday for the occasion of the tenth anniversary of the death of Grand Duke Sergei Alexandrovich.

When shall you receive communion, on Thursday or Saturday? If on Thursday, then I congratulate you and the Grand Duchess on your partaking of the Holy Mysteries.

Goodbye, my dear Tatiana Nikolaevna, dear, I kiss you very, very firmly.

Loving you with all my heart

Your

Olga Voronova


## Fund 651, inventory 1, file 103

Petrograd 4 February 1915

My dear Tatiana Nikolaevna,

Can you imagine how happy I am? I just got a telegram from my husband. He has called me to Warsaw. I will leave, God willing, tomorrow at 1 in the afternoon. Supposed to arrive at 6pm, but they say there are big delays on the way. I hope I shall be there by 7. I want to stay at the Hotel Bristol. So it shall be good if I get to Warsaw and see my husband! I also got a sweet telegram from Anna Alexandrovna. I kiss you, my own one, very firmly and warmly. Yours, with all my soul, Olga Voronova

**Fund 651, inventory 1, file 48**

Tsarskoe Selo. February 6th, 1915

My dear darling Olga,

Thank you very much dear for the two letters. I am terribly glad for you that you have again managed to go see your husband. I will remember you both tomorrow from that day a year ago. I wish you all the best.

I hope that you arrived on time so that you can spend the 7th together.

We will receive communion tomorrow. Thank you very much for your congratulations. I hope very much that this letter will reach you.

Unfortunately, we had to work less in the infirmary this week due to the fact that we had to go to church. Well, goodbye, my dear Olga. Please give your husband my warm greetings. God bless you. I kiss and hug you firmly and tenderly, my dear. With all my heart

Tatiana


**Fund 651, inventory 1, file 103**

Petrograd

February 16th, 1915

My dear Tatiana Nikolaevna,

I received your sweet letter in Warsaw before I left and was terribly touched by what you wrote to me there. I arrived in Warsaw in the morning of the 7th, just in time, so that was good. There was an awful lot of people on the train – even in the first class, soldiers stood in the corridor the whole way. I came back home via Moscow and stayed there for 3 days to see my friends. Yesterday I went to the church of the Holy Martyr St Tryphon there. You know there is a miraculous icon there. There was a moleben service and I prayed very ardently for all of you.

My husband asked you to thank you very much for your greetings and asked me to give you a bow. I hug you firmly and warmly, my dear.

Warmly loving you with all my heart

Your

Olga Voronova

## Fund 651, inventory 1, file 48

February 18th, 1915

My dear Olga,

Thank you very much for your letter. I am glad that you have returned safely. I hope that you got to see your husband often. How is he and all the others?

Anya moved back to her house on Sunday; she is scared enough to be at home. But she is still lying down with a starched dressing and in traction.

Yesterday a very badly injured man came to us. Today, in our attendance, one of his legs was amputated. I am so sorry for these poor young people who have been crippled for life. Then one had to take away his right hand.

The Commander of the Life Guard Izmailovsky regiment, T. M. Kruglovsky, was brought to our infirmary as well. His left arm is cut off above the elbow, and on the right he is wounded in the hand, the poor thing, I am so terribly sorry for him, and he probably feels so helpless.

Gen[eral] Po. had lunch with us today.

Well, how are you, what are you up to and when will you return?

Do you ever see A.O. Butakova? How is she, the poor thing, very sad? I really want to see you.

Well, goodbye. God bless you. I kiss you firmly and gently my dear darling Olga and hug you.

Loving you with all my heart,

Your Tatiana


## Fund 651, inventory 1, file 103

Petrograd
20th February 1915
My sweet Tatiana Nikolaevna,
Thank you very much for your dear letter. You ask what am I doing now. Of course, I have a cough again. I'm just desperate that I can't completely get rid of this nasty cough that seems to want to become chronic. They keep me at home. On the third day I was vaccinated for smallpox, which seems to have taken. It's awful what happened with Tata and Ella's hands.

The other day, Nolde came here from the 2nd battalion, do you know him? He brought me a letter from her husband. My husband writes that on the night of the 14th a zeppelin flew over Warsaw and threw 6 bombs, and an aeroplane flew over his village, which ours soon drove away. My husband and the others see each other rarely now, because they are scattered about in different places a few miles from each other, but there are telephones everywhere. Their affairs are now greater than at the beginning, since they are in charge of the crossings.

My husband's brother was involved again several times. He writes that the prisoners say that they are terribly afraid of being taken prisoner by us, as they were told that a huge flour mill was arranged in Moscow, where all the prisoners are turned into flour. Horror, what nonsense, and really everyone believes it!

Before I left for Warsaw, I saw A.O. Butakova several times. How awful, the poor thing, it's such a pity. Every day it becomes harder for her and the only thing that keeps her going is the presence of her little Nikita. On the 10th, she was supposed to go with him to her mother in Vladivostok. What do they write to you from the Crimea? It seems that they promised to write to you what damage there was from shelling by the Turks.

I firmly, firmly hug you, my dear. Loving you, with all my heart

Your Olga


**Fund 651, inventory 1, file 103**

Petrograd

20 March 1915

My dear Tatiana Nikolaevna,

There's a light rain, yesterday and today, and its leaves begin to dissolve (as it's written in the text). So finally, spring is so pleasant.

My husband was on duty at the battalion yesterday and now I am waiting for his return. The officers are allowed to leave now, and today I am going to leave for Petrograd. Kozhevnikov, Rodionov, Khvoshchinsky and Kublitsky may be relieved from my husband.

Then it will be terribly fun to travel together.

Yesterday I went around the city a lot, which I really liked. So clean and pretty.

Well, goodbye, my dear Tatiana Nikolaevna.

I firmly, firmly kiss You. Warmly loving you

Your Olga Voronova, London Hotel. Odessa.

## Fund 651, inventory 1, file 48

Tsarskoye Selo, April 16<sup>th</sup> 1915

My dear Olga, darling,

Thank you very much for your sweet letter. I was very glad to receive it. Papa sent Mama a telegraph after leaving Odessa that he was terribly glad to see all of ours there. It's very cold lately, so tedious.

How do you live, are you alone with your husband in the hotel, or is everyone with you? How is your health? When we were in Petrograd yesterday, we met your sister Ella on a motor. Now we have a bit of a lull and very few wounded officers. There's only 12 left in the infirmary where we work. Many are leaving. It's so sad to part with them because you don't know whether you'll see each other again. Please convey my warm greetings to our friends in Yalta.

I am sending you my warmest congratulations and wish you all the very, very best for your birthday. We went riding once, and then the weather turned bad and it's tiresome to ride when the wind is cold and strong. Well, goodbye, Olga darling. A heartfelt bow to your husband. I kiss you firmly and tenderly and congratulate you once again.

Loving you with all my heart

Tatiana

## Fund 651, inventory 1, file 103

My dear Tatiana Nikolaevna,

I thank you sincerely for your congratulations and for the letter I received in Odessa. I was so awfully glad to see you yesterday!

I kiss you very firmly. My husband asks you to convey to you and Their Highnesses his deep bow.

Warmly loving you

Olga Voronova

April 21, 1915

**Fund 651, inventory 1, file 103**

April 22, 1915

My dear Tatiana Nikolaevna

I do not dare to directly congratulate Her Imperial Majesty on her name-day, so I decided to write to you to congratulate you and Their Highnesses on this day and ask you, if possible, to pass the loyal congratulations of my husband and I on the name-day of the Empress to Her Imperial Majesty. I kiss you, my dear Tatiana Nikolaevna firmly, firmly.

Warmly loving you

Your Olga Voronova


**Fund 651, inventory 1, file 48**

Tsarskoe Selo

1915

My dear darling Olga,

Thank you very much for your sweet letter, I was terribly happy to receive it. I was all set to answer you straight away, but I didn't have time, I had no time at all. I was so glad to see you both here before your departure. Today it is cold and it has been raining almost all day, but the trees are blooming.

Today, 70 new wounded arrived at our soldiers' department. There are some terrible wounds in some of them, and several wounds on each one, the poor things! They suffer so much during the dressings. No matter how hard you try to bandage them carefully, you still hurt them involuntarily. The poor ones, I am so sorry for them.

There are still very few officers, because they bring 3 or 4 in by trains, but our ones, thank God, are getting a little better.

Well, goodbye Olga darling. Write sometimes.

Warm greetings to your husband, etc.

I firmly and tenderly kiss you, as I love you.

Your

Tatiana


**Fund 651, inventory 1, file 103**

April 28th, 1915

My dear, dear Tatiana Nikolaevna,

I sincerely thank you for your sweet letter, which was waiting for me here and for your remembering me.

My husband and I now live by ourselves in the hotel. Everyone else, except married couples who rented dachas, have moved to the barracks. They come only sometimes for lunch.

The other day we wanted to go to the estuary, it's a kind of resort (they have mud treatment there it seems) 6 miles from here. They say the swimming's good there. As soon as it gets warmer, I terribly want to go swimming in the sea.

On the 30$^{th}$, my husband is on duty at the battalion. I brought my work here. I will do lace and read, so that the day will pass quickly.

I warmly embrace you, my dear Tatiana Nikolaevna. My husband asks to give you a deep bow.

With all my soul, your

Olga Voronova

**Fund 651, inventory 1, file 103**

Odessa

London Hotel

May 19$^{th}$, 1915

My dear Tatiana Nikolaevna

My husband and I ask you to accept, and to convey to Their Highnesses, our warm congratulations on the birthday of Her Imperial Majesty.

I beg you, dear Tatiana Nikolaevna, if possible, to pass on our loyal congratulations to Her Imperial Majesty.

It's been quite summery here. It's hot, the lilac has faded and the fragrant acacia is blooming now.

How is Anna Alexandrovna's health now? Please give her my sincere greetings.

I strongly and firmly kiss you, my dear Tatiana Nikolaevna, and bow deeply to Their Highnesses.

Passionately loving you, your

Olga Voronova

## Fund 651, inventory 1, file 48

Tsarskoe Selo.

May 24th, 1915

My dear Olga, darling,

Thank you very much for your sweet letter which I just received.

Mama and all of us thank you very much for you and your husband's congratulations.

Have you received the two letters that I wrote to you there? I will send this letter with Molokhovets since it will be quicker and will definitely arrive. We have only just had lilacs begin to bloom in some places – it's so late, it's awful that it is still cold. Yesterday it was warm, but today it is cold again. Poor Anastasia is terribly sad, because her little dog *Shvybzik* died from a brain inflammation, it's so sad. Yesterday, an officer was brought to the infirmary, who was wounded for the third time and was lying with us all the time. The first time he was wounded in his right hand. Then on the left and to the chest. He was sent to the Crimea, and now again in his left hand. – Poor fellow. He's very young, 22 years old.

How sad it is for poor Tatyana Konstantinovna, but she is surprisingly cheerful and so restrained. She left for the Caucasus where he will be buried and she will remain there for a little while. Her children are terribly cute, such darlings. How are you feeling? What are you doing? Please pass on my regards to our Yakhtinsky. Well, goodbye. I firmly and gently kiss you my dear Olga darling. Say hello to your husband.

Loving you with all my heart, Tatiana.

## Fund 651, inventory 1, file 103

My dear Tatiana Nikolaevna,

My husband and I ask you to accept our warm congratulations on your birthday and the most cordial wishes for a bright and joyful day. I sincerely wish you a fun and good day.

Yesterday we went to the resort of Lustdorf, which is about fifteen miles from here. There is a very good beach and, they say, a lot of people come to be treated here in summer. We swam in the sea for the first time. The water is very warm, I think no less than 19. Now the heat has started here, so you can only go for a walk after 4 o'clock. Do you have a lot of work in the infirmary at the moment?

Goodbye, my dear and darling Tatiana Nikolaevna. Strongly and firmly I kiss you and ask you to convey my heartfelt greetings to Their Highnesses.

Yours with all my heart

Olga Voronova

**Fund 651, inventory 1, file 103**

Odessa

London Hotel.

May 29th, 1915

My dear, darling Tatiana Nikolaevna,

Thank you very, very much for the letter that Molokhovets brought to me. Can you imagine one of your letters to me didn't arrive! Upon returning from Petrograd, I received only one letter from you. Apart from the one that was waiting for me here – your congratulations on April 21st. I answered you immediately.

It is very hot here, and every day I swim in the sea.

The other day, the Medzhidie arrived in port, but I did not see it, because it is still forbidden to go to it.

I'm terribly sorry for poor Benckendorff. Is it true? He was so sweet.

Now I'm going to buy books. In the hottest hours of the day and when my husband is in class, I read a lot. Lately I read a lot in French. I kiss you firmly, firmly my dear. I am thinking about you especially today. My husband asks to convey his deep bow to you. With all my heart

Your

Olga Voronova

**Fund 651, inventory 1, file 48**

Tsarskoe Selo. June 2, 1915

My dear Olga,

I'm sorry that I did not answer you with a letter, but I did not have time at all. Your sweet letter has just been brought to me, for which I kiss you deeply and thank you very much. I was awfully glad to receive it. The weather is still not settled and it is cool. So tedious. They have arranged tennis for us in our garden, the same as on the Standart on the boards, it's very good. Because we are spending this summer here in Tsarskoe, Papa and I have decided to play. We are terribly pleased about it. This is the first year that we will not stay at Peterhof, but it is not convenient to go there, leaving the infirmaries and our work. It would even be sad to live there, because you know that there will be no dear yachts and skerries awaiting. But it's a bit boring here without the sea. Olga kisses you and thanks you for your greetings, the sisters too. Do you have friends in Odessa or is there no one? Soon O. Byutsova arrives there, to her Papa-Feod. The wedding will be there too. I wonder how it will all be. If it's not to troublesome, write sometimes.

Well, goodbye. Greetings to your husband. Firmly and gently I hug you my dear darling.

Loving you with all my heart

Tatiana

**Fund 651, inventory 1, file 103**

Odessa

London Hotel.

June 9$^{th}$, 1915

My dear Tatiana Nikolaevna

I sincerely thank you for your sweet letter, which I was terribly delighted to get.

O. Ev. Byutsova has not arrived yet. I did not know that the wedding would be in Odessa. If they call us, I will certainly write to you how it went. The other day we had our photos taken by one of the local photographers. No doubt they will be awful, how poorly done.

We have very few friends here. Admiral Khomenko is very sweet, cheerful and lively, and Count Sollogub, a senior officer of the Guards Crew. I don't think there's anyone else.

Of our ladies, only Filatov's wife stayed on here. V. G. Lukina left for Petrograd, because her husband was sent to Kovna. N. L. Knyazhevich came here for three days. I have not seen him since my wedding day. He said that he was very busy. He's building a railway in the Tauride region and in general there's a massive amount of work to improve the outskirts.

Yesterday, my husband and I caught some mice in our room. For some time now they have been eating all of our sweets. We set up a mousetrap and watched them exit a hole in the floor. Finally, we caught a tiny mouse with a huge head. I've never seen such a darling.

Bye bye, my dear, darling Tatiana Nikolaevna.

I firmly kiss you and bow deeply to the Grand Duchesses.

My husband also asks very much to bow to you and Their Highnesses.

Loving you with all my heart.

Your

Olga Voronova.

**Fund 651, inventory 1, file 48**

Tsarskoe Selo. June 14, 1915

My dear Olga,

Thank you very much for your sweet letter. I was awfully glad to receive it. Finally, thank God, the weather has settled down and it is warm. It's wonderful to ride around the park here in Pavlovsk. We go kayaking. Did the photo you wrote about to me come out or not? We are getting more wounded. One young warrant officer, 19 years old, got tetanus and was terribly unhappy, one leg was injured and the bone was broken, so that his leg was stretched out and the other leg was cramping. He is feeling a little better, yesterday and today. In the Grand Palace Infirmary there is a wounded officer, Lieutenant Dietrichs, from the Tuzemny Division of the Tatar Cavalry Regiment during wartime. Maybe your husband knows him. He was in our guard on the Standart in 1911 and commanded one cyclops, but I don't remember which number. It is strange that the lieutenant is not only on land but in such a division. How is your health? Well, goodbye. Write. Warm greetings to your husband and our Yakhtinsky. I tightly, tightly hug you my dear.

Loving you with all my heart

Tatiana.

**Fund 651, inventory 1, file 48**

Tsarskoe Selo. 4 July. 1915.

My dear Olga,

I am sending you my warmest wishes and congratulations for your Angel Day and wish you all that is joyful and bright. I'm afraid this letter will not get to you in time. Did you receive the letter that I sent with O.E. Byutsova? I sent it to her before she left and asked her to take the letter with her, but I haven't had a reply from her, so I don't know.

How are you? What are you doing? Today we will have the wedding of one of our wounded officers. He is from Mama's 21st Sib[erian] Regiment. This is the second wedding. Now they have organised croquet in the infirmary's small yard, and when we have time after dressings, we play with them. And, of course, everyone is arguing terribly and cheating terribly. Even those on crutches play. Well, goodbye Olga darling. Warm greetings to your husband and the others. I hug you tightly and gently.

Lovingly yours, your

Tatiana.

**Fund 651, inventory 1, file 103**

Petrograd

July 10th, 1915

My dear Tatiana Nikolaevna

Now I've arrived in Petrograd and I hasten to write to thank you for your sweet letter of June 14$^{th}$, which I received on the day of our departure from Odessa.

O. V. Byutsova brought me to the station. She herself spent two weeks in the countryside and had just arrived in Odessa, so she wasn't able to give it to me earlier. How fresh it is here after Odessa!

We are both resting. It took a dreadfully long time to get here because the train was delayed. I have not yet seen any of my own family, because everyone left for the funeral of our old nanny, who died on the third in an almshouse.

Goodbye for now. I kiss you firmly, dear Tatiana Nikolaevna. My husband bows to you very much.

Yours with all my heart

Olga Voronova

**Fund 651, inventory 1, file 48**

Tsarskoe Selo. July, 12. 1915.

My dear Olga, darling.

Thank you very much for your sweet letter. Not knowing that you had left Odessa, I sent you my congratulatory letter there yesterday. We've just returned from Peterhof, where we 5 had been with Papa, via Krasnoe Selo and Ropsha. There i.e., in Peterhof, we went swimming in the sea. It was wonderful, so good. Then we drank tea there, played a little and on the way back we got caught in a terrible thunderstorm and heavy rain. It was nice to see the sea again, though it was dirty, but even so. How long are you staying here? A wounded man was brought to the infirmary [illegible]. You know him, I guess. Write to me sometime Olga darling if it's not too tiresome. Well, goodbye. A warm bow and hello and thank him for remembering me. Tightly, tightly I hug you my dear.

Loving you very much.

Your Tatiana.

**Fund 651, inventory 1, file 103**

Petrograd

July 16th, 1915

My dear, sweet Tatiana Nikolaevna,

I sincerely thank you for your sweet letter.

We are leaving for Sevastopol tonight, all of ours left for there the other day. I don't know how long I'll stay there.

Yesterday they brought many wounded to Petrograd, and in almost all the hospitals they are increasing the number of beds. Mama seems to have more too. Perhaps they brought a lot to Tsarskoe too? You wrote that you have a sailor Dietrix. My husband does not remember him. Did he only visit the skerries or did he also come to Crimea? Our photo came out disgusting of course, just as we expected.

The other day I received a letter from my brother in Kislovodsk. He feels terrible. Almost unable to walk, very weak and so deafened that the doctor says that he hears 12 times worse than normal. So scary! It is completely incomprehensible why this happened. I think he was shell-shocked and did not notice. This often appears only after a while. Right?

Goodbye, my dear Tatiana Nikolaevna. I firmly, firmly kiss you.

I will stay at the hotel *Kista* in Sevastopol. I'd be terribly glad if you wrote to me somehow. My husband asks you to give you a deep bow and we both bow to the Grand Duchesses.

Loving you with all my heart,

Your Olga Voronova

## Fund 651, inventory 1, file 48

Tsarskoe Selo. 1915. 20 / VII

My dear Olga, darling,

Thank you very much for your letter. I was very surprised to hear that all of ours are in Sevastopol. What is the weather like there? We now have many wounded and all the infirmaries are increasing the number of places – so much is needed now. In the infirmary of the Gr[and] P[alace] instead of 45, now there are about 60 officers. We will probably also increase the number of beds, but at the soldiers etc there will be beds in the corridors as there is no place. What are you doing now in Sevastopol? How do you spend your time? We traveled with Papa to the launch of the Borodin. It was the first time I have seen a launch and I enjoyed it awfully much. It was terribly beautiful. And such an incredible length. Then we had breakfast at the Naval Minister on the Neva and it was so nice but sad to pass by our yacht and not be on it and see it empty. Awful! This is the first time in ten years that we are not swimming. So sad. Sorry for the chatter, but I looked at the photo of the yacht and thought about everything.

Well, goodbye. Warm greetings to your husband, Kazhevnikov and Rodionov. I strongly, firmly kiss you as I love you.

With all my heart

Tatiana


## Fund 651, inventory 1, file 103

My dear, sweet Tatiana Nikolaevna,

I thank you with all my heart for your letter.

Kazhevnikov and Rodionov, just like my husband, were terribly pleased with your greetings which I conveyed, and send you their deepest gratitude for your remembering them and the attention you showed them. We are all moving to apartments here today, we found a suitable one for ourselves and move in tomorrow. Our new address: Catherine 85 sq. 4.

Every morning I take a sea bath at the Romanovsky Institute (medical). The last few days, I examined the city a bit and now I would go to see the surroundings. Yesterday we went to the theatre. They played pretty well. Sometimes we visit the seaside boulevard in the evening, where music plays.

The other day I met my husband's uncle, Admiral Petrov-Chernyshin, who is the chief of staff of the port here. He seems very sweet, but since he now has a lot of work, I have not seen him much yet.

Sorry, my dear Tatiana Nikolaevna, for such a boring letter, but at this time we have nothing new.

I warmly embrace you, my dear. I ask you to convey my heartfelt greetings to the Grand Duchesses. Loving you with all my heart

Olga Voronova

Sevastopol

July 25th, 1915

## Fund 651, inventory 1, file 48

Tsarskoe Selo. 8 August, 1915.

My dear Olga.

Thank you very much for your lovely long letter. I terribly envy Nikolai Pavlovich that he saw you all. He told us a lot of interesting things and was terribly pleased to see everyone! How did you get a new apartment? Yesterday we saw our poor wounded with Papa. The poor ones are brought from captivity. A mass of them without both legs or without arms, but for the most part without legs. They said that the Germans simply threw them into the dugouts (those who had typhoid fever) and they lay there without any dressings and in the end, they all froze and their legs fell off, and then of course they had to do amputations. It was terribly sad to see them. Another party is being brought in today. It will now be several times a week. We have a rather severely wounded one in the infirmary, shot in the lung, he had surgery and they took out part of a rib, now it's a little better, but the dressings are very painful. We are now arranging a hospital for 1000 lower ranks at the Winter Palace. And it will be ready in a month. It will be in some of the halls.

Well, goodbye my dear Olga. I firmly and gently kiss you as I love you. Say hello to your husband.

With all my heart. Tatiana

## Fund 651, inventory 1, file 103

My dear Tatiana Nikolaevna

I sincerely thank you for your letter, as well as for the congratulations for my name day, which was finally sent to me.

I feel so sorry for our poor invalids, about whom you write, how awful! The poor things!

My husband was sick for a week. He developed inflammation of the periosteum on his leg, and so he had to stay in bed. Yesterday he was able to go out for the first time and we went to

Balaclava. You must have been there. It's really beautiful, isn't it? We came back home in the moonlight. How dreadfully good it was!

Today, Kazhevnikov, Rodionov and Khvoshchinsky will come visit us in the evening.

Some days ago, Khvoshchinsky left on one of the destroyers for several days at sea and, on his return, told us many interesting things. They sank 60 Turkish boats. They went to Batum. They say it's remarkably beautiful there.

Goodbye, my dear Tatiana Nikolaevna. I tightly and firmly kiss you and ask you to convey my heartfelt greetings to the Grand Duchesses. My husband asks you to give a deep bow from him. Loving you with all my heart,

Your

Olga Voronova

Catherine 85. Apt. 4

Sevastopol

August 12th, 1915

**Fund 651, inventory 1, file 48**

Tsarskoe Selo, 24 August 1915

My dear, darling Olga,

Thank you very much for your letter, I can't remember if I thanked you for it, but I think that I didn't. The weather today is disgusting – raining since morning. So dreary. Papa departed from us on the evening of the third. Have you been to Yalta yet or not? It must be so nice there. Groten is recuperating at Mama's Red Cross infirmary there. You probably knew him when he was a Life-Hussar. He was wounded in the leg but without damage to the bone. And how is your brother, and where is he? With the regiment at the war or here? And where is Tata? I often think about you and your husband. We haven't seen each other for so long, it's awfully sad. But I am so awfully happy for you that you are able to spend this whole time with him. How have you arranged your new dacha? At the moment, we have two officers from my regiment in the infirmary. I'm terribly happy to have them here. We saw Rita Khitrovo yesterday at A.A.'s. Do you remember her from Crimea? She is going to start working at an infirmary somewhere here now. How is your health and how is your husband's leg? Tell him how sorry I was to hear of his leg's illness.

Well, goodbye, darling Olga.

I firmly, firmly kiss you and bow to Pavel Alekseevich.

Your

Tatiana

## Fund 651, inventory 1, file 103

Sevastopol

Ekaterinsky 84

2nd September 1915

My dear Tatiana Nikolaevna,

I thank you from my heart for your sweet letter. I was so happy to receive it. My husband thanks you from his heart for your attention and asks me to convey to you his deepest bow. His leg does not hurt at all anymore. I don't feel so good myself, I frequently get very tired and have severe headaches.

My brother went back to his regiment a few days ago. He is completely better, just some deafness remaining. They say that will need treating now, or his hearing might not return. Tata is in Petrograd and is very busy in the community.

Yesterday we saw sharpshooter Atyatin here. He told me he'd been hospitalized at Tsarskoe, just where Groten had also been at Her Majesty's infirmary.

How are you doing, my dear Tatiana Nikolaevna? Do you have a lot of work?

If you do me the honour, I very firmly embrace you and ask you to pass on my heartfelt greetings to the Grand Duchesses.

My husband asks you to receive his deep bow

Sincerely and warmly loving you

Olga Voronova

## Fund 651, inventory 1, file 48

Tsarskoe Selo. Sep 7, 1915.

My dear Olga,

Thank you very, very much for both of your letters. I did not immediately answer the first one, because I thought that our letters would cross. I saw Apukhtin twice at the Red Cross community here in Tsarskoe. Now they have brought in Putyatin, wounded. A lot of the *Preobrazhentsy* [Regiment] were wounded, but it seems they were taken to Petrograd. We either leave or the wounded arrive. Several of them went to

Yalta for treatment. Including Bar[on] Taube L[ife] Gu[ards], 1 sharpshooter from Papa's regiment. He was in our infirmary himself the first time, and now, he is wounded for a second time and his right leg is again injured above the knee. What is your weather like in Sevastopol? It is awful here. Today, only 5 degrees and a strong wind. On September 1 we began lessons on the winter schedule. Pretty boring! Rita Khitrovo works in our infirmary and is very good. She helps with dressings, removes dressings, etc. And what are you doing all day?

Well, goodbye my darling Olga dear. The sisters thank everyone for the bow and kiss. I bow very much to your husband and our people. I hug you tightly and kiss you as much as I love you.

Your Tatiana

**Fund 651, inventory 1, file 103**

September 17th, 1915

Sevastopol

Ekaterinskaya 84

My dear Tatiana Nikolaevna,

I thank you very much for your sweet letter and ask you to forgive me for being so slow in responding. We went for 2 days to Evpatoria, because we had heard a lot of good things about this place. Have you been there?

Both of us really enjoyed it. The coast is wonderful, sandy and in summer, they say, perfect swimming. At the moment, there are very few people and it was mainly only the wounded who were there, of whom there are quite a few.

We drove from Simferopol to Evpatoria by car (65 versts), but, they say, the railway will be ready soon.

After some very cold days, summer weather came again. It was so good!

You ask, dear Tatiana Nikolaevna, what I do every day. Alone at home, the wife of flügel adjutant Pogulyaev, whom I met here, asked me to help her sew warm clothes for sending to the army. I'm terribly glad that I found at least a little thing to do here. The other day, this lady arranged a charity lottery and asked me to take part in that as well. Tata entered the $2^{nd}$ year of her courses and wants to become a real Sister of Mercy indeed. In spring, she will have exams. I really envy her and am so sorry that I cannot do this too.

Goodbye, my dear Tatiana Nikolaevna. I kiss you very firmly. My husband asks to give you a deep bow.

Lovingly yours, with all my heart, Olga Voronova

**Fund 651, inventory 1, file 48**

Tsarskoe Selo. October 10th, 1915.

Dear Olga,

Thank you very, very much for your letter and please forgive me for not having thanked you earlier, after I heard about the death of your *beau-frère*, I thought that you would probably come here and I did not want to bother you with my letters. How is your poor sister now? Tata told me that she was in an awfully bad way. I am so sorry for her. I am writing to you here again as I don't know where you are. If you are here, how much longer will you be here? In a couple of days, we are going with Mama to Stavka to get Alexei. I expect that he probably doesn't want to come back home, because he is terribly happy being there with Papa. He wrote to Mama that he hoped to stay there for a long time. And here we are still working every day in the infirmary. There's a lot of wounded. Well, goodbye Olga darling. I kiss you very firmly my sweet and bow to your husband.

Your Tatiana.

I bow to all of ours in Sevastopol.

**Fund 651, inventory 1, file 103**

Hotel Kista Sevastopol

October 14th, 1915

My dear Tatiana Nikolaevna,

Thank you very, very much for your sweet letter. Yesterday I arrived in Sevastopol with Tata, who is not feeling well and very tired.

My husband and I went to Petrograd for several days and convinced Tata to return with us to rest up for a bit. Unfortunately, my husband had to leave us on the way, to join ours, who had left from here. You probably already know that. We'll stay here for a few more days, and then think about returning to Petrograd if my husband doesn't write to me. I know that one of ours wanted to leave his wife.

Of course, I am terribly sad that we had to leave, but we have been together for so long that I am ashamed to complain. Ella returned from Diveyevo. She is in a terrible state and looks like a shadow. Mama and my older sister, Clara, are with her now, and yesterday her daughter was brought to her from the countryside. We all hope terribly that the presence of the little one will help her to endure the most difficult time.

Tata bows very much to you, and, if you will allow it, I kiss you firmly, my dear Tatiana Nikolaevna, and a warm thank you again from all of us for your deep sympathy. We both ask you to convey our heartfelt greetings to Their Highnesses.

With all my heart, loving you, yours

Olga Voronova

**Fund 651, inventory 1, file 48**

Tsarskoe Selo. October 19, 1915.

My dear darling Olga,

Thank you very much, my dear, for your letter that I received here when I got back from Stavka, where we were for 4 days. It was very good. Before we went there, we were with Mama in Tver, Ryazan, Velikie Luki and Orsha. Then to Papa. It was very good in Mogilev, Alexei is so happy being there and told us a lot of interesting things, all his impressions. Papa gave him the St. George medal of the 4$^{th}$ degree at the request of Gen. Ivanov and his western army, who they had visited. They were 5 versts from the trenches and heard artillery fire and saw the troops. Papa and Alexei are terribly happy and said that it was wonderful. The troops were convened for a parade and after that, they went back to the trenches. They cheered so loudly that the soldiers in the trenches said that the enemy must have heard everything. It was that close. Write to me, Olga darling, if you move from Sevastopol. I'll wait for you to write so that letters won't cross paths. My sisters kiss you and Tata and thank you for the greetings. I hope Tata has a good rest. How fortuitous it turned out that she is now with you, otherwise you would have been very sad and bored being alone without your husband. Well, goodbye my dear. God bless you. Kisses for Tata. I kiss you firmly as I love you.

Your Tatiana.

**Fund 651, inventory 1, file 103**

Fontanka 54, Apartment 207

Petrograd

October 29, 1915

My dear Tatiana Nikolaevna,

I sincerely thank you for your sweet letter that was sent to me today from Sevastopol.

We stayed there for only three days, because they told us that there would no longer be a direct train and we took the last one. The other day, my husband arrived here. So good! He was sent to train new recruits, as such, he will stay here for more than a month.

We have Tata here for now, and Mama has my elder sister, Clara, because Mama moved to Petrograd and she will live on the French Embankment. The apartment is not yet ready and we are all taking part in putting it together. I really love it.

Ella is still here, but will probably leave for the south with her little one in November. She looks very poorly.

I think that Grand Duke Alexei Nikolaevich must be very pleased with his medal, right? Well it must be sweet to see it on such a wee one.

Will you go to Stavka again soon?

Do you still work at the infirmary?

Goodbye, my dear, sweet Tatiana Nikolaevna. I tightly, tightly hug you and ask you to convey heartfelt greetings from Tata and me to Their Highnesses.

Tata and my husband ask Everyone to accept their bow.

My *belle-soeur* Nina Voronova said that she saw you at the Winter Palace. My husband and I are deeply grateful and endlessly moved by Her Majesty's and Your Highnesses gracious attention to us.

Once again, if I may, my dear Tatiana Nikolaevna, I kiss you tightly. God bless you!

Loving you with all my heart

Your Olga Voronova

**Fund 651, inventory 1, file 48**

Tsarskoe Selo

3 November 1915

Darling Olga,

Thank you for your letter. I was very happy for you when I heard that your husband has been appointed here. How good it is that you are together so much. Alexei writes that he is terribly happy to be with Papa again, and that he is awfully pleased and proud with the medal. We are so happy for Papa too that he received the cross. These days I work alone in the infirmary. Mama was tired again and her heart hurts, but Olga seems to be simply burnt out and was put to bed for several days. But it's nothing, however she's tired from standing and has been put to bed so that she will recover quicker. But now, we do not have much work at the infirmary, just a few officers and not all need dressings. Well, after dressings, if there is time, I play some games with them, for about an hour. We have a living room attached. Previously, everyone had to sit in the corridor and it wasn't so comfortable and everyone has lunch there as well.

This house was built for infectious patients and it was ready just in time for the war and because it was new and clean, Mama chose it for the wounded. What are you doing? How many are with Ella and how is she, the poor thing? Are your brother and *beau-frere* in good health? I guess you will be very happy to get back to your old apartment? It is so sad here without Papa and Alexei. But I'm glad that they are together, at least it is not so tedious for Papa. They live together in the same room, shared bedroom and study. Papa has a large desk, and Alexei has a small one, at which he is engaged with his French tutor, Mr Gilliard. I think you may have seen him in Livadia? Alexei loves him very much. In the afternoon, Alexei goes with Papa and the rest for a walk out of town or by the Dnieper. They go for walks and make bonfires. He has breakfast there independently with the mass of people and foreigners. He does not embarrass them at all and speaks French with them. He doesn't use English much, but it's nothing. Well, goodbye Olga darling. Warm greetings to your husband. I kiss you firmly as I love you.

Your Tatiana.

**Fund 651, inventory 1, file 103**

Fontanka 54 Apartment 207

Petrograd

November 13th, 1915

My dear Tatiana Nikolaevna,

I am terribly ashamed that I have not answered your sweet letter for so long. I hope you will forgive me. Thank you very much for your lovely, interesting letter. I was so pleased to get it.

How is Olga Nikolaevna's health now? I sincerely hope that the overwork has passed and that Olga Nikolaevna is now feeling quite well.

Please convey to all three Grand Duchesses my most cordial greetings.

These days we have spent a particularly long amount of time with Ella since she is leaving tomorrow with her girl for the Caucasus. She will probably be there for a long time.

Now I'm off to see her again and taking a small toy.

My brother is currently in the fields with sick horses.[18] My husband's brother will probably be on holiday soon if the regiment is taking a break. For the whole time of the war he has come but once for 6 days. Mama and Tata have already moved to the French Embankment, although not all the rooms are ready there still.

Goodbye, my dear, sweet Tatiana Nikolaevna. I kiss you very, very firmly.

My husband asks to pass on to you and Their Highnesses his deep bow.

Loving you with all my heart

Your

Olga Voronova

**Fund 651, inventory 1, file 103**

November 1915

Petrograd

My dear Tatiana Nikolaevna,

I am sending you my contribution of things for the poor. Yesterday and today I have been sitting at home because I have a terrible runny nose.

Ella left on the 14th to Gagra, where she will stay, most likely, until spring.

We got news from her from the road.

How is Olga Nikolaevna's health now?

I kiss you very, very firmly my dear Tatiana Nikolaevna and ask you to convey my sincere greetings to Their Highnesses.

Loving you with all my heart

Your

Olga Voronova

---

[18] Dima served in His Majesty's Life Guards Hussars Regiment. The "fields with the sick horses" is a literal translation most likely meaning he was transferred to the Regiment's Luga garrison where injured horses were looked after.

**Fund 651, inventory 1, file 48**

Tsarskoe Selo. November 24$^{th}$, 1915.

Olga darling,

Thank you very much for your letter, money and things. And also for the letter which I have not yet answered. I am so sorry. I hope that Ella will be well in Gagra. Will your husband stay here a while or is he leaving soon? Can you let me know a few days before his departure? Anya V. wanted to write letters to the equipage. Olga feels better, she comes to the infirmary, but not for long, and she still does not work, but rather sits with them. There is not much work now because there are few wounded. I make arsenic shots for some, then I sit with them in the parlour, knit stockings so as not to waste time. Olga and my sisters kiss you and bow to your husband. Well, goodbye Olga my darling. Kissing you very firmly. Say hello to your husband.

Your Tatiana.


**Fund 651, inventory 1, file 103**

Petrograd, Dec 8, 1915

Dear Tatiana Nikolaevna,

My husband was told today that in a few days he would need to return to his battalion. Probably it will be in 3–4 days, at the most 6–7 days. Please tell this to Anna Alexandrovna.

When my husband leaves, I am thinking of moving to Mama and Tata's, because it will be very sad to be on my own.

I was very glad to see you at Sonia Orbeliani's funeral. Both of us were there, and we also went to one of the evening requiem services.

Ella writes that Gagra is warm, but it is raining. The little one is recovering and gets rosier every day.

She doesn't write much about herself.

Well, goodbye, my dear Tatiana Nikolaevna. I kiss you very, very firmly. My husband sends you a deep bow, and we both ask you to convey our sincere greetings to the Grand Duchesses.

Loving you with all my heart,

Your Olga Voronova

**Fund 651, inventory 1, file 48**

Tsarskoe Selo. December 16$^{th}$, 1915.

My dear Olga,

I was terribly glad to see you both, it had been such an awfully long time since we saw each other. Thank you for the letter for which I have not yet thanked you. I'll be thinking about you tomorrow, Olga darling. Please convey our heartfelt greetings and best wishes to your husband. And ask him to greet all of our people. Well, all the best. God bless you.

I kiss you very firmly as I love you.

Your Tatiana.

**Fund 651, inventory 1, file 103**

Petrograd

Dec 17, 1915

My dear Tatiana Nikolaevna,

I sincerely thank you for your sweet letter. We were both very touched by it. My husband says to warmly thank you for your attention and greetings.

He will pass on your regards to everyone. My husband left this morning and I am so awfully sad about it! I have already written to him, so he will no doubt receive my letter, soon after he arrives.

My dear Tatiana Nikolaevna, thank you once again from the bottom of my heart for your kind words. I hug you very, very tightly.

I'm afraid that the news will not be good, they say it has been difficult lately to maintain orderly messages. If you learn anything about ours, will you write to me? Yes? I will be infinitely grateful.

My husband asked me to convey, and I join him, heartfelt greetings to Their Highnesses.

Once again, my dear, I kiss you firmly.

With all my heart

Your

Olga Voronova

**Fund 651, inventory 1, file 103**

My dear Tatiana Nikolaevna,

Please accept my warmest congratulations and I wish you all the very best.

My husband writes and asks to congratulate you very much. Thank you very much for your sweet congratulations. I am thinking of moving to Mama's on the French Embankment, 18, on either the 28th or 29th.

I hug you very, very tightly

Loving you, with all my heart

Your

Olga Voronova

Dec 23, 1915


**Fund 651, inventory 1, file 48**

Tsarskoe Selo. December 30, 1915

Darling Olga, my dear,

I am sending you my warmest wishes for all that is bright and joyful in the New Year. God grant that this one will bring you a lot of happiness and an end to this terrible war. Thank you for your letter and congratulations. I wanted to write and congratulate you yesterday, but I didn't get time. It is very sad that Papa left today. But it was so good that he was here for the Christmas party. Does your husband often write to you? We have Midshipman Sekerin – I don't know how to spell it – in the infirmary. He has a dislocation of his right shoulder, but glory to God is already better. The bandage has already been removed and massage has started, so he will probably leave soon. I had never seen him before. There are now many new ones who we did not know before. We go to Christmas parties in different infirmaries during the day.

Well, goodbye Olga darling. When you write to your husband, please greet him from me. I kiss you very firmly.

Your Tatiana.

## Fund 651, inventory 1, file 104 (all of the 1916 letters to Tatiana Nikolaevna)

Petrograd

2 January 1916

Dear Tatiana Nikolaevna,

I thank you wholeheartedly for your lovely letter and your warm wishes for the New Year. I'm also sending you once again my warmest wishes of happiness and joy. I'm so touched that you remembered about the birthday of my husband. Yesterday I received two long letters from him that he had sent with one of the personnel accompanying the new conscripts. On the 27th he just arrived in Volochysk and was about to start off to join the battalion that was stationed more than 50 miles away from there. Fortunately, it was not cold there but it was terribly muddy.

From the time of my husband's departure, I have received about 20 letters from him, but now he will be writing once a week, when the opportunity comes to pass a letter, because the post service is problematic there. He writes that the wounded whom he had met on the way were reporting very good news from the battlefront.

I'm thinking of moving to the waterfront around the 5th. These days Clara, Tata and I are visiting our aunties with the New Year greetings. Yesterday my brother came from Luga for one day, and all of us visited the New Year party of my older sister's children. They are so funny. The youngest girl is 3 years old. She knows by memory some long verses and yesterday was reciting them to us. We could not stop laughing because it was impossible to understand anything because she can't pronounce some letters properly yet.

So long for now, my dear Tatiana Nikolaevna. I kiss you very warmly, please pass my best regards to Their Highnesses.

Loving you with all my soul and faithfully yours,

Your Olga Voronov

11 January 1916

Dear Tatiana Nikolaevna,

I'm congratulating you wholeheartedly with your Angel's Day and sending you my warmest wishes for all the best. My husband was very touched by your kind attention and asked me to pass to you his congratulations and best wishes.

The other day I moved to the waterfront. My room is very nice and has a wonderful view to Neva.

I hug you very tightly, if I may, my dear Tatiana Nikolaevna.
Loving you very much and faithfully yours,
Olga Voronov
18, French Waterfront.
Petrograd


7 February 1916
My dear Tatiana Nikolaevna,
First of all, I wanted to thank you from the bottom of my heart for your forever kind attention, which touches me deeply. I hug you very warmly. It is truly precious to me that you are thinking about me on such a day. I was incredibly happy to receive your lovely letter. I'm sorry that I have not written for so long to you. I had an influenza and then I was in bed again for several days because of a severe nerves-related headache.

I'm feeling very sad without my husband, especially today. In a couple of days it will be already 2 months since he has left.

My sister Ella has gone to the Seraphimo-Diveyevsky convent, where her husband is buried. Her little daughter is here, and Tata was asked to look after her, so Tata can't resume her studies in the commune now. Besides, she has not yet completely recovered and regained strength.

How is the health of the Grand Duchess Olga Nikolaevna?

My *belle-soeur* Nina Voronov told me that she had seen His Majesty and all of you in the Winter Palace hospital.

I kiss you very warmly, my dearest Tatiana Nikolaevna, and once again thank you wholeheartedly for your attention that is very dear to me. Please pass my heart-felt regards to Their Highnesses.

Loving you with all my heart and truly yours,
Olga Voronov


3 March 1916
Petrograd
My dear Tatiana Nikolaevna,
Thank you very much for your lovely, warm letter. Please forgive me that I'm replying only now. I'm very touched that you are asking about my health. My headaches are now gone, hopefully for a long time. On the 25th my husband came here and on Monday went back. He was allowed to have 3 days leave

to visit a doctor. He had a severe throat inflammation and apparently, they will have to cut out or scrape something out of his throat. So terribly unpleasant!

On the 22nd, Tata went to Diveyevo to stay with Ella for a while. She will probably come back next week. Ella's little girl is not living with us, she has stayed in Ella's house with two nannies and Tata was there every day from the morning. Now I'm going there every day. Little Elena is 2.5 years, she is so sweet and lovely! Sometimes she is brought to us, and she likes this very much.

All this time I have been busy with taking apart our previous flat. All furniture has been taken to the warehouse. In this flat not everything has been arranged yet either.

I congratulate you, and I'm sorry that belatedly, with the Holy Communion. I will probably be fasting and preparing for the Holy Communion on the 4th week. My husband was asking to pass his heartfelt thank-you to you for your attention and his most respectful regards to you and Their Highnesses. He was terribly touched that you remembered about us on the 7th of February.

You probably already know that our forces are now close to Dvinsk and apparently have accommodated quite well in some estate.

Goodbye for now, my dear Tatiana Nikolaevna. I kiss you tightly and tenderly, please pass my warmest regards to Their Highnesses.

Loving you with all my heart and truly yours,

Olga Voronov

Petrograd 16 March 1916

Dear Tatiana Nikolaevna,

The other day my husband arrived. He has been assigned to a combined regiment. This was very unexpected for both of us. I'm very happy that he is here, especially because many practical matters have accumulated for us lately, and it's very hard to deal with them by myself.

Tata is coming back from Diveyevo tomorrow. Ella feels a little better but is not planning to return from there any time soon.

How are you doing, dear Tatiana Nikolaevna?

I kiss you warmly. My husband is asking to pass his most respectful regards to you. Please pass our regards to Their Highnesses.

With all my heart loving you, Your Olga Voronov.

21 April 1916

Petrograd

My dear Tatiana Nikolaevna,

I thank you from the bottom of my heart for your congratulation. I'm so touched that you have not forgotten. My husband and I are asking you, dearest Tatiana Nikolaevna, if possible, to bring to the feet of Her Majesty our allegiant congratulations with Her Imperial Majesty's Name-Day.

Recently I have been to Tsarskoye Selo and paid visits to the regiment's ladies. I only found one of them at home – Sapozhnikova, the fat one, you know? I also saw Korobchook (!) at her place.

I will probably remain in Petrograd because in summer Pavlik will go the headquarters and I will go to Clara, to the country estate near Moscow. Ella is still in Diveyevo and is thinking to stay there for the whole summer. The little girl is here. She has had a very mild case of canker rash, now she doesn't have to be in bed anymore, but we have not seen her yet because the quarantine has not yet finished.[19] She lives in Ella's flat. Tata wanted to move in there to look after the little one, but the doctor banned her because the little girl had a very mild case of the disease and excellent care, while for adults the disease is dangerous.

Clara is taking her children to the country estate tomorrow and Tata will probably join them there in the end of May.

Goodbye for now, my dear Tatiana Nikolaevna. I kiss you very warmly. Please pass my most heartfelt regards to Their Highnesses.

My husband is thanking you very much for remembering and asks you to accept, and pass to Their Highnesses, his most respectful regards.

Loving you with all my soul and truly yours,

Olga Voronov.

---

[19] Canker rash – a form of scarlet fever.

22 May 1916

Imatra[20]

My dear Tatiana Nikolaevna,

Please bring to the feet of Her Imperial Majesty, if you find it appropriate, my and my husband's allegiant congratulations with Her Majesty's birthday.

I thank you from the bottom of my heart, my dear Tatiana Nikolaevna, for your lovely, interesting letter. I'm writing to you from Imatra where my husband and I arrived today. We too have been travelling all this time. We spent a week in Chernigovskaya gubernia[21] and from there went to Kurskaya gubernia.[22] We were there when you were passing on your way back from Crimea. This was *Rzhava* station (formerly 'Kleinmichel's').[23] You probably have not noticed it because you didn't stop there. We were there only for two days. We had a wonderful time in Chernigovskaya gubernia. I was collecting masses of lilies of the valley and violets in the forest and bringing them home. Apple trees and lilacs were in bloom. It was so lovely that we didn't want to leave. Here at Imarta we didn't like it that much at first. We expected it to be much more beautiful but now we have gone to the second waterfall and it was stunningly beautiful! We are thinking of staying here for a day or two longer and to return to Petrograd on the 25th, where we will probably stay until the beginning of June. My husband will go to headquarters, and I will join my older sister at her country estate near Moscow. The address there is station *Skhodnya* on *Nikolayevskaya* railway, Estate *Znamenskoye* of Martynovs family. I thank you very much for your kind wish to write to me there. I'm always so happy to receive your letters!

Recently little Elena Puschina had an operation – they removed her tonsils and adenoids. She was so good, extremely patient and after the operation thanked the doctor. He was totally charmed by her. Now she has completely recovered and in the next few days will be going to the country estate.

Bye for now, dear Tatiana Nikolaevna. I'm kissing you very warmly. My husband is thanking you wholeheartedly for your attention and is asking you to accept and pass to the Grand Duchesses his most respectful regards, and I do too.

Yours, loving you with all my heart,

Olga Voronov.

---

[20] A town in Finland.

[21] An area around Kyiv, now in Ukraine.

[22] An area around Kursk, near the border with Ukraine.

[23] A train station in Kursk, probably close to Ivnya.

27 May 1916

Petrograd

Dear Tatiana Nikolaevna,

My husband and I are warmly congratulating you with your Birthday and asking to accept our most heartfelt wishes of happiness and all the very best and joyous.

Thank you very much for your lovely letter which made me so happy.

I spent the whole day today with the little Elena. She is so funny, it's impossible to feel bored being with her. Tata is still here with us but around the 3rd she is going to go to Clara at the country estate. The three of us will be together in summer while Ella wants to stay in Diveyevo (Clara is with her now). In July the little one will go there to join her.

So long for now, my dear Tatiana Nikolaevna. I kiss you very warmly.

With all my soul faithfully yours,

Olga Voronov.


Estate "Znamenskoye" of Martynovs family
13 July 1916

Station Skhodnya of Nikolayevskaya railway

My dear Tatiana Nikolaevna,

Thank you from the bottom of my heart for your sweet letter and congratulations. I was so happy to receive your letter, even more so after not having heard from you for a very long time.

I came here on the 9th. I was so glad that my husband could spend the 11th with me. It's just a shame that it rains here all the time, for the last 4 days already so there is almost no chance to go out. My headaches are not so frequent now, I will try to get better here and relax, so that they don't come back. I thank you very much for your attention to me.

Has Alexey Nikolayevich come back with you? What have you been doing? I so much would love to see you.

I brought many books with myself, some work and also want to do some drawing. I like drawing very much, but I'm terribly lazy and because of this have not really learned much of it.

How is your singing?

So long for now, my sweet and dear Tatiana Nikolaevna.

I kiss you very warmly.

Truly yours and loving you very much,

Your Olga Voronov.

Znamenskoye

22 July 1916

My dear Tatiana Nikolaevna,

I was delighted to receive your lovely letter for which I thank you very much.

What a great man Khvoschinsky is! I'm so happy that our forces have done so well and proved themselves so brilliantly! Isn't it pleasant? Though I always knew that they were great.

Recently my husband's relative was killed, the Imperial Rifleman Voronov. I feel incredibly sorry for his parents. He was their only son and such a young boy.

I don't know Girse but I've heard about this misfortune. It is so good that he is getting better now. I've heard that the poor man has been suffering terribly.

I have to finish this letter now because letters need to be delivered to the train. I will write more to you in the next few days, if I may, my dear Tatiana Nikolaevna.

I'm kissing you very warmly and sending my regards to the Grand Duchesses.

Yours with all my heart,

Olga Voronov.

My sisters are thanking you very much for your attention.

27 July 1916

Znamenskoye

My dear Tatiana Nikolaevna,

Thank you very much for your lovely letter which I have just received. I congratulate you with the birthday of Nikolay Alexeyevich and ask you to pass my congratulations and best wishes to His Highness.

The weather has improved a little and now we go to search for mushrooms in the forest every day. This is a great fun, each of us is trying to collect more than others, we are all in a mad hurry, this is so funny. There has been no opportunity to play tennis because the grounds cannot dry up. My husband is going to come on the 29th, not sure for how long, but probably for 2–3 days.

Have your heard that poor Apoukhtin (Nikolay) is seriously wounded, apparently he had his arm amputated up to the shoulder. This is so awful, poor guy!

It is very nice here. Wonderful garden with masses and masses of flowers. There is a river – *Klyazma*. Near the estate there is Klushino village, where the armed forces of General Zholkevsky were stationed, when he was advancing to Moscow.[24] There is a very big mount there, and in winter it is a great fun to slide from it on a sledge or skis.

I kiss you warmly, my dear Tatiana Nikolaevna. I'm also sending my warmest regards to the Grand Duchesses. My sisters are thanking you wholeheartedly for your attention and are sending their most respectful regards.

Loving you with all my heart,

Your Olga


6 August 1916

Petrograd

Dear Tatiana Nikolaevna,

Today my husband passed to me your letter for which I thank you very much. I'm thinking of going to *Znamenskoye* on Tuesday.

Yesterday I was in Tsarskoye Selo, I was visiting the mother of the killed Imperial Rifleman Voronov. I feel so awfully sorry for her. She has changed so much and is completely unable to cry – this is the worst.

How are you doing, my dear Tatiana Nikolaevna?

My husband is asking to pass his most respectful regards to you, and I'm hugging you tightly, if I may.

Our warmest regards to the Grand Duchesses.

Very much loving you,

Your Olga Voronov

---

[24] Most likely refers to the events of 1610.

10 August 1916

Petrograd

My dear Tatiana Nikolaevna,

I have just received your letter that was forwarded to me from *Znamenskoye*. Thank you very much for it. I have decided to stay here, probably until the end of August and after that I don't know yet what I will be doing. Tata has gone to Chernigovskaya gubernia to visit Sonya Dunin-Borkovsky. I think I probably have written to you that this is a big friend of ours who lived with us this winter.

Ella is still in Diveyevo. Now her little girl is there with her too.

I have not seen my brother for a very long time. He is in Luga.

I'm very happy for you that you enjoyed yourself and had a good time at headquarters. Will you go again? How is the health of Anna Alexandrovna now? Is she walking better now?

I kiss you very warmly, my dear Tatiana Nikolaevna. Please pass my warmest regards to the Grand Duchesses.

Loving you with all my heart,

Your Olga Voronov

My husband is asking to pass his most respectful regards to you.

23 August 1916

Petrograd

My dear Tatiana Nikolaevna,

Thank you very much for your letter. In three days, I'm going to *Znamenskoye* for several days and will be back on the 1st or 2nd of September. My husband is leaving today to go to Chernigovskaya gubernia for the same period, to attend to some business.

Is it nice now at the headquarters? Here it's so terribly cold!

On 6 September Clara with her children and Tata are going to Crimea. My husband very much wants me to enjoy some sun too and is sending me there together with them. If I go, I will live in Simeiz. It must be very nice there now, but it's sad to part with Pavlik.

I kiss you very warmly, my dear Tatiana Nikolaevna. My husband is thanking you very much for your attention and is sending his warm regards to you. Our heartfelt regards to Their Highnesses.

Very much loving you and truly yours, Olga Voronov.

7 September 1916

Petrograd

My dear Tatiana Nikolaevna,

Thank you so much for your lovely letter.

Tata and Clara left for Crimea yesterday and I have decided to stay. The reason is that communications with Simeiz, and with the southern coast in general, is very problematic, and I don't like going so far away without having an option to come back at any time.

I thank you very much, my dear Tatiana Nikolaevna, for your attention and your concern about my health. I'm feeling not very well. The headaches are much less frequent, but I feel weak and become tired quickly after any effort. I might go somewhere not far away for some treatment. In general, I don't have anything specific, apart from the usual anaemia.

How are you doing, dear Tatiana Nikolaevna and the Grand Duchesses? Please pass my heartfelt regards to them.

I have read a lot this summer and also have been doing embroidery. In the next few of days, I will finish the pillow that I'm embroidering for Mama.

How is your singing?

So long for now, sweet and dear Tatiana Nikolaevna. I'm kissing you very warmly.

My husband is asking you to accept and also pass to the Grand Duchesses his most respectful regards.

Very much loving you,

Your Olga Voronov.


13 September 1916

Petrograd

My dear Tatiana Nikolaevna,

Thank you so very much for your letter. My husband is on duty today and has just told me over the phone that he must go to the headquarters on Saturday. I decided that while he is away, I will go to Finland to Rauch's medical resort. We have been there for 2 days in spring. It is very nice! If there is an opportunity, I will go to headquarters for several days.

Ella is still in Diveyevo and is not going to move out of there yet. My brother is in Luga. I have seen Sofka Ivanenko in summer. I think she has matured very much and became somewhat serious. For the whole winter she was working in Oppel's clinic as the operation theatre nurse. Isn't she amazing?

I have been incredibly surprised by the wedding of Kitty Golitsyn. It was rather unexpected, wasn't it?

I will write to you from the Rauch's resort, if I may, my sweet Tatiana Nikolaevna. For now, I kiss you very warmly, please pass my sincere regards to the Grand Duchesses.

Very much loving you and truly yours,

Olga Voronov.


28 September 1916

Petrograd

Dear Tatiana Nikolaevna,

Thank you very much for your lovely letter. I received it upon my return from the Rauch's medical resort in Finland where I went to have some rest and ended up spending only three days. My husband was meant to leave on Saturday to go to headquarters. Two days before that he took me to Rauch's and upon coming back found that he was going to leave the regiment and was being assigned to the battalion. In view of this I immediately came back, to be with my husband until his departure. So now I will just stay here. After all, the correspondence is delivered to Petrograd in the quickest and best way, while in Finland the post service is sloppy and I would have been only worrying more, receiving the news belatedly.

It was very nice in Finland, the weather was wonderful. The sun was so warm that despite the cold, the windows in my room were open for the whole day.

Poor Verkhovsky is apparently better now, isn't he? He is not a relative to my husband but a regiment mate and a good friend of my *beau-frère*.

It just so happens that my *beau-frère*, the brother of my husband, has arrived for leave today. I have not seen him yet, he is coming to visit us soon.

Tata is writing that it's very hot in Crimea. They are baking in the sun and have become very tanned. The children have turned into real little Arabs. Tata met *hussar* Maltsev there, you might remember him from Crimea, and his sister whom we have known for a long time. She is being treated there for exhaustion and overstrain, because during the war she worked as a nurse for the whole time, and lately was working in Persia where conditions were so harsh that she even became sick with scurvy. Horrible!

You know, the other day Pavlik met Kitty Golitsyn–Foster with her husband, both looked very cheerful and happy.

So long for now, my dear Tatiana Nikolaevna, I kiss you warmly. My husband is asking to pass his most respectful regards to you. We both are sending our best regards to Their Highnesses.

Loving you very much and truly yours,

Olga Voronov

29 September 1916

Petrograd

My dear Tatiana Nikolaevna,

Thank you very much for your letter that I have just received. The other day we received a letter from Ella where she told us she had taken the veil. It was very unexpected for us, and we are all terribly emotional, but Ella is writing that she made this decision a long time ago and had been preparing for this but was not telling anyone because she didn't want us to try to dissuade her. She says that she feels calm and happy now and believes that she would find solace there. We all are hoping with all our hearts that the God helps her on this difficult path and gives her inner peace and a consolation in her grief, and we are praying eagerly that He give her the strength and bless her for the new life.

I don't know for sure when my husband is leaving but probably on 4th or 5th, or around those dates. It seems that Klyucharev still needs to arrive to the regiment.

Sonya Dunin-Borkovskaya will move in with me, so I will not be alone.

Tata and Clara are coming back here on 27 October. They only managed to get the tickets for the 25th. Nothing was available for earlier.

My husband thanks you very much for your regards and asks to pass his most heartfelt regards to you and Their Highnesses. I will be definitely writing to you to headquarters, my dear Tatiana Nikolaevna.

I kiss you very warmly. My heartfelt regards to Their Highnesses.

Loving you with all my heart,

Your Olga Voronov

9 October 1916

Petrograd

My dear Tatiana Nikolaevna,

I thank you wholeheartedly for your letter. Ella wrote to us that she wanted little Elena to stay in Diveyevo for now, so that she could keep an eye on her upbringing. While she is little, it is probably even better that she doesn't live in the city. After all, there is good country air there.

Tata is writing that it is still nice and warm in Crimea, and they have become very tanned and gained some weight. What a difference with the weather in here! Today it's so foggy that the Petrograd side cannot be seen.[25] Terrible!

How are you doing, my dear Tatiana Nikolaevna? Is it still as nice at headquarters? Are you doing fun trips on the Dnepr River?

The other day my Aunt Volkonskaya visited us and brought along her young protégée, a girl of 15 with an amazing voice, for us to listen to. I don't remember where my Aunt found her, but she has a remarkably strong and pleasant voice. She is small, with a very childish face and a tiny plait, and it is so strange to hear this very adult voice and manner of singing.

My husband thanks you for the bottom of his heart, dear Tatiana Nikolaevna, for your kind wishes and sends his most heartfelt regards to you. We are sending our warm regards to Their Highnesses.

Loving you very much and truly yours,

Olga Voronov


20 November 1916

Petrograd

Dear Tatiana Nikolaevna,

I thank you wholeheartedly for your lovely letter that I was very happy to receive. Tata and I apologise profusely that we still have not sent you things for the poor. We were waiting for your return from headquarters to send you the package that we have already prepared. I'm very happy for my husband that he has seen you. He probably told you about Natasha's wedding and that I was her 'Step-in Mother'.[26]

---

[25] One of the districts of St Petersburg.

[26] Step-in Mother and Step-in-Father are very close relatives or friends of the bride and groom who act as their parents at a Russian wedding ceremony.

I'm hoping that I will also go to Odessa – I would really love to. Tata is thinking of going to the country estate to my older sister Clara for Christmas. For the period before Christmas, we are organising our former governess, who was with us in Crimea in 1913, to come here from Moscow, so that she could chaperone Tata while we are away. I'm also happy that my cousin Marusya Kleinmichel lives with her family in the same building, on the floor below ours, so Tata will be often with them and will not feel lonely.

My little *belle-soeur* is writing from Sochi, where they went after the wedding, that the weather is very much summer-like and they are walking just in a dress. It's almost hard to believe, isn't it? She asked me very much to thank you and Olga Nikolaevna for the congratulation, that you asked me to pass, and which touched her greatly.

So long for now, my dear and sweet Tatiana Nikolaevna. I kiss you very warmly. Please pass my heartfelt regards to the Grand Duchesses.

Very much loving you,

Your Olga Voronov.

P.S. I thank you once again for the lovely letter and your attention. I was happy to receive news about Pavlik. I'm greatly touched that you swiftly wrote to me about him.

I'm hugging you tenderly once again.

Olga.

The things and money are from both of us.

29 November 1916

Petrograd.

(*On the front of the letter, vertically:*)

Tata is asking very much to pass her regards to you, and my husband is also sending his most heartfelt regards.

Dear Tatiana Nikolaevna,

Thank you very much for your lovely letter. We are leaving on 1 December and will probably be in Odessa on the 4th. We will be staying in the London Hotel again. You know, we persuaded Tata to come for the Holidays to Odessa. It will be such fun. My little *belle-soeur* is returning from Sochi on the 1st or 2nd, I think. She was very pretty in the wedding dress. She is so funny with her joy to be a grown-up lady! In her heart she is still such a child.

Today we visited poor Vladimir Alexandrovich Komarov. He is better now but he still can't move his left leg and only a little of the hand. I feel so sorry for him!

My husband is attending the farewell breakfast today that the regiment has organised for him.

I kiss you warmly for now, my dear Tatiana Nikolaevna. Please pass our heartfelt regards to the Grand Duchesses.

Very much loving you and truly yours,

Olga Voronov.


20 December 1916

Odessa, The London Hotel

My dear Tatiana Nikolaevna,

I congratulate you warmly with the coming Holidays and wholeheartedly wish you much happiness in the New year.

I'm by myself in Odessa now. My husband was here only for 6 days. I'm receiving letters from him while he is on the road. I'm so happy that there is an opportunity to frequently send letters to him. Tomorrow I'm sending him various food supplies for the Holiday. I'm thinking of staying here for a while longer, seeing I receive letters from my husband much quicker here.

On the 24th Tata will come here to spend Holidays with me. She will stay with me in my hotel room. I have been seeing Olga Evgenyevna here. They have a very nice and cosy flat. Olga Evg. looks very content and happy, but unfortunately, she still feels unwell. I'm going to her for a tea today.

The weather is nice here. It's warm, but yesterday there was frost. I walk a lot but otherwise sit in my room and read or work.

How are you doing, dear Tatiana Nikolaevna? I would be incredibly happy if you write to me. There are very many people in Odessa. A large number of foreign officers, Romanians, Serbians and others.

I kiss you very warmly for now, my dear Tatiana Nikolaevna.

Very much loving you and truly yours,

Olga Voronov.

P.S. My husband is asking to pass to you and Grand Duchesses his greetings for the Holyday and best wishes for the New Year.

Olga.

**Fund 651, inventory 1, file 105 (all of the 1917 letters to Tatiana Nikolaevna)**

Odessa, 1 January 1917

Dear Tatiana Nikolaevna,

Thank you very much for both your lovely letters. The day after tomorrow, in the morning, my husband and I are going unexpectedly to Petrograd. My husband is feeling unwell and is being sent to see specialists. His throat illness has worsened and, separately, there is apparently something wrong with his heart. We don't know yet how long we will stay in Petrograd and when we shall go back. We both feel so sad to leave. The weather here is magnificently warm, you can walk around just in a suit. Flowers are being sold on the streets, while in Petrograd I've heard it's very cold.

Tata didn't come to Odessa because she could not buy any tickets. We have a small Christmas tree in our room which we lit up yesterday on New Year's Eve. It was very cosy.

I kiss you very warmly, dear Tatiana Nikolaevna.

Loving you,

Your Olga Voronov


Petrograd

11 January 1917

Dear Tatiana Nikolaevna,

My husband and I are asking you to accept our heartfelt congratulations and best wishes for your Angel's Day.

We arrived in Petrograd a few days ago. My husband has been visiting doctors. They told him that he needed to have an operation in the throat and are also sending him to Caucasus for treatment. Now he is waiting for a panel assessment in the navy hospital.

It feels so cold to me here after Odessa, and there is no sun at all.

Poor Tata was sitting at home for the whole time during the holidays because she had a very bad cold.

How are you doing?

I kiss you very warmly, dear Tatiana Nikolaevna.

Loving you,

Your Olga Voronov

P.S. Unfortunately, we don't have a photocard of Tata and myself together at the moment, but we are very touched that you would like to have it.

15 January 1917

Dear Tatiana Nikolaevna.

Nikolay Pavlovich Sablin has passed an invitation to us to come to the palace today. To our chagrin, we will not be able to come because on Tuesday my husband became ill with influenza. He was in bed for three days and only today started walking around in the rooms. We have just asked a doctor if my husband can go out and go to Tsarskoye. He unequivocally forbade him to go out, let alone go out of the city in an open carriage. We are so terribly upset.

We are asking you, my dear Tatiana Nikolaevna, if possible, to bring to Their Majesties our deep gratitude for their gracious attention.

I kiss you very warmly, dear Tatiana Nikolayeva and ask to pass our heartfelt regards to Their Highnesses.

Loving you and truly yours,

Olga Voronov

22 January 1917

Petrograd

My dear Tatiana Nikolaevna,

Please forgive me that I'm only now responding to your lovely letter that I received the other day. I thank you very much for it.

The medical panel that assessed my husband found that he needs treatment for at least two months and are sending him to Kislovodsk.[27] We are going to go there in the next few days. Meanwhile they are doing some cauterising in his throat and will probably operate upon his return.

When we go, our French companion lady will stay with Tata, the one who was with us before.

It is so terribly cold here!

You know, in Odessa there have been also heavy snowfalls and terrible cold.

---

[27] A famous spa resort with natural mineral springs, in southern Russia.

Tomorrow we are going to the *Mariinskii Theatre* for a charity play, the proceeds of which go towards patriotic schools. Are you going to be there?

I kiss you very warmly, dear Tatiana Nikolaevna. My husband is sending you his kind regards and we both are asking to pass our regards to the Grand Duchesses.

Loving you, Olga Voronov


11 February 1917

Kislovodsk

My dear Tatiana Nikolaevna,

I thank you very much for your lovely letter which I received before the departure from Petrograd.

We arrived several days ago and there have been no warm days yet. It has been frosty, down to minus 14, and today it's snowing so heavily, that large snow mounds have formed. Just terrible! They are saying, before our arrival there had been hot days here.

We both have already started treatment. My husband is taking *Narzan* baths and I will start too in the next few days.[28] They are forcing me to eat a lot and drink two glasses of cream a day!!! I terribly dislike all these dairy things and I really struggle to do this. On the brighter side though, I will probably gain weight.

For now, we are staying in *Villa Retvizan* but want to move to the Grand-Hotel in the next few days. It is convenient that you can take the *Narzan* baths inside the hotel.

There are quite a few familiar faces here, and every day all these people meet and spend much time together. We have been to the theatre several times in the last few days. It is organised in Kursaal and after the show everyone is having dinner at the restaurant in the same building.[29]

The shows finish at 10pm, so we can go to bed early. During the lent there will be apparently no shows at all. The troupe that has been performing here, is leaving.

I'm seeing Urusov girls here. Do you remember them from Crimea? Also, the little Krusenstern girl is here who is now married to Keller. Tomorrow we are having breakfast at their and his mother's place. Picnics are often organised here by everyone, and despite the cold weather, they go for rides quite far away, but we refrain for now, because we are still getting

---

[28] Narzan bath is a natural mineral spring that has medicinal properties.

[29] Kursaal is a public building at a spa where entertainment is provided.

tired quite quickly from everything. The whole Kislovodsk is situated on the mountains, and walking is very tiring.

The locals are saying that the warm weather is coming but we are finding it hard to believe, looking at the snow falling in thick clumps. The air is indeed wonderful here, so clean and invigorating, amazing!

When it's sunny, we are sitting in the morning in the park and enjoying the warmth. There are very many people here. All the hotels and dachas are full and it's hard to find a room. We are still waiting for a free room in Grand-Hotel so that we could move there. It should be possible in 2–3 days.

How are you, dear Tatiana Nikolaevna? What have you been doing?

If you write to me, which would make me very happy, my address here is: Kislovodsk, Grand-Hotel.

I kiss you very warmly. My husband is asking to pass his regards to you. Our heartfelt regards to the Grand Duchesses.

Loving you,

Your Olga Voronov.

APPENDIX III
# SOURCES FOR NOTES

## FOREWORD

1. https://www.theromanovfamily.com/journal-of-a-russian-grand-duchess-complete-annotated-1913-diary-of-olga-romanov-eldest-daughter-of-the-last-tsar/

2. https://www.theromanovfamily.com/romanov-family-friend-anna-vyrubova/

3. https://www.theromanovfamily.com/romanov-family-games/

4. Google Maps

5. See family tree

6. https://www.restcrimea.com/en/article/kosmo-damianovskij-monastir/

7. In Russian, Чемодан – my grandmother taught me to play this game and I, in turn, have taught my sons how to play

8. Note by Helen Azar

## CHAPTER 1

1. Google maps https://www.google.com/maps/place/Pochep,+Bryansk+Oblast,+Russia/@52.924787,33.4517715,13z/data=!3m1!4b1!4m5!3m4!1s0x46d2d3274657300d:0xfb282e1caeef53c7!8m2!3d52.9291372!4d33.4540551

2. Solovyov, Yuri. 'Good People of the Bryansk Land: Count Alexei Kirillovich Razumovsky.' Bryansk Tema, 6 (116) 2017

3. Roosevelt, Priscilla R. Life on the Russian Country Estate: A Social and Cultural History, UK: Yale University Press 1995

4. https://www.britannica.com/technology/iconostasis

5. Solovyov, Yuri. 'Good People of the Bryansk Land: Count Alexei Kirillovich Razumovsky.' Bryansk Tema, 6 (116) 2017

6. Kleinmichel family tree – A de Fircks collection

7. https://www.geni.com/people/Andreas-Kleinmichel/6000000087422923902

8. Kleinmichel family tree – A de Fircks collection

9. Lyashenko, Leonid. 'Random Railroad Worker.' Историк https://xn--h1aagokeh.xn--p1ai/journal/21/sluchajnyij-zheleznodorozhnik-2c.html and Troubetskoy, Helen (Elena). Helen Troubetskoy to Tatiana de Fircks, March 5, 1974. Letter. From A de Fircks collection.

10. Chmieliauskas, Alfredas, Emile J. L. Chappin, Chris B. Davis, Igor Nikolic and Gerard P. J. Dijkema, 'New Methods for Analysis of Systems-of-Systems and Policy: The Power of Systems Theory, Crowd Sourcing and Data Management,' in System of Systems, ed. Adrian V. Gheorghe, 77-98. Croatia: IntechOpen, 2012

11. Lyashenko, Leonid. 'Random Railroad Worker.' Историк https://xn--h1aagokeh.xn--p1ai/journal/21/sluchajnyij-zheleznodorozhnik-2c.html

12. https://vk.com/@priseforthelosers-stalnoi-taran-derzhavnoi-voli-graf-petr-andreevich-kleinmihe

13. Hughes, Lindsey, Peter the Great: A Biography, United States: Yale University Press, 2008

14. Woronoff, Olga. Notes on memories. From A de Fircks collection.

15. Troubetskoy, Helen. Helen Troubetskoy to Tatiana de Fircks, March 5, 1974. Letter. From A de Fircks collection.

16. Troubetskoy, Helen. Helen Troubetskoy to Tatiana de Fircks, March 5, 1974. Letter. From A de Fircks collection.

17. Kleinmichel family tree – A de Fircks collection

18. Kleinmichel family tree – A de Fircks collection

19. Original note from *Upheaval*

20. Woronoff, Olga. Notes on memories. From A de Fircks collection.

21. Woronoff, Olga. Notes on memories. From A de Fircks collection.

22. https://kehilalinks.jewishgen.org/pochep/kehilalinksPochepHist1.html

CHAPTER 2

1. Clay, Eugene. Review of A Prodigal Saint: Father John of Kronstadt and the Russian People, by Nadieszda Kizenko, The journal of modern history, Vol. 74:3 (2002): 685-687

2. https://tj.sputniknews.ru/20190910/dom-nikitskaya-moscow-1029635582.html

3. http://socialdance.stanford.edu/syllabi/russian_mazurka.htm

CHAPTER 3

1. http://xn-----7kcba7baaefibfzhiq2begimk2mwc1a.xn--p1ai/

2. Kleinmichel family tree – A de Fircks collection

CHAPTER 4

1. Original note from *Upheaval*

2. Original note from *Upheaval*

3. Starkova, Svetlana. 'Ancestors'. Email, 2023

4. Starkova, Svetlana. 'Ancestors'. Email, 2023

5. https://xn--80aabjhkiabkj9b0amel2g.xn--p1ai/materials/places/details.php?page=1996

6. https://xn--80aabjhkiabkj9b0amel2g.xn--p1ai/materials/places/details.php?page=1996

CHAPTER 5

1. http://www.unofficialroyalty.com/grand-duchess-maria-pavlovna-the-younger-of-russia/ and http://www.unofficialroyalty.com/grand-duke-dmitri-pavlovich-of-russia/

2. http://www.unofficialroyalty.com/grand-duke-sergei-alexandrovich-of-russia/

3. https://www.rbth.com/multimedia/pictures/2014/08/18/10_kremlin_monuments_weve_lost_39083

4. https://www.rbth.com/multimedia/pictures/2014/08/18/10_kremlin_monuments_weve_lost_39083

5. From the memories of A de Fircks who helped her mother make Koulitch and Paskha for many Easter celebrations.

6. Woronoff, Olga. Notes on memories. From A de Fircks collection.

7. Kleinmichel family tree – A de Fircks collection

8. Woronoff, Olga. Notes on memories. From A de Fircks collection.

9. My grandfather's Russian name which was Anglicised when they immigrated to America

10. http://www.antver.net/history/standart.html

11. Azar, Helen. Journal of a Russian Grand Duchess: Complete Annotated 1913 Diary of Olga Romanov, Eldest Daughter of the Last Tsar. Great Britain: Amazon 2015

12. Personal note A de Fircks

13. See Appendices

14. Translation from the French


CHAPTER 6

1. More about ladies in waiting can be found in: Russian Women, 1698-1917: Experience and Expression, An Anthology of Sources. Ukraine: Indiana University Press, 2002.

2. The year has been calculated based on the date of the wedding of my grandparents

3. MacMillan, Margaret. The War that Ended Peace: How Europe Abandoned Peace for the First World War. London: Profile Books Ltd, 2013

4. http://www.unofficialroyalty.com/grand-duke-alexander-mikhailovich-of-russia/

5. Starkova, Svetlana. 'Citation required'. Email, 2021 which included excerpts from the Feodorovsky Cathedral Registry Book 1914, ЦГИА СПб Ф.19 Оп.128 Д.1686 Л.11

6. Starkova, Svetlana. 'Citation required'. Email, 2021 which includes the transcription of an article from the Петербургский листок, translation reads:

A high-society wedding in the Highest presence

Yesterday, February 7, at 2 p.m., in Tsarskoye Selo, in the Feodorovsky Cathedral, the marriage of Lieutenant of the Guards crew Voronov with the lady-in-waiting of the Empress Countess Kleinmichel took place.

The wedding was attended by Their Imperial Majesties the Emperor and Empress Alexandra Feodorovna with Their August Children the

Heir Tsarevich and Grand Duke Alexei Nikolaevich and daughters Grand Duchesses Olga Nikolaevna, Tatiana Nikolaevna, Maria Nikolaevna, Anastasia Nikolaevna, Princess Marina Petrovna, Grand Duke Alexander Mikhailovich, the duty Wing-Adjutant Grand Duke Kirill Vladimirovich, Grand Duke Dmitry Pavlovich, who was the Best Man from the side brides.

The planted mother of the groom was the Empress Alexandra Feodorovna.

The Minister of the Imperial Court, Adjutant General Count Fredericks, the retinue of the Empress Empress Maria Feodorovna Countess Mengden, the retinue of the ladies-in-waiting of the Empress Alexandra Feodorovna, Princesses Obolenskaya and Orbeliani, and Ms. Bulova, the chief administrator of His Majesty's Own Office for the institutions of Empress Maria, State Secretary Bulygin, the flag captain of His Imperial Majesty, Adjutant General Nilov and his wife, General - Adjutant Nikolayev, head of the Tsarskoye Selo Palace administration, Major General Prince Putyatin. Officers of the Guards crew, led by the commander of His Majesty's retinue, Rear Admiral Count Tolstoy.

7. Woronoff, Olga. Notes on memories. From A de Fircks collection.

8. Woronoff, Olga. Notes on memories. From A de Fircks collection.

9. Woronoff, Olga. Notes on memories. From A de Fircks collection.

10. Capo, Ava Laboy, Wedding Traditions from Around the World, United Kingdom: AuthorHouse, 2013

11. Starkova, Svetlana. 'St Petersburg birth records'. Email, 2021 which included a translation of the journal entry of Nicholas II

12. https://www.retronews.fr/

13. Woronoff, Olga. Notes on memories. From A de Fircks collection.

14. There is nothing on Trotsky which I can find which indicates he was connected to Ivnya, which does not mean it is not true.

15. Voronoff, Olga. Olga Voronoff to Grand Duchess Tatiana Nikolaevna, 29 July 1914, Petersburg. Letter. Central State Archive in Moscow, Department of personal fun[ds], F[und] 651, Storage Unit 102

CHAPTER 7

1. https://www.historyplace.com/worldhistory/firstworldwar/index-1914.html

2. Voronov, Pavel Alexeyevich. Pavel A Voronov to his parents, 30 August 1914, Letter. From A de Fircks collection

3. Voronoff, Olga. Olga Voronoff to Grand Duchess Tatiana Nikolaevna, 29 July 1914, Petersburg. Letter. Central State Archive in Moscow, Department of personal fun[ds], F[und] 651, Storage Unit 102

4. Voronov, Olga. Olga Voronov to Grand Duchess Tatiana Nikolaevna, 22 September 1914, Department of personal fun[ds], F[und] 651, Inventory 1, File 102

5. Globachev, Konstantin Ivanovich. The Truth of the Russian Revolution: The Memoirs of the Tsar's Chief of Security and His Wife. Albany: State University of New York Press, 2017 muse.jhu.edu/book/51778

6. Personal note by A de Fircks

7. https://www.newworldencyclopedia.org/entry/Dmitri_Merezhkovsky

8. https://alphahistory.com/russianrevolution/nikolai-tchaikovsky/#:~:text=Nikolai%20Tchaikovsky%20(1851%2D1926),became%20involved%20in%20radical%20politics.

9. Personal note by A de Fircks

10. Google maps

11 Google maps

12. https://vladnews.ru/ev/vl/4718/127439/polkovodcem_byt

13. https://www.geni.com/people/Prince-Vladimir-Galitzine-Golitsyn/6000000002188612064

14. https://www.prlib.ru/en/node/437715

15. http://xn----7sbbj3bk0auv.xn--p1ai/luga-v-fevrale-marte-1917/

16. http://xn----7sbbj3bk0auv.xn--p1ai/luga-v-fevrale-marte-1917/

17. http://xn----7sbbj3bk0auv.xn--p1ai/luga-v-fevrale-marte-1917/

18. Personal note by A de Fircks

19. Medical Certificates for Lieutenant Pavel Alexeyevich Voronov from A de Fircks collection

20. Google maps

21. https://www.gctm.ru/en/event/song-of-the-revolution-by-feodor-chaliapin-sevastopol-1917/

CHAPTER 8

1. Medical Certificate Pavel Alexeyevich Voronov from A de Fircks collection

2. With the assistance of Svetlana Starkova who pointed out that Nikolay Kleinmichel owned an estate near Evpatoria, the deduction was made.

3. Kleinmichel family tree – A de Fircks collection

4. https://rosgenea.ru/familiya/dumbadze

5. http://swolkov.org/doc/kt/20.htm


CHAPTER 9

1. Google maps


CHAPTER 10

1. https://www.husj.harvard.edu/articles/wartime-occupation-and-peacetime-alien-rule

2. Google maps

3. Google maps

4. Braithwaite, Rodric. Across the Moscow River: The World Turned Upside Down, London: Yale University Press, 2002

5. Braithwaite, Rodric. Across the Moscow River: The World Turned Upside Down, London: Yale University Press, 2002

6. https://www.historytoday.com/archive/months-past/murders-ekaterinburg

7. Google maps

8. Google maps


CHAPTER 11

1. Original note from Upheaval.

2. Google maps

3. http://soviethistory.msu.edu/1917-2/treaty-of-brest-litovsk/

4. https://www.historytoday.com/archive/nestor-makhno-and-russian-civil-war

5. Kenez, Peter. Civil War in South Russia, 1919-1920: The Defeat of the Whites, California: University of California Press, 2021

6. Google maps

7. https://knigaread.com/dokumentalnye-knigi/biografii-i-memuary/page-167-40245-irina-knorring-povest-iz-sobstvennoi-zhizni-[dnevnik].html

8. https://www.learnrussianineu.com/russian-izba-its-origin-and-interior

9. Personal note A de Fircks

10. Voronov, Pavel. Pavel Voronov to Olga Voronov, 5 April 1919. From A de Fircks collection.

## CHAPTER 12

1. https://russianlife.com/stories/online/reds-whites-greens-and-blacks/

2. Woronoff, Olga. Notes on memories. From A de Fircks collection.

3. Woronoff, Olga. 1919 Diary from A de Fircks collection.

# Discover more books from

# downingfield.com

We accept manuscript submissions

**COUNTESS OLGA KONSTANTINOVNA KLEINMICHEL** was born into an aristocratic Russian family with close ties to the monarchy. Her grandfather was a close friend of Tsar Nicholas I, and Olga became acquainted with the daughters of Tsar Nicholas II. In 1914, Olga married Lieutenant Pavel Alexeievitch Woronoff, a naval officer on the Tsar's personal yacht, the Standart, and one of the love interests of Grand Duchess Olga. Their wedding was attended by the Imperial family.

**ALEX DE FIRCKS** is a family historian, writer, and scholar. Her academic awards include two Bachelor of Arts degrees (one with Honours), a Diploma of Family History, and a Master of Research, where her thesis examined how to narrativise family history ethically and authentically. She has written several short stories and articles. In 2013, Alex was the highest-placed Monash University student in the Monash University Undergraduate Prize for Creative Writing, as part of the Emerging Writers Festival. Her entry was published in the anthology "Promise: Monash University Undergraduate Prize Shortlist" 2013. In 2020, Alex was shortlisted for both the St Kilda Short Story Competition and the Genealogical Society of Victoria Writing Competition. Her story for the latter was published in the GSV's Ancestor magazine. Alex is passionate about research, history, genealogy, and family stories. Her ancestors originate from Russia and the Baltic States, and she is especially interested in the conflicts that helped shape their lives. Alex's research into her family history is ongoing, and she writes stories about her ancestors on her website www.alexdefircks.com.

www.ingramcontent.com/pod-product-compliance
Lightning Source LLC
Chambersburg PA
CBHW030305080526
44584CB00012B/443